D1575466

Appreciative Intelligence

Seeing the Mighty Oak in the Acorn

Appreciative Intelligence

Seeing the Mighty Oak in the Acorn

Tojo Thatchenkery & Carol Metzker

BERRETT-KOEHLER PUBLISHERS, INC.
San Francisco

Copyright © 2006 by Tojo Thatchenkery and Carol Metzker
All rights reserved. No part of this publication may be reproduced, distributed, or transmitted in any form or by any means, including photocopying, recording, or other electronic or mechanical methods, without the prior written permission of the publisher, except in the case of brief quotations embodied in critical reviews and certain other noncommercial uses permitted by copyright law. For permission requests, write to the publisher, addressed "Attention: Permissions Coordinator," at the address below.

Berrett-Koehler Publishers, Inc.
235 Montgomery Street, Suite 650
San Francisco, CA 94104-2916
Tel: (415) 288-0260   Fax: (415) 362-2512   www.bkconnection.com

Ordering Information
Quantity sales. Special discounts are available on quantity purchases by corporations, associations, and others. For details, contact the "Special Sales Department" at the Berrett-Koehler address above.
Individual sales. Berrett-Koehler publications are available through most bookstores. They can also be ordered directly from Berrett-Koehler: Tel: (800) 929-2929; Fax: (802) 864-7626; www.bkconnection.com
Orders for college textbook/course adoption use. Please contact Berrett-Koehler: Tel: (800) 929-2929; Fax: (802) 864-7626.
Orders by U.S. trade bookstores and wholesalers. Please contact Ingram Publisher Services, Tel: (800) 509-4887; Fax: (800) 838-1149; E-mail: customer.service@ingrampublisherservices .com; or visit www.ingrampublisherservices.com/Ordering for details about electronic ordering.

Berrett-Koehler and the BK logo are registered trademarks of Berrett-Koehler Publishers, Inc.

Printed in the United States of America

Berrett-Koehler books are printed on long-lasting acid-free paper. When it is available, we choose paper that has been manufactured by environmentally responsible processes. These may include using trees grown in sustainable forests, incorporating recycled paper, minimizing chlorine in bleaching, or recycling the energy produced at the paper mill.

Library of Congress Cataloging-in-Publication Data
    Appreciative intelligence : seeing the mighty oak in the acorn / by Tojo Thatchenkery and Carol Metzker.
        p. cm.
Includes bibliographic references and index.
ISBN-10: 1-57675-353-0; ISBN-13: 978-1-57675-353-8
1. Creative thinking.   I. Metzker, Carol, 1960–   II. Title.

BF408.T42 2006
153.3'5—dc22   2005057040

First Edition
12 11 10 09 08 07   10 9 8 7 6 5 4 3 2

Interior production by Publication Services, Inc.

To Tessy, Sruthi, and my parents
— T.T.

To Eric, who sees infinite wonderful possibilities
— C.M.

Contents

Elevating and Extending Our Capacity to Appreciate the Appreciable World

 Imagine what would happen to you if you had the ability to see consistently, and connect with, every strength—every one of the capacities—inherent in the world around you; or to see every positive potential in your son or daughter; or, like Michelangelo, the intellectual ability to "sense" the towering, historic figure of David "already existing" in the huge slab of marble—even before the reality.

Indeed, the appreciable world—the universe of strength, value, and life-generating potential all around us—is so much larger than our normal appreciative capacity. Yet there are some—we all know them—who seem to have a special knack for seeing, noticing, and connecting with ever-expanding domains of positive potential. There are great coaches who see extraordinary things in their players, hidden strengths no one has ever seen. There are grandparents who "know" the specialties of their grandchild, intuitively it seems, long before those potentials are nurtured or even recognized by others. Could such appreciative capacity explain, for example, the success of leaders who have ranked relatively low on traditional measures of IQ but have gone on to change human history or reshape entire industries?

In late 2005, two years after the publication of the human genome, a global team of scientists published a new map of human genetic variations that will enable scientists to begin to answer many questions related to health, longevity, and aging. The map was catalogued by the HapMap Project, involving scientists from Japan, the United States, Canada, China, and Nigeria. Francis Collins, director of the Human Genome Research Institute, said, "I have dreamed of the day when we would be able to apply the tools of genetic analysis to the . . . prevention of common diseases. . . . [This announcement] brings us a step closer to that dream."[1] Speak to anyone involved in the human genome work and one thing is clear: The work is thrilling.

Something similar is happening in the field of human intelligence. Today we know with full clarity that there are multiple kinds of intelligence. Although many in our culture continue to adhere to the assumptions that intelligence is a single, general capacity that every human being possesses to a greater or lesser extent and that, however defined, it can be measured by standardized verbal instruments, such as short pencil-and-paper tests, today we know that these assumptions are theoretically untenable and developmentally confining. In the introduction to the tenth-anniversary edition of his classic *Frames of Mind: The Theory of Multiple Intelligences*, Howard Gardner indicated that all the groundwork is now laid and that we stand poised at the beginning of mapping the codebook for thinking about intelligence, including everything the term implies, from the creation of classrooms to the cultivation of leadership. Many asked whether additional intelligences were added—or original candidates deleted—since the early work on multiple intelligence in 1983; although Gardner chose "not to tamper *for now* with the original list," he stated unequivocally his conviction that there are in fact others, from "intrapersonal intelligence" to some form of "spiritual intelligence" to a kind of meta-intelligence that can "yoke all the intelligences together and mobilize them for constructive ends."[2]

Appreciative Intelligence, I believe, is about this, the latter. It's about the kind of intelligence that not only can "yoke" but elevate and extend the intelligence of the wide variety of known intelligences: linguistic and logical-mathematical intelligence, musical intelligence, spatial intelligence; bodily-kinesthetic intelligence; and the types or forms of personal intelligence, one directed toward other persons, one directed toward oneself. The subtitle in this scholarly and captivating work by

Tojo Thatchenkery and Carol Metzker says it all. Put in the most concise, metaphorical way, Appreciative Intelligence is "the ability to see the mighty oak in the acorn"; that is, it's all about the ability to perceive the positive *inherent generative potential* in the present. And, as the reader will soon see, it's a powerful construct. Immediately upon turning the book's pages I began to understand things about my sons and daughter I had not noticed before and began to understand puzzles about tremendously successful leaders who literally had flunked out of grade school, yet today stand poised to change human history. Let me share a quick story, for, as we all know, sometimes a short anecdote can express more than many words. It is an unlikely story, but now I think I understand it.

At the time of this writing the situation in the Middle East appears more unstable, some say hopeless, than ever. It appears that nobody can find a solution to the bloody bombings, the conflicts and bitterness between Arabs and Jews and others, the suffering and distress, and the spreading of terror around the world. It's precarious. It's dangerous. And nobody sees an easy solution.

Nobody?

A few months ago I had the opportunity to speak as an invited guest at the dedication for the new Arison School of Management in Israel. During the talk I raised questions about where the peace is going to come from. From the lawyers? Not likely. From the military? Not likely. From governments? From the religious leaders—Muslim, Christian, Jewish, and so forth? My proposition, tentatively offered, was that it would be none of these. The best place to look, I argued, would be the world of business—that business could be the most important ground and force for peace. Forget about the major headlines of Enron and WorldCom, I said, because the 21st century is going to be a time when we learn to unite the dynamism and entrepreneurial capacities of good business with the global issues of our day. I did not have many examples, but made the argument anyway.

After the talk a stranger came up to me. He said: "I'd like to invite you to meet me at my helicopter tomorrow morning at 8:00. I want you to see this thesis in action—business as a force for peace." He went on: "It's a story of human imagination and the capacity to make something from nothing except hard work." The next morning we flew to the Galilee region, across the desert to an area without any natural resources. It is called Tefen, and later I discovered that this unassuming man was perhaps the wealthiest person in Israel; his worth was estimated to be over four billion dollars, and what he has created now accounts for over 10% of Israel's export GNP. His name is Stef Wertheimer. And for what he has accomplished, he honestly deserves to be nominated for the Nobel Peace Prize.

When I got out of the helicopter, I could not believe my eyes. Up until the mid-1980s Tefen was a barren hilltop grazed by local herds of goats. Today the scope of industrial exports manufactured at Tefen equals that of the entire Jerusalem area. Beautiful homes and neighborhoods surround what Wertheimer calls a "capitalist kibbutz"—with four Tefen Model Industrial Parks that have given birth to more than 160 new businesses and schools for all the children that now populate the area. Most surprising: the whole thing is based on the principle of coexistence, Arab and Jewish—living together, going into business together, building schools and art museums together, and dramatically transforming entrenched conflicts into collaborative energies for economic empowerment, development, and peace.

Stef Wertheimer is literally igniting a revolution in hope by harnessing the best in business to melt frozen animosities easily and rapidly, and in the process create islands of peace and shared prosperity. His theory: Create 100 more of these islands—a distinct and special kind of entrepreneurial industrial park modeled after the "Tefen Miracle"—and strategically locate them throughout the eastern Mediterranean. It's literally this region's version of a Marshall Plan and one that, growing numbers of supporters from Turkey, Jordan, Israel, and the Palestinian Authority believe, could lift the region out of poverty and take the biggest step toward finishing terrorism. It's something all of us should take notice of. In his book *War and Anti-War: Survival at the Dawn of the 21st Century*, the prolific author Alvin Toffler cites Wertheimer's example as one of the most important quiet revolutions in the world today.

Many are now calling the 79 year-old Wertheimer a genius, but most do not know that this genius dropped out of grade-school. He couldn't cut it. He failed in most classes. For survival he created his first business, and the first two people hired were an Arab and a Jew, respectively. A seed vision was born and was motivated, as he puts it, "by the metaphysical concept of survival" and his growing conviction that creativity and entrepreneurship *together* were the only things that could create conditions for lasting peace, dignified lives, and eradication of strife. "A booming industrial base will provide more security than any military outpost." Today Wertheimer is working tirelessly to establish 100 of these industrial parks throughout the non-oil-producing parts of the Middle East—his version, as mentioned above, of a Marshall Plan for the region.

The most exciting part of my visit? I was sitting in on a class of Jewish and Arab 10-year-old children—laughing and playing and singing—learning together in a region of the world most define as hopelessly entrenched in hatred. It's a story that, with the click of the button, should be shared with everyone everywhere in the world.

Traditional IQ tests cannot explain—and never would have predicted—what I saw from the helicopter that day in Galilee. The present articulation of the concept of *Appreciative Intelligence* is indeed a cutting edge-work. It illuminates.

Stef Wertheimer could see the mighty oak in the acorn. Where there was desert, he could see vast neighborhoods. Where there was poverty, he could see the unlimited human resource of collective imagination. One part of his brilliance is that he *reframed* everything. For example, Stef was ecstatic that there were no natural resources in the area such as oil—"the Arab world, alas, has been cursed with oil," in his words. Along with such reframing, this genius selectively noticed everything of value worth valuing, *appreciating positive possibility* in every person and situation he was engaged with. He is proof that we can live with a positive love of life amid onslaughts of torment. Another part is his capacity to see the future-ideal interwoven in the texture of the actual—he *knows* peace will prevail and he sees a Marshall Plan for a whole region, simply from the demonstration of going beyond "what works" in Tefen. This is what Appreciative Intelligence is all about, Thatchenkery and Metzker propose. Its code has three dimensions and can be mapped out clearly: the power of *reframing* (the capacity to see one's view of the world *as* a view is, perhaps for the first time, articulated as a signature mark of contemporary intelligence); *appreciation of positive possibility*; and seeing how *the future unfolds from the present*.

If it were up to you, how would you cultivate Appreciative Intelligence—with our young people and schools, in our leaders, our media, or perhaps most important, in yourself? To be sure, a good place to start is right here with this volume. Tojo Thatchenkery, a brilliant colleague and former doctoral student from Case Western Reserve University (where I continue to teach), and Carol Metzker have written a delightful book with insights that ring true and are deeply important. Drawing from disciplines such as the neurosciences to the breakthrough research in positive psychology and social construction, the authors make complicated ideas both accessible and applicable for every aspect of our lives. You will love this book and find it difficult to set aside. The book is lucid in its storytelling, pragmatic in its exercises, and rich in its intellectual integration. It's is the kind of book you will want to share with family, colleagues, and friends.

I enjoyed reading Tojo's sharing of how he came up with the concept of Appreciative Intelligence and the role he acknowledges that the intellectual climate our department of Organizational Behavior has had in shaping his thinking. Tojo and many alumni like him continue to remind us that one thing we are good at in the Organizational Behavior department is in creating scholars who go on to plant the seeds for new ideas in their fields. I also remember Tojo saying that using the Appreciative Inquiry methodology for working with an exceptionally innovative organization called the Institute of Cultural Affairs (ICA) for his doctoral dissertation opened up his horizon of thinking. The ICA is a unique organization gifted with Appreciative Intelligence. I recall Tojo calling me once in the middle of his data collection to say, "David, everything is going so perfect here that I don't know what to do!"

See things differently—it's clearly a message for our times. May this daring book open new options for cultivating research, education, and practices for developing Appreciative Intelligence, and may it help us magnify our capacity to *appreciate the appreciable world* all around us. My son Matt came up the other day and asked me about our troubled world. He asked what to do. I suggested firstly, that he read this book, and then search for people like Stef Wertheimer and learn exactly how it is that they are able "to see the mighty oak in the acorn," in times of both trouble and success.

It's a learning journey with vast implications—and the domain of our own lives is an optimal venue for letting the journey begin!

David L. Cooperrider
Case Western Reserve University
Cleveland, Ohio
November 6, 2005

Preface

One doesn't discover new lands without consenting
to lose sight of the shore for a very long time.
—*André Gide (1869–1951)*

There was something unique about the way I (Tojo Thatchenkery) approached seminar discussions in the doctoral program in organizational behavior at Case Western Reserve University during my student days. Having grown up in a different cultural setting, I was very good at "constructive criticism," which I understood as pointing out holes in my classmates' arguments. With the best intentions, I happily highlighted what was missing in their presentations. When my turn came to do a seminar, however, it was pay back time! I got a taste of my own medicine! That was the first time I experienced the powerful differences in individual ability to bring out the best (or the opposite) in others.

A few years later (the late 1990s) I got absorbed in understanding the phenomenal growth of information technology–related entrepreneurialism in the Silicon Valley and the rest of America. I came across entrepreneurs who had a unique ability to recognize hidden talent in individuals and seize business opportunities in the market. These individuals also knew how to put the pieces together to make their vision a reality. Having trained in the field of psychology and been mentored by faculty who created the Appreciative Inquiry methodology, I began to see an Appreciative Intelligence in these entrepreneurs. I believed they have an ability or capacity to reframe reality to bring out the best from others and the environment. Once I conceptualized this notion of Appreciative Intelligence, it was easy to see how it differed from other types of intelligences and abilities. This book, co-authored with Carol Metzker, says it all and more.

Someone asked us recently whether people really need to know about another type of intelligence. It was an interesting and unusual question that seemed analogous to the question, "If a botanist sees that a new plant has popped up in the garden, should he or she look at it?" The short answer is yes. Why not?

There is also a longer answer. Using the metaphor of the plant, we believe better questions might be: What is the plant? What role is it serving in the garden? Is it a weed that will use up the soil's nutrients or block important crops from getting sunlight? Or is it like a legume that puts nutrients back into the soil, or an herb that acts as a natural insect repellent for itself and the surrounding plants? What are its characteristics? Does it bear fruit that is edible by humans, or does it have a bloom that is lovely to look at? Has anyone identified it before? How does it grow? Where else might we find it growing naturally? Can we transplant it or grow more? How can we fertilize it, cultivate it, and apply it? What will change if we do nothing, and what will change if we do something?

Likewise, these are better questions to ask about a new intelligence, specifically Appreciative Intelligence. They are also questions that we have begun to answer. We have identified Appreciative Intelligence, named it, learned to recognize it and described it. We have determined that it is useful—it leads to innovation and success. We provide other people with the tools to recognize it, describe it, apply it, and cultivate it. Now, using techniques laid out in this book, you, the readers, have the opportunity to explore your own Appreciative Intelligence, look for it in people around you, nurture it, enhance it, and use it for personal and organizational success.

Success comes in all shapes and sizes, just like the people who create it. It can be defined as any or all of the following: financial well-being; healthy personal and professional relationships; effective leadership; ability to achieve goals; ability to bring out the best in others at work and at home; social status or recognition and personal fulfillment. *Appreciative*

Intelligence: Seeing the Mighty Oak in the Acorn provides real-world stories about a variety of successful people and their winning ventures, the secrets behind their innovation and leadership, and concrete steps for you to take to create your own success. Regardless of your definition of success, this book could make a difference in the possibilities you see today for the future that is rushing up to greet you.

For individuals, this book offers a myriad of possibilities. Developing and enhancing your Appreciative Intelligence could mean that you learn how to reframe situations for better negotiating or solving problems in a creative way. You may begin to lead more effectively or to see innovative solutions. You might find that you are less often involved in situations of blaming or finger pointing and more often involved in getting what you want or where you want to go. You may find yourself bringing out the best in others; finding happiness, appreciation, or fulfillment where you hadn't before; or seeing connections you had never noticed.

Although Appreciative Intelligence is an individual ability, it significantly affects groups and organizations because they are composed of individuals. For businesses, applying Appreciative Intelligence can lead to a competitive advantage: creative solutions, new products, ability to achieve goals, and a better work environment that leads to productive and satisfied organization members and higher member retention, all which eventually affect the financial bottom line. For teachers, families, and caregivers, applying Appreciative Intelligence could have a profound effect on the next generation. This book provides examples and approaches to help children find their talents and strengths. As one of the leaders cited in this book suggests, our task is not simply to be "nice" to young people; it is to provide them with an environment where they can have real successes to learn and to build real self-esteem and the conviction that their actions matter.

For policy makers and government agencies this book provides a new context to understand the significance of their contribution. By resisting the temptation to define public policy challenges as crises or irresolvable problems, government agencies and policy makers can do something different. They can reframe the challenges as opportunities, look for possibilities that are inherent in the system but not yet recognized or tapped, and build on the collective good of the citizenry.

In the same way that individuals have an impact on organizations, organizations have an impact on society. By applying Appreciative Intelligence to create thriving businesses and organizations, more effective schools, better leaders, solid connections between groups, and healthier relationships among people, we build stronger communities and a healthier economy. In short, we build a better future.

Appreciative Intelligence: Seeing the Mighty Oak in the Acorn is written to guide you through what Appreciative Intelligence is, how it affects our lives, and how it can be used to change the future. Chapters 1 through 3 introduce the construct of Appreciative Intelligence, its components, and its ensuing qualities. Chapters 4 through 6 provide details about its components. Chapter 7 discusses the results of Appreciative Intelligence at work. Chapter 8 lays out steps to identify and enhance your personal Appreciative Intelligence for your own success and personal fulfillment. Chapters 9 and 10 discuss details of our methodology and the psychology and social cognitive neuroscience studies that we use to make a case for Appreciative Intelligence. The eleventh and final chapter discusses the implications of Appreciative Intelligence and provides initial steps for moving forward after reading the book.

We invite you to read this book and realize something you have always known but did not quite know to how to articulate: the power of your own Appreciative Intelligence in making a positive difference in your life, the lives of others, groups, organizations, and communities around you.

Chapter 1

Appreciative Intelligence: The Missing Link

A fool sees not the same tree that a wise man sees.
—William Blake (1790)

When the Hubble Space Telescope was launched in 1990, the general public, as well as scientists in the aerospace field, held high hopes. The world waited expectantly for discoveries and answers to riddles of the universe that would be revealed by the telescope's views of space.

But blurry images caused by a flawed mirror sent those hopes crashing down to earth. Congress demanded an explanation for the failure. The project and its creators became the butt of late-night television jokes. Stress was high among NASA engineers, as were health problems.

"It was traumatic," said Charlie Pellerin, the former director of NASA's astrophysics division, who oversaw the launch of the Hubble. Nobody could see how to fix the problem, which many seemed afraid even to address.

Well, nobody except Pellerin. He not only had the initial insight to solve the problem but also found the funding and the resources to repair the telescope, for which he received NASA's Outstanding Leadership Medal. The ultimate reward was that over the next decade, the telescope provided spectacular images and important discoveries of stars, galaxies, and other cosmic phenomena.

What was behind Pellerin's success? There were dozens of other people at NASA with high IQ and world-class technical knowledge—they were, after all, rocket scientists. They could perform the same analysis, use the same logic, and wield the same models and mathematical formulas. So what gave Pellerin the insight to help the telescope get a metaphorical pair of eyeglasses? What made him persist until the telescope was fixed when others felt overwhelmed by the challenge?

Pellerin possessed something more than the others did: Appreciative Intelligence. While he lived with the same conditions and circumstances as everyone else, his mind perceived reality very differently than others did. He reframed the situation as a project that was not yet finished, not as a completed product that had failed. He saw the potential for a positive future situation—a working space telescope. He saw how that positive future could happen as the result of technical solutions—a corrective optics package and repairs performed by a crew of astronauts[1]—that were already possible with a rearrangement of funding and resources that already existed within NASA. By reframing, recognizing the positive, or what worked, and envisioning the repaired telescope, he was able to help orchestrate the unfolding of a series of events that changed the future.

Consider another story. In 1979, after participating in a project to immunize children in the Philippines against polio and reading about the worldwide eradication of smallpox, Clem Renouf, then president of the civic organization Rotary International, telephoned John Sever, then chief of the Infectious Diseases Branch at the National Institutes of Health and a fellow Rotarian. Renouf asked Sever to find out whether Rotary could help eradicate a disease. A month later, Sever recommended pursuing polio eradication.

For the next two decades, a group of key stakeholders, backed by a million Rotarians, overcame challenge after challenge to battle the disease. They reassured the medical community that focusing on polio wouldn't take away from the battle against other diseases such as measles, tuberculosis, or HIV/AIDS. Rotarians raised millions of dollars to buy polio vaccine. They persuaded reluctant government health ministries in many countries to help the cause and invited the World Health Organization, UNICEF, and the U.S. Center for Disease Control to join Rotary as its program partners. They motivated volunteers who transported vaccine in developing countries where there were few roads and who found ways to keep the vaccine vials cold where there was no electricity. Rotary provided infrastructure, organization, and helping hands worldwide to deliver and administer the oral polio vaccine to millions of children, many whose parents were impoverished, illiterate, and afraid that the vaccine was voodoo or a disguised attempt by culturally or politically different organizations to sterilize or harm their children. With the audacious goal of eradicating the virus, the program raised awareness of immunization and disease prevention for illnesses beyond polio. It spurred the allocation of government funds for vaccines in certain countries and improved disease surveillance processes. At the same time the program was changing the world's response to disease, it reduced the incidence of polio by 99%, from over 350,000 cases in 125 countries in 1988 to 1,255 cases in 2004.[2]

What was behind the string of creative and innovative solutions behind the polio eradication project? What differentiated this project from the medical community's attempts to eradicate other diseases such as malaria and yellow fever? What was behind more than 20 years of persistence? If the same vaccine, medical knowledge and expertise, challenges, and conditions existed for others who looked at the situation, what ability made the difference for this group of Rotarians—a volunteer group of predominantly business and community leaders—to face polio and reduce its incidence by 99%?

The opening for a different outcome was created when Rotarians reframed the challenge of eradicating polio. Renouf, Sever, Herb Pigman, and Carlos Canseco, with the help of Dr. Albert Sabin, who had developed the oral polio vaccine, reframed polio as an organizational challenge instead of a medical problem. They focused on Rotarians' organizational skills, leadership, talents, and resources as the key to the solution. They saw a positive future—a world without polio—and envisioned a string of managerial decisions and organizational operations—transportation, refrigeration, finances, communication, and education provided by Rotary's established worldwide network of volunteers—that were already possible at that time.

What did Charlie Pellerin and the leaders of Rotary have in common that led to their projects' success? What is the ability that enables some people to take new or challenging circumstances and turn them into golden opportunities and enriching experiences for themselves and those around them, while others falter at similar situations? It is Appreciative Intelligence, the ability to perceive the positive inherent generative potential within the present. Put in a simple and metaphorical way, Appreciative Intelligence is the ability to see the mighty oak in the acorn. It is the ability to reframe a given situation, to appreciate its positive aspects, and to see how the future unfolds from the generative aspects of the current situation.

Appreciative Intelligence: Seeing the Mighty Oak in the Acorn offers a new perspective on successful people and provides a road map for those who want to realize their full potential. It offers an explanation of a unique ability of those who formally or informally lead projects and people and who make a difference in their small groups, organizations, the larger community, and the world. It provides a new answer to what enables successful people to dream up their extraordinary and innovative ideas; why employees, students, partners, colleagues, investors, and other stakeholders join them on the path to their end goals; and how they achieve those goals despite obstacles and challenges. It shows how a new type of intelligence, not traditional IQ or other types, links to success. In the next ten chapters, this book introduces Appreciative Intelligence, a new construct that explains a competitive advantage possessed by exceptional leaders in business, education, government, and nonprofit organizations.

Appreciative Intelligence also offers another perspective on what it means to be smart or intelligent. Ask a group of people what it means to be intelligent, and their answers might vary considerably. Several people who spoke with us during our research told us that they weren't sure they were *that* smart—smart enough to have created such success. They felt that luck was certainly a factor in their progress. Yet in every case, the people we interviewed were leaders or participants in exceedingly effective projects with innovative solutions and far-reaching outcomes. Their definition of smart or intelligent was too narrow to encompass the ability that allowed them to see the possibilities that "luck" provided—a notion described by the nineteenth-century scientist Louis Pasteur, when he said, "Chance favors the prepared mind." Their definition excluded the mental processes that resulted in ideas and outcomes that amounted to what others would call "brilliant" or even "genius."

When Carol, one of the authors, was in grade school, her entire class "knew" what it meant to be intelligent. "Intelligent" meant a classmate Chris (not his real name)—sometimes called by his nickname "Brains"—who earned top grades and quickly understood lessons from teachers and from books. He had a solid grasp of academic fundamentals in math, English, and science. Chris grew up to be a successful Wall Street executive. At a high-school reunion the graduates all knew that our old friend was still just plain smart.

In the same grade school, students also considered who wasn't as intelligent. Surely the girl who sat in the back of the class chatting away with her friends, paying less attention to class work than to the behavior of classmates around her, was less intelligent. At a later school reunion, a few alumni overheard her talking about her work. When her father passed away, he left her a piece of property in our small town. She had noticed that as the tiny town grew, more traffic passed by the corner where her property was located, so she opened a convenience store on the corner. Noting new needs and desires around town, she rented her extra space to a startup limousine service. In a relatively short time, she became a successful businesswoman.

Both classmates drew upon their abilities—one upon mathematical, analytical cognitive thinking, the other upon the ability to notice people's behaviors and recognize opportunities inherent in them—to become successful business people. The successful businesswoman used her Appreciative Intelligence to see hidden potential in a piece of property and a situation of changing needs to realize business value.

Defining Appreciative Intelligence

Appreciative Intelligence is the ability to perceive the positive inherent generative potential within the present. Put in a simple way, Appreciative Intelligence is the ability to see the mighty oak in the acorn. Metaphorically, it is the ability to see more than the present existence of a small capped nut. It is the capacity to see a strong trunk and countless leaves as emerging from the nut as time unfolds. It is the ability to see a breakthrough product, top talent, or valuable solution of the future that is currently hidden in the present situation.

There are three components of Appreciative Intelligence:

- Reframing
- Appreciating the positive
- Seeing how the future unfolds from the present

Like a three-legged stool that cannot stand if a leg is missing, Appreciative Intelligence is not present without all its components. Each part is essential to the construct.

Reframing

The first component of the intelligence we discuss in this book is the ability to perceive—to see, to interpret, to frame or reframe. Framing is the psychological process whereby a person intentionally views or puts into a certain perspective any object, person, context, or scenario. One of the most common examples of framing is that of calling a glass half empty or half full. Regardless of how the glass is described, the amount of water is the same; it is only the perspective that is different.

In any act of perception or reframing, a person is faced with a series of choices. He or she chooses to pay attention to one stimulus and, at least for the time being, to ignore the remaining stimuli. That decision is a judgment call, value-based in the sense that what gets focused on must have more value than what does not. Consider the scenario of the half-glass of water. Factors, such as whether the perceiver is an optimist or pessimist, dying of thirst or attempting to bail out a boat that is about to sink, will affect his or her value judgment of the amount of water. Using Appreciative Intelligence, the person consciously or unconsciously reframes what is in the present, thereby shifting to a new view of reality that leads to a new outcome, just as the Rotarians reframed polio eradication as an organizational, not medical, challenge.

Appreciating the Positive

Ask several people what it means to be appreciative. Some may refer to rising property value; another may recall that a "thank-you" note or recognition speech needs to be written. But most will have an accurate sense of what the word means and that subjective value is at play. In this book, the term *appreciation* specifically refers to a process of selectivity and judgment of something's positive value or worth. This is the second component of Appreciative Intelligence.

Consider the following scenario: You are browsing through an art exhibit at a museum while your friend is checking out a few paintings at a nearby flea market. You both see similar paintings by the same artist.

Assuming neither of you is an art critic, you are more likely to have a better appreciation of the painting than your friend has at the flea market. Because you are in the art museum, you have an appreciative mindset. Aware that an expert might have picked the painting as worthy of being displayed in the art gallery, you are intentionally looking for beauty in the painting. As you look intently, you see aspects of the painting you might have missed had you looked with a casual eye. Meanwhile, your friend might be looking for a bargain. She tries hard to discover some fault in the artwork in order to negotiate a lower price. It is reasonable to think that your friend is intentionally looking for deficits while you are trying to appreciate the picture. A cognitive psychologist would say that you are actually interpreting or reframing the details of the painting as beautiful or exquisite because of the appreciative context that has been created. In the end, both your friend and you find what you are looking for.

Similarly, successful people have a conscious or unconscious ability to view everyday reality—events, situations, obstacles, products, and people—with appreciation. Because they are reframing to see the positive, they often see talents or potential that others might miss.

Seeing How the Future Unfolds from the Present

The implication of the second component is that useful, desirable, or positive aspects already exist in the current condition of people, situations, or things, but sometimes they must be revealed, unlocked, or realized. People with high Appreciative Intelligence connect the generative aspects of the present with a desirable end goal. They see how the future unfolds from the present, the third component of Appreciative Intelligence. Many people have the ability to reframe and the capacity to appreciate the positive. Yet, if they don't see the concrete ways that the possibilities of the present moment could be channeled, they have not developed their Appreciative Intelligence.

Consider an instance in the story of Brownie Wise, the marketing genius of Tupperware, who was building a sales force in the 1950s to sell plastic home products through home parties. Once, a poorly dressed woman showed up in a coal delivery truck to talk with Wise about becoming a Tupperware dealer. Wise reframed the context by ignoring the appearance of the woman and intentionally focusing on the positive, the "desire in her eyes."[3] Furthermore, Wise had the ability to see how the future could unfold from the present as she saw what could generate success—the woman's strong determination—and a concrete way to realize it—by booking parties, demonstrating products, and selling Tupperware.

The following real-life examples, historical and present-day, have characteristics in common with Charlie Pellerin and the Hubble Telescope repair, and Rotary International's and their partners' 99% reduction of polio worldwide. They show Appreciative Intelligence and hint at the power and consequences of the three components working together.

1. Coca-Cola's Asa Candler saw the potential for a top-selling soft drink in a failing headache remedy.[4] He reframed the product as a beverage instead of a health product, focused on proving its great taste to other people, and set into motion what is now a multibillion-dollar business.

2. Cosmetic company founder Estee Lauder saw a shoeless woman who entered an upscale store as a possible good customer, and ended up selling two of each cosmetic product to her and more to her relatives the next day.[5] Lauder saw beyond the outward appearance of the woman and reframed her as a potentially good customer, rather than as a poor visitor to the store. She treated her as someone of value, thus creating a dramatically different sales transaction from what would have occurred had Lauder listened to the employee who suggested ignoring her.

3. At W. L. Gore & Associates, founder Bill Gore sparked the idea for Glide Floss, shred-resistant dental floss, when he attached a ribbon of Gore-Tex fabric to his toothbrush and began to floss his teeth. Company associate (Gore's term for an employee) Dave Myers had a flash of insight that led to Elixir guitar strings after coating his mountain bike gear cables with a thin layer of slick plastic material. Since Gore's inception in 1958, its innovators have dreamed up and

realized a range of other products, including wires and cables that have gone to the moon and a waterproof cast lining that allows patients to swim or shower while their broken bones heal. The company is best known for Gore-Tex fabric, used in sportswear and outdoor clothing. By reframing the uses of their plastic materials, seeing the positive value in their products and people, and connecting technology and materials possible in the present with the vision of better products for the future, the company has enjoyed a long tradition of bringing original products to the market.

4. In response to concerns that the number of U.S. students earning engineering degrees has declined in the past decade, Dean Kamen, inventor of the Segway Human Transporter, founded FIRST (For Inspiration and Recognition of Science and Technology). He formed the organization to address the decline as a cultural issue, rather than as an educational problem. FIRST introduced math, science, and engineering principles to 73,000 high-school-aged students in 2005, not through additional classes or science fairs but through a giant robotics event akin to an "Olympics for Smarts,"[6] featuring games, music, and cheering spectators at the Georgia Dome.

The leaders in these stories have commonalities—persistence, big dreams, passion, conviction that their actions matter, ability to overcome obstacles, creativity, innovation, and a knack for persuading people to share their goals and hard work. They also created significant business and organizational success.

At the same time, we all could also point to examples of leaders, and their organizations, who couldn't overcome obstacles or change their circumstances; couldn't disentangle themselves from a web of difficulties; couldn't attract and hold talented employees, loyal customers, or investors; and couldn't accomplish goals. In short, we all know people who didn't succeed.

The Genesis of Appreciative Intelligence

What is the ability that enables some people to take new or challenging circumstances and turn them into successful experiences for themselves and those around them, while others waver at similar situations?

That was the question that Tojo Thatchenkery, one of the authors of this book, asked shortly after he arrived in the United States in 1987. While working on his doctoral studies in organizational behavior, he observed that in the culture of his university department, leaders possessed a distinctive manner of dealing with fellow faculty, students, and their environment. They were constantly looking for ways that others' ideas might work, how their proposed concepts might be realized and developed. He also noticed an aura of success among the faculty that, in turn, led to successful graduates. This was in marked contrast to a culture of critique he was previously familiar with, where it was assumed that if the gaps and deficiencies in ideas were pointed out, it would lead to improvement. It quickly became apparent to him that a culture that appreciatively framed others' ideas into possibilities led to more original and more rapidly generated concepts and discoveries.

On a larger scale, Tojo noticed a high incidence of innovation in the United States, such as that associated with the phenomena of Silicon Valley. The technology center in California that originated as Stanford's University's solution to financial shortages ultimately became the birthplace of many of the world's computers, semiconductors, electronics, and software inventions. During the late 1980s and early 1990s, Silicon Valley produced a significant quantity of intellectual capital that resulted in the phenomenal growth of the Internet and the subsequent Information Technology revolution and globalization. As he witnessed a pervasive attitude of looking for the next nugget of gold in the pan of dust, Tojo began to perceive that there was a link between entrepreneurs' and leaders' positive and appreciative approach, innovative and creative ideas, and successful organizations. He also noticed that such people had a unique ability to perceive opportunities, talents, and innovative ideas and to bring them to fruition when others didn't. Tojo coined the term *Appreciative Intelligence* to capture this ability.

After studying hundreds of stories of real-life leaders and talking with additional ones (in a methodology described in Chapter 9 of this book), and examining research from the new field of social cognitive neuroscience (discussed in Chapter 10), we found evidence to explain what Tojo previously had intuitively perceived. A common characteristic of many successful leaders and innovators is a unique way of thinking—the newly identified intelligence called Appreciative Intelligence.

Appreciative Intelligence is a new construct. Different from a concept, which "expresses an abstraction formed by generalization from particulars," a construct is a "concept that has been deliberately and consciously invented or adopted for a specific scientific purpose."[7] Constructs are developed to help us make sense of various phenomena in our world. They can be observed and measured, thus allowing us to make predictions about behavior. Development of new constructs can also lead to theory development, research, and practice.

The new construct of Appreciative Intelligence helps explain the thinking behind success. Behind top leaders', inventors', and innovators' achievements, it shows up in a myriad of ways, foremost in the perception of products, places, people, events, and situations. In each case, reality is seen as possessing high value, regardless of its face value. In much the same way that Coca Cola's Asa Candler saw possibilities for a popular beverage in an unpopular health product, an architect with high Appreciative Intelligence may see a quaint historic home in what others view as a rundown house in a depressed neighborhood. A sports or talent scout might see a future star in an amateur athlete or actor. Or another person might see a catastrophe as an opportunity for change. Appreciative Intelligence encompasses the capacity to appreciate people, to see and reveal the hidden value in others, and to look past stereotypes, as did Estee Lauder, who saw the shoeless woman as a potential customer, and Tupperware's Brownie Wise, who saw a successful salesperson in an untested, unremarkable-looking job candidate with few credentials. Such leaders see positive endings to stories where others might not even perceive a story exists.

This ability is followed by persistence, the conviction that one can achieve a goal or perform a task as a result of one's own actions, tolerance for uncertainty, and "irrepressible resilience," the ability to bounce back from a crisis or difficult situation. Appreciative Intelligence is associated with uncommon perceptions and beliefs about accomplishing a task that rely less on the extent of abilities or resources available as how abilities and resources available can be utilized. This notion is expressed in the famous American scientist and inventor George Washington Carver's explanation for creating his own lab apparatus for experiments from bits of trash—"Equipment is not all in the laboratory, but partly in the head of the man running it."[8]

Unlike other models of intelligence, Appreciative Intelligence is linked to humans' need for meaning, vision, and value. There is intentionality about it. Appreciative Intelligence is behind creating new possibilities and helping see the steps necessary to realize them. It allows us to dream and to strive. It keeps humanity's desire for continuous improvement alive by generating new opportunities. Appreciative Intelligence is also about a way of knowing and interpreting situations. It is similar to what Viktor Frankl, survivor of a German concentration camp, wrote in his classic book, *Man's Search for Meaning,* about the power of looking horror in the face and finding leverage in it to survive. It is that capacity not to flinch or deny but to learn from failure and the things we fear. To quote Frankl, "everything can be taken from a man but one thing: the last of the human freedoms—to choose one's attitude in any given set of circumstances, to choose one's own way."[9]

Those with high Appreciative Intelligence have a capacity to endow everyday activity with a sense of purpose. Because they can reframe, they are flexible and actively and spontaneously adaptive. Seeing a situation from a new perspective allows them to deal with obstacles with courage and resilience. Because they can see what is positive and how the future unfolds from the present, they have a capacity to face adversity without letting it destroy them. They are predisposed to see the larger picture and the connections between diverse things because they can shift their frames of reality to see possibilities, not boundaries. Due to their higher capacity to embrace ambiguity, or shades of gray in situations, they can live in uncertainty without knowing the answers. Because they see how a positive future can come from the present, they live their lives with a sense of realistic optimism.

Those who possess a high level of Appreciative Intelligence lead organizations to higher incidence of innovation and creativity, more productive members, and greater ability to adapt in a changing environment. Hence, their organizations enjoy a competitive advantage, greater financial success, and greater world impact.

The identification and development of Appreciative Intelligence has far-reaching implications for individuals, organizations of all types and sizes, and our society as a whole. As we discuss further in subsequent chapters, everyone has Appreciative Intelligence to a greater or lesser degree. The most recent understanding of intelligence as a changing capacity that can be enhanced and nurtured, rather than as a static entity, leads to the conclusion that Appreciative Intelligence can be developed and enhanced. Recognizing and cultivating it means the ability to affect prosperity, health, and success on individual and organizational levels. Further ramifications are that we can shape the future we desire by choosing and grooming leaders and innovators who possess high Appreciative Intelligence and helping expand its application.

The most effective and successful people exhibit the ability to reframe, appreciate the positive, and see how the future unfolds from the present. They have Appreciative Intelligence, the ability to see the mighty oak in the acorn.

Ahead in This Book

The following ten chapters of this book are designed to walk you through a deeper introduction to the core of Appreciative Intelligence and its components through a variety of studies and real-life stories.

Chapter 2 discusses the application of this new intelligence. Appreciative Intelligence leads to four qualities—persistence, conviction that one's actions matter, tolerance for uncertainty, and irrepressible resilience—as shown in this chapter through stories of real-life leaders and innovators.

In Chapter 3, we look at Appreciative Intelligence in action by examining a school whose leaders, teachers, and mentors use their Appreciative Intelligence to shape the next generation.

Chapters 4, 5, and 6 take a closer look at the three components of Appreciative Intelligence. Chapter 4 discusses reframing. It also discusses the mysterious quirks of human perception and the effect of conscious and unconscious choices we make as we see reality. Chapter 5 further probes the second component, appreciating the positive. It includes information from the fields of Positive Psychology and Positive Organizational Behavior and discusses the methodology and technique of Appreciative Inquiry. Chapter 6 discusses the third component, seeing how the future unfolds from the present.

Chapter 7 explores the organizational effects of leaders and members with high Appreciative Intelligence. Whether an organization is a for-profit corporation or a not-for-profit institution, whether it works with adults or students and sells products or services, an organization that weaves its members' Appreciative Intelligence into the fabric of its culture displays some extraordinary practices and results.

Chapter 8 provides a Personal Appreciative Intelligence Profile and practical, concrete exercises to develop your own personal Appreciative Intelligence. The profile and exercises spring from the notions that everyone has Appreciative Intelligence to a greater or lesser degree, that intelligence isn't static, and that because our brains are continually evolving, our intelligence and behaviors can change, too.

For those of you curious about how Appreciative Intelligence came about or others who are looking for the technical background, Chapters 9 and 10 provide explanations and studies of intelligence, Positive Psychology, and the brains behind the mental processes we call Appreciative Intelligence. They discuss others' studies from the field of social cognitive neuroscience, as well as some of our analysis and insight from reading about and interviewing successful leaders and innovators.

Finally, Chapter 11 concludes with a deeper look at possibilities and implications for the future and an invitation to develop further practices and approaches to evaluation, development, and predictions of the construct. We invite others to plant their own acorns from the knowledge of this intelligence.

Leveraging Appreciative Intelligence

*The real act of discovery consists not in finding
new lands but seeing with new eyes.*
—*Marcel Proust (1871–1922)*

When people see the mighty oak in the acorn, they can change the future. They find innovative solutions. They bring out the best in people. They invent new products. Often, they and their successful ventures become magnets for other people. In our interviews with organizational leaders and innovators, we found that the ability to reframe, appreciate the positive, and see how the future unfolds from the present consistently led to the four qualities shown in Figure 2.1:

- Persistence
- Conviction that one's actions matter
- Tolerance for uncertainty
- Irrepressible resilience

Because the people we interviewed could reframe, appreciate the positive, and see how the future could unfold from the present, they could see how their end goal was possible to accomplish. Thus, they were willing to persist and to believe that their own actions and abilities would take them to a successful conclusion. Because they could envision the way a positive future could unfold from the present, they could deal with the uncertainty that often accompanies a new venture, product development, or a crisis. They exhibited irrepressible resilience, the ability to bounce

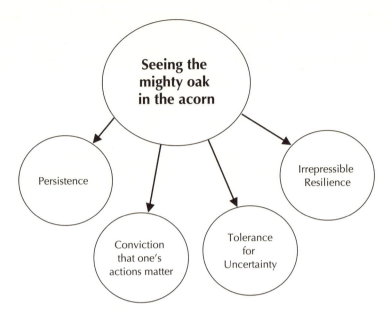

Figure 2.1: Appreciative Intelligence leads to four qualities.

back from a difficult situation, as the result of reframing, seeing what was positive in the situation, and understanding that a better future could come about despite a crisis or setback.

Consider the following business case of W. L. Gore & Associates. It illustrates the core ability of Appreciative Intelligence and the four ensuing qualities of persistence, conviction that one's own actions matter, tolerance for uncertainty, and irrepressible resilience. W. L. Gore & Associates' story of innovation and success has few parallels.

In 1958 Bill Gore, a research chemist at DuPont,[1] saw vast potential in a nonstick plastic material. Exploring its possibilities would move DuPont in a direction it did not want to pursue. So he left the company to start his own.

What began as a small business in the home of Gore and his wife Genevieve (Vieve) became an internationally known private company with 6,000 associates in 25 countries. Their initial product, insulated cables, expanded to include the fabric Gore-Tex and a vast range of goods in the automotive, electronics, music, healthcare, and aerospace industries. The last several years have seen annual sales revenue of over $1 billion. In the past two years, it has been recognized as one of the top companies to work for in Italy, Germany, the United Kingdom, and the United States.[2]

Company leaders and associates began at square one with an unusual ability to frame or reframe in positive, creative ways. Bill Gore framed corporate communication as the type of conversation that happens in a carpool, where people discuss ideas openly and candidly without the constraints of hierarchy or divisional boundaries.[3] To accomplish this, he and other early associates reframed the workplace as a flat lattice organization rather than as a typical hierarchy, and they allowed natural leadership and associates' choices to determine who led and who followed. They replaced *bosses* with *sponsors* and the term *employee* with *associate*. Early team members even reframed Vieve's kitchen appliances and utensils as lab equipment, once co-opting her eggbeater as a tool to coil cables.[4]

They also worked at seeing the best in their fellow workers, a virtue that was articulated in Gore's second guiding principle, "to encourage, help, and allow other associates to grow in knowledge, skill, and scope of responsibility."[5] Business leaders at Gore upheld that guideline as they helped product associate Matt Schreiner switch from an early work situation in which he was struggling to one where his talents were fully exercised and appreciated. According to Schreiner, their interest in his success amazed him at first. But it was that level of attention that helped him blossom and bring about business results for the organization.[6]

At any given time, the company might have hundreds of new products on the burner. Sales associate George Shaw estimated that only one in six ideas makes it to the market and becomes profitable. In various stages of development, products face technical hurdles, market changes, and a variety of other impediments. "So we need to start with a lot of ideas," Shaw added.[7] Gore encourages its associates to persist and take the risk that accompanies entrepreneurship by providing a corporate culture that accepts failure and success as part of the process. It provides support for about ten percent of their time to dabble in new ideas and money to follow through with their creative hunches.

Numerous company practices reflect Gore's acceptance of the uncertainty that is part of research and development. A "passionate champion" (Gore's term for the associate who has seen an oak in an acorn or an idea with future potential) conveys the value of the idea to other associates and enlists their help in bringing it to fruition. When a developing idea or product encounters setbacks, its champion leads the charge for finding creative solutions. Each new product goes through a "Real, Win, Worth meeting," during which associates evaluate its viability. Products deemed prospective winners continue to receive money and support; those that don't are dropped so that the company doesn't waste further resources. When initiatives fail, associates still celebrate with beer and champagne. Gore also applies lessons learned from the experience to subsequent projects. When ventures fail, associates are offered new career opportunities with other teams. In the same way associates share in the consequences of products that don't pan out, they share the financial reward of company stock when ideas become blockbusters. Gore's associates demonstrate persistence to bring a product to market, conviction that their efforts will help the company meet its objectives, and irrepressible resilience in their practices.

Persistence

The history of Glide Floss is a remarkable example of persistence in individuals and a corporation. More than 30 years passed between the day in 1971 when Bill Gore first flossed his teeth with a strand of Gore-Tex[8] and September 2003, when consumer products company Procter & Gamble bought Gore's Glide Floss business.[9] Gore associates tried unsuccessfully five times over 20 years to sell their idea of nonshred dental floss to various health care product companies. In 1991, an associate named John Spencer framed the dental floss as a medical technology product rather than as another type of consumer good. He tested the product in a clinical trial, earning the product approval of the American Dental Association.[10] Spencer then framed the initial sales campaign as one of direct marketing to local drugstores and dentists, instead of through the typical channel of a distributor. Within two years, Glide Floss had achieved enormous consumer popularity. When the company sold Glide Floss to Procter & Gamble, it was the top floss used in dental offices and the number two retail brand in the United States.[11] Without persistence in keeping the idea in company associates' minds and persistence in talking to consumers, dentists, drugstore personnel, and corporations, the product would not have survived, not to mention earning annual sales of more than $45 million.

Persistence is one of the key qualities in individuals having high Appreciative Intelligence, as exemplified in the comment of Ed Hoffman, director of NASA's Academy of Program and Project Leadership: "Success is just having the fortitude to keep going."[12]

Although academic researchers and practitioners may approach the concept of persistence and its application to daily life in slightly different ways, they concur that persistence, perseverance, or the ability to stick with a project or problem to its end, is crucial for its success. According to psychologist Jonathan Schooler, "One critical attribute involved in actively finding an alternative approach [to solving a problem] is simple perseverance. . . . because the direction in which one needs to go is unclear, one may have to search a long time before getting anywhere."[13] Similarly, according to consultant Eric Metzker, long chains of problems can seem daunting to people, and without persistence, workers may prematurely stop looking for solutions.

There are two types of persistence: behavioral and cognitive (thinking). *Behavioral persistence* is the external manifestation of concrete visible actions that are sustained over a period of time to accomplish a stated or implied goal, such as a young child's repeated walking up and down a step for 30 minutes until climbing stairs is nearly mastered. Most research conducted on persistence is on behavioral persistence, though cognitive persistence is also important. In *cognitive persistence*, an individual continues to think about a goal that may continue long after behavior to accomplish it has stopped. For example, Gore associates continued to think about developing nonshred dental floss during the 20-year period between their attempts to sell the idea to consumer product companies. Kurt Lewin, widely regarded as the founder of organizational development, and Bluma Zeigarnik, a Russian psychologist and originator of the Zeigarnik effect ("the psychological tendency to remember an uncompleted task rather than a completed one"[14]), conceptualized persistence in the early 1930s. They showed that if a goal-directed behavior is interrupted, a state of psychological tension persists, keeping the goal and goal-related thoughts activated in memory.

In the case of an architect the author observed, during renovation of an old home Greg Radford was at the top of a ladder wielding a paintbrush or tape measure hours after other workers had left the site. He described his mental tenacity during a project: "Perseverance is a virtue. It's a virtue to keep going even when you don't want to keep going."[15] Without simultaneous behavioral (continuing to paint) and cognitive (thinking about the project in between work sessions) persistence, the home would not have been completed.

Similarly, in the case of the polio eradication program, Rotarians exhibited both behavioral and cognitive persistence. They repeated requests for support and the act of immunization, examples of behavioral persistence. After a setback, they mentally grappled with issues and problems until they found a solution along each step of the way, an example of cognitive persistence. Had either type of persistence been missing, the outcome of the program would not have been so successful.

"Persistence was my job," said Rotarian Herb Pigman. "There were discouraging moments."[16] For example, in the early years of the program, there were 4000 new cases of polio in India per week. It took a few years to persuade officials to institute National Immunization Days on which all children under the age of five would receive the vaccine.

After reducing the number of polio cases in India to 258 in 2001, Rotarians learned of the resurgence in the number of cases to 1600 the following year. Again, they pushed on and brought the figure back down to 134 in 2004.[17]

According to another Rotarian, while he wouldn't have said that he or Rotary were persistent by nature—they like to "win the game and move on"—the strong vision of the end state, a world without polio, kept him at his role for more than a decade. The vision kept the program going after 20 years.

Persistence is influenced by the self-esteem of individuals. As early as 1890, well before psychologists used the term *self-esteem*, philosopher William James wrote about it as a "self-feeling that in this world depends entirely on what we back ourselves to be and do."[18] In simple terms, it is the degree to which we perceive our self positively or negatively. It is our attitude toward our own self.

Overall, high-self-esteem (HSE) individuals have a greater tendency to persist in the face of failure and obstacles. At the same time it is not blind persistence. University of British Columbia psychologists Adam Di Paula and Jennifer Campbell studied this issue in more depth, examining self-esteem, persistence, and rumination—prolonged deep thought—when encountering failure. Their experiments revealed that after a single failure, high-self-esteem participants persisted longer toward a goal than those with low self-esteem. But HSE individuals spent less time seeking a solution after repeated failure. On the other hand, LSE participants reflected on their failure longer than HSE participants did. Di Paula and Campbell concluded that people with high self-esteem tend to make more efficient use of environmental cues and deploy more effective strategies in deciding when to persist. They also concluded that individuals with high self-esteem are more likely to see the presence of alternatives, even when faced with failure, than low-self-esteem individuals.[19]

Taking cues from studies such as those just described, we believe that individuals with high Appreciative Intelligence tend to persist longer—behaviorally and cognitively—than people with low intelligence, but not indefinitely. They know when to quit and look for alternatives, as Gore did when it pruned its idea for producing coated bike cables and sprouted its guitar string business from the same coating. In the end, individuals with high Appreciative Intelligence succeed in their objectives either by perseverance or by adjusting their goals and ensuing strategies.

Individuals with high Appreciative Intelligence pay better attention to the cues in the environment and know that persevering for a goal is more important than persevering for a particular approach or task. The resulting flexibility gives rise to more ways to succeed in a project or goal. Some of the heads of the Rotarians' polio eradication program moved in and out of positions of responsibility and leadership over the 20-year period. They also changed strategies or tactics, shifting focus on cultural, organizational, or logistical issues depending on what segment of a population needed persuasion to join the efforts, donate money, or immunize their children. In other words, they paid attention to the changing environmental challenges and cues for solutions and adapted the program to fit a dynamic context. But according to Rotarian Bill Sergeant, what made the project survive was the long-lasting goal "to protect those who can't protect themselves—little children," he said. "It helped the project survive. [It] was going to help the most beloved part of human society."[20]

Conviction That One's Actions Matter

Psychologists refer to the belief or judgment that one can achieve a goal or perform a task as a result of one's own actions as "self-efficacy." It is the confidence that a person has in his or her abilities to bring about the motivation, mental resources, and plan of action needed to accomplish a particular task in a given situation.[21]

Stanford University Psychologist Albert Bandura first introduced the construct of self-efficacy in 1977 and later showed that individuals create their own belief systems that allow them to be more proactive and in control of their own lives.[22] Accordingly, how individuals behave is more dependent on the beliefs they hold about their capabilities (self-efficacy beliefs) than by what they are actually capable of accomplishing. These self-efficacy beliefs exercise a measure of control over individuals' thoughts, feelings, and actions. They influence the choices they make and determine how much effort they will expend on an activity or how resilient they will be when confronted with challenges. The higher the self-efficacy, the greater the persistence and resilience.

Bandura also introduced the concept of "reciprocal determinism," the notion that thoughts, feelings, and environmental factors influence one another, creating an interdependent system.[23] In other words, people evaluate their experiences through self-reflection. Their reflections may match closely to what others may have observed, perceived, and described. Sometimes, however, because of factors such as mood or physical wellness/illness, their evaluations may be quite different from others'. These reflections then lead to beliefs about their competencies or abilities, which, in turn, influence the ways in which they behave.

For example, Rotarians' beliefs that they were effective in maneuvering through bureaucracies, diplomatic communicators, and competent problem-solvers influenced their actual abilities to take action. Bill Sergeant remarked, "Usually in Rotary, we start with something that we can accomplish."

Psychologists Frank Pajares and Dale Schunk have pointed out that self-perceptions of capability help determine what individuals do with the knowledge and skills they have. More important, their beliefs about their abilities are critical determinants of how well knowledge and skills are acquired in the first place. The process of creating and using self-beliefs is an intuitive and appreciative one: Individuals engage in a behavior, interpret the results of their actions, use these interpretations to create and develop beliefs about their capability to engage in subsequent behaviors in similar domains, and behave in concert with the beliefs created. Pajares and Schunk also indicate, following Bandura's findings, that it is therefore not surprising that people with strong self-efficacy take on more challenging tasks, increase their efforts if they think they might fail, and recover quickly after unexpected failures. Furthermore, if individuals with strong convictions in their abilities fail, they assume that they failed because they did not try hard enough or did not have the relevant knowledge. So in further attempts, they try harder after acquiring the knowledge they believed was necessary for success. People with low self-efficacy, on the other hand, often exaggerate the perceived difficulty level of the job demands around them.[24]

Closely related to self-efficacy is the construct of self-fulfilling prophecies, a term coined by sociologist Robert Merton in 1948.[25] Self-fulfilling prophecies are predictions or expectations that, irrespective of typical cause-effect relationship, come true. As an illustration, Merton pointed out that during the depression era of the 1930s, many banks collapsed despite being solvent because large numbers of customers withdrew their money after hearing rumors that the banks were going to become insolvent. As we know now, the banks eventually failed because of these large-scale withdrawals. In this case, the expectation (fear) of the account holders came true because of their own actions.

Self-fulfilling prophecies work for positive expectations, too. Gore's business leaders told Matt Schreiner that he had talent and asked whether he would like to switch projects, thus creating positive expectations that contributed to Schreiner's own belief in his abilities and his actual success. In the best-selling book *Organizing Genius*, authors Warren Bennis and Patricia Ward Biederman described the mindset of collaborative groups that changed the world by accomplishing huge feats (such as the Disney animators who created the film *Snow White* and the young technologists who invented the Macintosh computer): "Not knowing what they can't do puts everything in the realm of the possible."[26]

In a battle against the odds, a friend recovered from a rare and life-threatening condition in great part because of his self-fulfilling prophecy that he would survive. After a 67-day hospital visit, he went home for further recuperation looking like a healthy person. "Denial would have been not acknowledging that I was going to die," he said. But the possibility of death wasn't even in his mind to refute. "I knew I was sick, but I really believed I would live," he said. His understanding of the power of such beliefs was first learned as a young boy in an experience that many readers might recognize as familiar. During his first attempt at riding a bicycle, he realized halfway down the street that he couldn't hear his sister's footsteps as she ran alongside and held up the bike. Although he had been pedaling and balancing successfully on his own for a while, when he discovered she was no longer there, he and the bike ended up on the ground. He now works with cancer patients and others to learn how to mentally reframe their notions of disease, treatment, or any other challenge in a positive light. He also helps them build their own positive self-fulfilling prophecies.[27]

In the words of American sociologist and educator William Isaac Thomas: "If men define situations as real, they are real in their consequences."[28] As the leaders whom we interviewed believed they could accomplish tasks and achieve their goals, they could and did.

Feeling confident and competent to achieve a task may stem, in part, from positive self-talk, an occurrence reported by a number of leaders we interviewed. Whether aloud, inside their heads, or even by affirming one's abilities to a group, they spoke about the ways they *could* find a solution or achieve a goal.

According to Charlie Pellerin, when the Hubble telescope was found to be flawed, he first felt anger. But his anger gave way to a feeling of proactive ability. "What matters is the story in your mind," he said. Whether a person feels powerful, aggressive, or victimized is largely shaped by the stories he tells himself, a principle that Pellerin tells his leadership session attendees and follows himself. The story that Pellerin said he tells himself is that of Davy Crockett—not the Hollywood version, he emphasized, but that of the successful and independent early American Congressman who said, "Be always sure you are right, then go ahead," Pellerin quoted.[29]

In another case, a dancer and choreographer who founded a troupe with the fundamental ideal of dispelling myths that dancers must look alike and women must be very thin to be beautiful said that each time she sees an advertisement that disturbs her, she thinks, "The students and dancers in my community won't feel that way," further motivating her to action.[30]

Pellerin and others whose positive self-talk took the form of stories were actually using a complex type of framing called story framing. According to Kirk Hallahan, "story framing involves (a) selecting key themes or ideas that are the focus of the message and (b) incorporating a variety of storytelling or narrative techniques that support that theme."[31] Any number of Crockett's positive attributes—independence, courage, or taking action after determining a correct path—could be selected as the focus of the message or the salient feature. The story itself, a narrative technique, was used to relay the key message and to move the listener, in this case Pellerin himself, to action.

As psychologist Albert Bandura also pointed out, "Unless people believe that they can produce desired effects and forestall undesired ones by their actions, they have little incentive to act. Whatever other factors may operate as motivators, they are rooted in the core belief that one has the power to produce desired results."[32] This proactive, positive conviction that their actions matter is very much present in people with high Appreciative Intelligence.

Tolerance for Uncertainty

Intelligence and insight experts Robert Sternberg and Todd Lubart contend that "the creatively insightful person seeks the paths that others avoid or even fear; he or she is willing to take risks and stray from the conventional."[33]

The ability to successfully reach toward the unknown, to take risks, and to grapple with the discomfort of uncertainty or ambiguity—even to feel comfortable with it—is the second quality that stems from Appreciative Intelligence. To understand how the two relate, first we need to explain the concepts of uncertainty and ambiguity.

Uncertainty and ambiguity are related to cognitive dissonance, a psychological term that refers to the discomfort people feel when new ideas or experiences seem to contradict what they already know or believe. To accept incongruous information, they must either find a way to relate the new and unfamiliar to something that is familiar or change their current belief or knowledge systems, the latter of which is no simple task. When the pain of accepting contradictory information is too great, people cannot accommodate it, and they reach a point of inability to learn the information at that time. Because of the mental struggle that occurs through this process, most people have a difficult time tolerating dissonance and make significant efforts to reduce it.

People can also experience uneasiness or pain associated with uncertainty or ambiguity during periods of change. During transitions caused by relocating to a new geographic area, switching jobs, changing family structures, or a variety of other reasons, familiar behavior patterns and relationships get replaced with new and different ones. People believe they know what to expect, or at least the range of possibilities, that occur under familiar circumstances. New behavior patterns and relationships that don't mesh with the old leave people confused, uncertain about what the future may hold, or struggling to make the contradictory old and new patterns fit together. To understand the strength of the discomfort with uncertainty, one need look no further than the victims of Hurricane Katrina and the devastation of New Orleans in 2005 who preferred to live in damaged houses amid bacteria-infested floodwaters over evacuating to locations far from home and with unknown consequences.

For the sake of this description and discussion of leaders with high Appreciative Intelligence, we refer to uncertainty or ambiguity as dealing with two seemingly contradictory ideas at one time, not knowing an answer, not knowing how to resolve a problem, or being unable to foresee the result of a given situation.

While ambiguity and uncertainty can lead to conflict and discomfort, there are benefits that arise from the process of resolving or making sense of contradictory ideas. Ambiguity can spark new ideas or products and generate mental energy, excitement, and creative tension.

One example of the benefits of new and conflicting ideas was a fresh set of work habits and co-worker interactions that followed the introduction of an unfamiliar technology tool. MIT researcher Wanda Orlikowski studied the early experimental use of the group collaboration software Lotus Notes at a large management consulting firm. "Notes," as the program was commonly called, sought to simulate a real-life organizational environment. It allowed its users to share information using features such as file replication and to collaborate virtually in real time. At the time (early 1990s), such use of groupware technology was "outside the box," a revolutionary concept. Although the use of e-mail was common, those who used software applications used personal tools such as spreadsheets or word processing documents in an individualized way, such as they would use a pen or stapler. The concept of collaborative technology tools seemed contradictory to some people—if one wouldn't use a stapler as a group tool, why would one use another tool that way? Employees began framing the product as "big e-mail" and "networks," or expanded versions of familiar products. As time passed and they became more comfortable with using Lotus Notes, their initial ambiguity was replaced by a better understanding and comfort level regarding the uses of the software. Eventually, use of Notes led to new practices and interactions.[34] Over the years, Notes has played a key role in helping computer users rethink how they send messages, synchronize calendars, and work together on projects regardless of geographic location.

Out of the messiness and chaos of ambiguity arise new knowledge, ideas, and opportunities to frame reality differently. Thus, it is no wonder that decades later, management and psychology experts are exploring the role of ambiguity in organizational leadership[35] and decision making.[36]

We found evidence of high tolerance for uncertainty, ambiguity, and dissonance in the leaders, inventors, and innovators we studied. While for many people the feeling of being "up in the air" is so difficult that they would rather deal with a negative conclusion than not know whether the ending will be positive or negative, the leaders we studied appeared to possess the ability to suspend those feelings of discomfort. Living one of the philosophies of Starbucks founder Howard Schultz,[37] they "risk more than others think safe."

Psychologist Joshua Correll and his research team suggested an explanation for dealing with ambiguity that relates to high self-esteem and self-efficacy, or the quality of conviction that one's actions matter. Through a study of students' attitudes toward an increase in tuition fees, their values, and their feelings of self-worth, the researchers found that the participants with the greatest levels of self-affirmation were able to pay attention to videotapes of persuasive debates about an increase in tuition payments that challenged their opinions. Correll and his team concluded that higher self-affirmation limited defensive reactions to conflicting viewpoints and enabled openmindedness.[38] We infer from their conclusions that individuals with high levels of Appreciative Intelligence are more open to challenging situations, contexts that are unfamiliar, or possibilities that seem threatening because they are new.

The ability to tolerate uncertainty allowed leaders with high Appreciative Intelligence to deal with new or risky situations on a number of levels. First, they were able to deal with their own dissonance long enough to investigate the seemingly contradictory pieces of information, thoughts, or beliefs until they made sense of the new with the old. For instance, Charlie Pellerin said he had never even considered the Hubble Telescope mirror flaw a result of leadership failure, as Congress deemed it. But he was able to consider the possibility to such extent that he went on to study leadership and apply his knowledge to the practice of benchmarking and diagnosing the strength of other organizations' teams.

Second, they had the ability to tolerate the longer periods of uncertainty that are required to develop innovative products or start a new organization—to take entrepreneurial risk. They were able to control or ignore the discomfort of not knowing whether or when a product or organization would become profitable or investments would be returned, long enough to innovate the product or start the new venture.

Beyond tolerating their own uncertainty, the leaders we interviewed coped with the reactions to uncertainty in others. By bringing new ideas into the open, leaders can cause discomfort in others by displacing old ideas and beliefs. Such discomfort in others could potentially take a toll on a leaders' or innovators' acceptance, credibility, or pocketbook. But they helped others deal with uncertainty, often by reframing situations to help them see what was positive, how the future could unfold from the present, and by encouraging persistence until what was unknown became known.

Dean Kamen, founder of FIRST and DEKA Research, has faced resistance to some of his innovative ideas. He discussed the exclusive relationship of stability and innovation. Managers seek stability, and in doing so they avoid risk and failure, he said. But for innovation to occur there must be some risk and the willingness to accept failure or setbacks as part of a learning process before finding a new solution. He related it to the field of medicine: "As you're going into surgery, you don't want to hear the surgeon say, 'I'm trying something new today,'" Kamen said. People want procedures that are proven successful.[39] His ability to deal with the contradiction of stability and innovation has allowed him to work with needs of the medical community and that of the general public for consistent success, while he and his company undertake the challenge to develop new medical devices. A high tolerance for uncertainty kept the door open for DEKA's invention of a new type of medical stent (a medical device to keep a blood vessel open) that was used in Vice President Dick Cheney's heart surgery.

In the case of W. L. Gore & Associates, company leaders codified strategies to help associates and the organization as a whole deal with entrepreneurial uncertainty. The company supports time for associates to work on new ideas, celebrates failures as well as successes, and helps find new positions within the company for associates whose projects have ended. When associates understand that an unsuccessful project or one that doesn't make it to market doesn't mean that their livelihood and well-being are threatened, much of the fear of uncertainty is replaced with a sense of curiosity and freedom to explore new ideas.

Irrepressible Resilience

The fourth quality, and the one we saw most often in stories and interview notes of people with superior Appreciative Intelligence, was that of irrepressible resilience, the ability to bounce back from difficult situations. The ability to reframe or reinterpret a given situation enabled them to perceive that a positive consequence could be built from even the most drastic or devastating circumstances. Rather than experiencing a position of impossibility, and therefore a situation without hope or remedy, intelligent leaders showed the capacity to see what is possible and to set a plan of action with concrete steps to create the envisioned positive state.

Irrepressible resilience is different from persistence. Persistence is perseverance or sticking with particular actions or thoughts until a goal is achieved, whereas resilience is a quality present in an individual that allows him or her to maintain a certain strength against adversity. A resilient individual makes positive adjustments when circumstances become challenging. Irrepressible resilience is the quality of not buckling under stress and returning to a state of strength despite weakening forces around.

One company president's comment reflected the sentiment of others we interviewed: "I honestly think we can turn almost any change into an advantage. That sounds unrealistic, but time bears me out. We got through the dot-com boom [and bust] fine. We got through the economic downturn fine. We're battle hardened—short of a neutron bomb, we'd be just fine."

Leaders with high Appreciative Intelligence showed a range of emotions when initially encountering a challenge. They felt anger, sadness, or betrayal, depending on the circumstances and extent of the challenge. But in a relatively short period of time, sometimes days or even minutes, they became flexible, adapted, and moved back into a positive emotional state as well as began work on the crisis or situation at hand. They ultimately survived regardless of the environment. They framed their situation for a better view of the future and addressed the present with the belief that they could achieve their goal. "I'm convinced there's almost nothing you can't work your way out of. It's just problem-solving," said architect Greg Radford.

Further than simply surviving, some leaders and innovators bounced back higher from challenges than the position from which they began. Embodying the philosopher Nietzsche's quotation, "That which does not destroy [or kill] me, makes me stronger," they turned challenging situations into opportunities to thrive.

Gore associate George Shaw discussed the irrepressible resilience of the leaders who helped the company through unforeseen disappointments. People may initially feel upset when things don't go right, he said, "but the group moves on." In an early company story of resilience, some of the first Gore-Tex clothing leaked at the seams. Holes made by sewing had not been sealed, Shaw explained. The company replaced the garments. Then it bounced back from the setback with lessons about the value of its corporate reputation and retaining a stake in quality control when partnering with other manufacturers on Gore products, thus preventing future mistakes, said Shaw.[40]

The understanding of resilience has received renewed attention in recent years and appears in a variety of publications. A recent doctoral dissertation by Michael Philip Hand, for instance, clarified the optimal levels of optimism, perceived locus of control (similar to self-efficacy), hope, and degree of adversity experienced in life, in the development and maintenance of psychological resilience.[41] Hand found that negative life experience, rather than positive life experience, was predictive of stronger correlations between optimism and hope, optimism and control, and hope and control. In the book, *The Beethoven Factor: The New Positive Psychology of Hardiness, Happiness, Healing and Hope*, Paul Pearsall, author and neuropsychologist, discussed the importance of resilience. He defined it as the ability to thrive in the face of adversity, as in the case of Beethoven, who wrote his Ninth Symphony (with Friedrich Schiller's "Ode to Joy" as the choral text of the last movement) after he became deaf.[42]

Another recent book, *Resilience at Work: How to Succeed No Matter What Life Throws at You*,[43] discusses the core elements of "hardiness." In this book Salvadore Maddi, a psychologist at the University of California, Irvine, and consultant, identified these elements in his 12-year research project at Illinois Bell Telephone twenty years earlier. The telephone company experienced significant organizational change and downsizing, which, predictably, produced severe emotional stress in most employees. Maddi and his research team examined the annual reviews and psychological evaluations of some 450 executives. Out of those employees, about half lost their jobs, and close to two-thirds were affected by stress-related disorders such as high blood pressure, psychological problems, or drug and alcohol abuse. Yet the researchers noticed one positive aspect amidst the misery: Approximately one-third of the executives experienced professional development (upward career mobility) and good mental health. The researchers referred to these executives as "the resilient group" and sought to explain the difference between its members and the others. Maddi's team isolated and identified three basic attitudes: commitment, control, and challenge. As authors Maddi and Khoshaba indicated in their book, the resilient group employed these attitudes and social support to make the best situation of their circumstances and to personally change for the better.

In yet another book entitled *The Survivor Personality: Why Some People Are Stronger, Smarter, and More Skillful at Handling Life's Difficulties . . . and How You Can Be, Too*, author Al Siebert discussed the answer to the question he posed about World War II survivors: When faced with adversity or tragedy, what makes one person crumble and another survive? Siebert discovered that World War II combat survivors were less like the bold, lone hero character played by Sylvester Stallone in the movie *Rambo* and more like the irreverent surgeon played by Alan Alda in the extremely popular television show of the 1970s and 80s, *M*A*S*H*. Years of subsequent research taught Siebert that those who survive (and thrive) often respond to challenge with humor, wisdom, and mental and emotional flexibility.[44]

Barbara Frederickson, researcher and director of the Positive Emotions and Psychophysiology Laboratory at the University of Michigan, and a team of researchers interviewed a group of people in early 2001 to learn about their optimism and resilience. As part of the study, they assessed individuals' resilience using a scale with items, such as "I quickly get over and recover after being startled," to which participants would respond. Only a few months later, the September 11 tragedy occurred. Her team contacted the earlier study participants and, in follow-up interviews, asked them what emotions they were feeling and what they had learned from the attacks. They found that while nearly every person interviewed felt angry, sad, or afraid, those who were identified as resilient in the earlier study were less likely to feel depressed, felt more positive emotions such as gratitude to be alive and safe, and reported that they had learned something from the crisis.[45]

In a range of studies researchers have found that resilience is related to the conditions that help individuals, like those in our Appreciative Intelligence interviews, succeed. People with resilience are perceptive, insightful, and open to new experiences,[46] factors that may allow those with Appreciative Intelligence to come up with and act on solutions that haven't been tried previously. Highly resilient individuals may have a greater capacity to learn from the lumps and bumps in the road and to use that knowledge to deal with future potholes.[47] According to Frederickson, people's positive emotions open the way for expanded cognition and behavior, which in turn build their "physical, intellectual, and social resources"[48]—one explanation of how leaders with high levels of Appreciative Intelligence are able to generate the future they see in the present.

People with high levels of Appreciative Intelligence see the oak in the acorn. They also go beyond—they plant their acorns and persevere to help them grow. While others may doubt the potential of the acorns, these leaders believe in their own and others' abilities to water and fertilize the plants from sapling to tall oak. They deal with the risk and uncertainty that comes with planting something new and hoping for growth. Finally, they find a way for the oaks to survive and thrive despite unpredictable circumstances or a challenging environment.

Chapter 3

Appreciative Intelligence in Action

The ultimate function of a prophecy is not to tell
the future, but to make it.[1]
—*W. Warren Wagar*

In the thick of our research and writing, a unique example of an organization "walking the talk" about Appreciative Intelligence emerged. It brilliantly exemplified the three components of Appreciative Intelligence and the four qualities that stem from it, and it highlighted the results of Appreciative Intelligence in action. It underscored the power of leaders with high Appreciative Intelligence to make a positive difference and change the future by applying Appreciative Intelligence to work with a younger generation.

Carol, one of the authors, walked into Delaware Valley Friends School (DVFS), an innovative college-preparatory school in the suburbs of Philadelphia for students who have learning differences. As she watched students make homemade pasta in a cooking class, study for a science exam, and talk with a teacher about geometric figures, it was difficult to comprehend that most of the teens she observed had floundered academically and personally at previous schools.

Because of challenges with dyslexia, other difficulties with reading and writing, or Attention Deficit Disorder, they had been incorrectly labeled as "lazy, stupid or crazy."[2] Most had initially arrived at the doorstep of DVFS carrying a legacy of failure. They failed at learning the first thing they had been taught publicly alongside their peers—to read and write. That early breakdown in education progressed to a downward spiral as each year of school required them to build further knowledge based on skills they had not acquired. Consequently, most students entered with learned strategies of avoidance and failure, reduced self-esteem, and limited curiosity. Katherine Schantz, head of school, described the students' mindset at the outset of their acceptance at DVFS: "All their hope has been dampened."[3]

From grades seven through twelve, the school works to turn that mindset around by turning the students' experiences around. Taking a multi-sensory approach to teaching and learning, and using an innovative and structured pedagogy, they teach students to read the same novels taught in other schools around the country and to write research papers as their peers elsewhere do. The school provides a wide variety of other learning experiences such as rock climbing, cooking, and digital photography in addition to traditional academics. Classes are taught by nontraditional teachers (some with learning differences themselves)—not necessarily those with special education degrees, but people who are intellectually curious and passionate about the subjects they teach and who have the ability to rekindle the love of learning in their students. Beneath it all is the school's appreciative philosophy: "to nurture the unique personal worth and potential good inherent in each individual."[4]

The history of the school itself is an entrepreneurial story of creative insight and reframing a need as an opportunity. It was begun in 1986 by heads of several schools who became concerned that there was no college-preparatory program serving students with reading and writing learning differences in the Philadelphia area. Flying in the face of traditional practice (their venture was described by some as a harebrained scheme, in fact) they did not start with an elementary school and expand to a secondary school. Starting with early grades would have been a less expensive proposition—fewer specialty educators required by the state would have meant fewer teachers' salaries to pay. Furthermore, filling the roll books would have been easier if they started with lower grades and naturally expanded to later grades as students grew older. Ignoring the obvious and traditional approach, however, the founders sought to start where they deemed the greater need. A principal (head of school), a few staff members, and five full-time teachers who left other teaching positions began the school by recruiting students in grades seven through eleven who needed a fresh start in the educational system.

The month before DVFS was to open, the founders hadn't enrolled enough students to meet their financial obligations. Since they had left their previous jobs, they decided to make a go of it anyway. The gamble paid off. By September, the beginning of the academic year, they met their minimum enrollment. Over the next decade, the school grew from 21 students to a steady enrollment of 150+ students. They moved from an old rented building to a permanent site with top-notch facilities and pleasant surroundings in a small, but bustling, community.

Nearly every inch of the Delaware Valley Friends School—its mission and principles, history, leadership, and student body—exemplifies the ability to frame appreciatively for a positive future and see that future unfolding from the present. DVFS reframes the entire notion of school and education for students as a place where they are successful and where they get "a jump-start on life,"[5] rather than as a place where kids fail and don't learn. DVFS is designed to help students and their parents see that they are at the heart of the organization, not at the periphery or at the left edge of a bell curve, as students had been at previous schools. Students who had been formerly labeled as learning disabled are taught that they have learning differences that can be overcome by remediation, compensation, and accommodation. In other words, they can succeed through taking new approaches for building skills, looking for compensating behavior to address needs, or simply refocusing on what abilities are at-hand, rather than abilities that don't exist.

The school is also a vivid example of an organization where Appreciative Intelligence is woven into the fabric of the larger group and community, so that appreciative behaviors perpetuate and success is generated beyond its walls. As described by Bill Keeney, the school's director of professional development and an English teacher, "the institution is the star—not the individual leader. [It] depends on commitment, loyalty and talents of many people. From its founding, our philosophy and focus have shaped the institution. That focus on the worth of every individual informs everything we do. It lets students see they are capable, valued and important members of the community. They will achieve. They're smart and capable and will find a way."[6]

Just as DVFS staff extends their Appreciative Intelligence throughout the student body, they teach what they know at workshops and training sessions in the school and at professional conferences. DVFS students also perpetuate the practices of reframing for possibilities and success, and seeing the best in others. After learning about Eye-to-Eye, a mentoring program that pairs college and elementary students who live with similar learning differences, DVFS students started their own mentoring program, the first of its kind for high school and elementary-aged students with similar challenges. Without formally addressing their differences, the mentors show younger students how to navigate school and social interactions by engaging in sports, games, and art projects and reading books together—by simply having fun. In another example of perpetuating success, graduates return on Alumni Day each year to share the ways they have overcome obstacles and won personal victories at college and in later careers.

The results speak for themselves: 98% of DVFS graduates go on to college,[7] a statistic way beyond the national average of 64%.[8] Students hold an impressive list of awards and recognition—National Merit Scholars, a Brooklyn Bridge Film Festival grand prize, and Most Creative in Show award at the Philadelphia Furniture and Furnishings Show. Graduates have gone on to become teachers and business owners. They hold positions in the fields of broadcasting and psychology. One graduate is pursuing her Ph.D. in Reading, Writing and Literacy; another has earned a law degree (J.D.) and is clerking for a judge. Another has helped found two schools in Ghana. Other success stories are invisible and have never received public recognition, but they cannot be underestimated. The yearbook of one teacher holds a rare end-of-year autograph from a high school boy—"Thanks so much for an excellent two years. . . . you helped me develop self-advocacy skills." The cycle of success that is begun at the school feeds itself and continues.

Using concrete examples from Delaware Valley Friends School, readers can see the highlights of Appreciative Intelligence in action. Readers can also use these main points to reflect, model, adapt, and enhance their own behaviors, thought patterns, qualities, and Appreciative Intelligence.

The Components of Appreciative Intelligence at DVFS

Appreciative Intelligence is the ability to perceive the positive inherent generative potential within the present. Its three components—the ability to reframe, to appreciate the positive, and to see how the future unfolds from the present—are very much evident in DFVS.

Reframing

Head of school Katherine Schantz concurs with students who wrote and designed a booklet about DVFS that said the school is about "seeing things differently." It reframes learning disabilities as learning differences, not disabilities or handicaps. It has selected the part of reality that is positive and allows opportunities toward progress in learning, rather than selecting the view that there are roadblocks (disabilities) to learning. What is salient, or most visible and important, to this view is that nontraditional paths to education can provide solutions when different learning styles exist.

English teacher and director of professional development Bill Keeney helps others understand the different view of learning. To help them reframe, he uses the following analogy and scenario with teachers, students, and members of the outside community to show them the importance of considering many possibilities when solving problems. Imagine that we're part of a basketball team, he says. We have a game at the end of the week, but we can't dribble the ball very well. We'll practice dribbling so we get better. But since we can't get really good at dribbling in less than a week, we must figure out how to get the ball up the court another way—by throwing, for example. Then Keeney applies the analogy to the skill acquisition at hand. There are strategies like this for writing, including technology—using electronic spelling checkers, for example, he says.

One of the more creative and unique examples of reframing by the school is that of the role of the library. According to DVFS's librarian/media center specialist, Dave Brubaker, for students with dyslexia or other reading challenges a library is a new place for exploration. If books are the media most difficult for students to access, there needs to be another way of addressing needs for finding information about a complex world or learning about different cultures.[9]

While the school was redesigning its library, the staff had a scary thought, said Schantz: "What if we built the library and kids didn't come?"

To address that concern, they designed the library to entice kids to enter and to make it their own space. Immediately inside the door, stacks of colorful, interesting, and age-appropriate magazines—*Surfer*,

National Geographic, *MAD*, *MacWorld*, *Imagine*, and *Sports Illustrated*, to name but a few—run the length of the wall. Comfortable chairs between bookshelves create a relaxed atmosphere; walls made of the type of glass used in discos reduce noise between library sections but provide a view of people and activity.

"The library is not just a place of reading," continued Brubaker. "It's a place of collaboration, a place to organize, produce and express ideas. This is a space for putting things together and practicing public speaking." Through careful design, the school reframed the library not as the traditional institution of the quiet place for reading and research but as a vibrant and vital learning space where students like to gather.

Appreciating the Positive

The school sees not just any oak, but the mighty oak. Rather than focusing on an ability that is not present, or focusing on the negative, Bill Keeney looks for an ability a student possesses—one that can help accomplish a task a different way. He looks for new ways to reach his students to teach them reading and writing. He doesn't simply repeat the approach used in traditional classes or expect students to learn the same way he did. He determines whether a student who hasn't completed an assignment "can't or won't," and figures out ways he or she "can" learn the skill. Ultimately, he respects the fact that they may not go to college to become English majors but will find their own unique specialties.[10]

Nearly everything the school does is for the purpose of bringing about the success of its students. Staff and administration look beyond the students' past academic records to see and show how bright the kids really are. They work from the understanding that the students have other intelligences and unique, special abilities. The school has designed a curriculum to reveal and enhance talents. Internships with local ad agencies, landscape designers, or carpenters, ABLE (Adventure Based Learning Experiences in bike touring, rock climbing, and ropes courses), and art classes help students learn their competencies.

"We make it clear to the students that what they've been beaten over the head with—that reading, writing and math are the most important things—isn't all there is. We honor other abilities, skills and intelligences," said Keeney. "[The head of school] reminds us that there is more to the students. We must keep other skills in view for them. We must help them develop so other paths will open for them. We can't predict what their paths will be, so we keep their opportunities available."[11]

The student-designed school booklet also quotes "Matt," a Northeastern graduate: "DVFS taught me to capitalize on my strengths which, fortunately, they recognized."

Seeing How the Future Unfolds from the Present

Appreciative Intelligence is about using what is positive in the present to connect with and build the future. The student-designed booklet about DVFS emphasizes, "It's about becoming the person you already are."[12] To help students achieve their greatest potential, faculty and staff—and eventually students themselves—look for learning abilities and skills already present in the students. Rather than seeking to create something where abilities don't exist because of neurological differences, they work with what abilities do exist in order to develop talents and find alternative strategies for learning necessary life skills.

The school Web site describes the institution. "It is a place where optimism—a dream for the future—is secured by the foundation of hope. Hope is the acquired belief that dreams can come true."[13] The pervasive mindset of the administration and faculty is that skills can be put into action and possibilities can be realized.

The Four Ensuing Qualities of Appreciative Intelligence

Appreciative Intelligence leads to four qualities: persistence, conviction that one's actions matter, tolerance for uncertainty, and irrepressible resilience. All four are evident at DVFS.

People with high Appreciative Intelligence show persistence of thought until a project or goal is achieved, and they show persistence in behavior until a task is completed. Teachers and administrators at DVFS exhibit both types of persistence and help students develop that quality. If a student at DVFS isn't completing homework assignments or is failing a subject, teachers continually try to determine what is behind the problem (persistence of thought). They figure out whether it's an issue of challenges due to learning differences, avoidance of an assignment, or something else that is preventing completion of a task. They determine whether it's a matter that the student "can't or won't" do the work, the same way Keeney determines whether a student is unable to write a paper because of obstacles with language skills or attitude. Teachers keep providing alternative methods or new strategies when working with the student (persistence of behavior). "We don't give up on them," said a teacher.

People with high Appreciative Intelligence also believe that they can achieve a goal or perform a task as a result of their own actions. They spend less time looking for the greener grass on the other side of the fence than they do making use of or fertilizing what is growing nearby.

According to the head of the school, "Self-esteem doesn't come from teachers being nice. It comes from successful experiences." While the faculty works with the students in supportive and caring ways, the school's observation that conviction in one's own actions stems from successful experiences supports the notion that what is "green" must ultimately be seen by the students as coming from within themselves, rather than elsewhere. The school's varied curriculum (such as the art and cooking classes, ABLE, and a new drama program in addition to traditional academics) and outside activities (such as the Eye-to-Eye mentoring program to help younger students succeed, photography contests, and sports) set up students to win and experience competency in numerous ways.

In a particular instance, one student wanted very much to go to college. But when she arrived at DVFS, she believed she would never be able to read and write competently. She assumed she would work in her parents' business, which required more physical labor than reading and writing. With hard work and a change in her self-fulfilling prophecies, she learned the necessary skills, graduated from high school, and entered college last year. During a break, she returned to DVFS to show a teacher a three-page paper she had written. She said she was confident she could survive in the academic arena although writing was not a natural skill for her.

People at DVFS also demonstrated the importance of positive self-talk. Whether aloud, inside their heads, or even by affirming their abilities to a group, they spoke about the ways they could find a solution or achieve a goal. When a student once told a teacher that she couldn't write an essay, Keeney told her, "If you say that, you won't be able to. Your brain heard that and it will believe it." By working with the student to change the story she told herself and others, as well as working on the necessary writing skills, the student was able to finish the paper.[14]

Like others with superior Appreciative Intelligence, a number of members of the DVFS community showed tolerance for uncertainty and helped others learn to deal with their discomfort. They helped them deal with seemingly contradictory information and risk. They used the chaos of ambiguous ideas to spark innovation and creativity. According to Katherine Schantz, Delaware Valley Friends School is a place where students "dare to be successful, one of the scariest dares in life because there is no more complex fear than the fear of success."[15] She explained that fear. Success is accompanied by expectations to be consistent and persistent and to demonstrate further success. To meet those expectations requires a high level of energy and focus, characteristics that students haven't necessarily shown in the past. Based on their history, they don't know whether they will be able to succeed in school. When they experience their first success at DVFS, they don't trust that success, Schantz continued. They believe that it was a fluke. They must first learn they can succeed in academic or other contexts. Then they must learn that they can experience a few failures along the way and still be an overall success.

When students believe they are academic failures, the first time they learn that they can succeed, the information contradicts everything they know. The school staff asks students to suspend that belief and to trust that teachers will help them learn and succeed. At the same time, the school provides opportunities for success and new strategies for acquiring skills. As students risk believing they can succeed in school, they find new ways for learning what they need to know and to strengthen their other talents. By daring to become successful, they find their own paths to personal success.

Graduates of DVFS also apply the ability to deal with uncertainty and risk to their ventures in later life. For instance, one alumnus opened a hair salon and subsequently started a successful salon franchise despite challenges in reading, writing, and math.

At each level of the school, people also exhibited irrepressible resilience. The founding teachers, who struggled when low enrollment nearly kept them from making payroll or opening the doors to the school on its first day, exhibited irrepressible resilience when they rallied and grew enrollment to more than 150 students over time. They fought self-doubt they might have had when enrollment was low or the necessary material and financial resources were not yet at hand.

The students at DVFS—despite failure in previous schools and past inability to function well in a regular academic environment—overcome their history, dyslexia and other learning differences, and low self-esteem. Using alternative strategies, such as technology, collaborative learning, talking with friends, and developing strategic thinking, they succeed. They channel their energy with focus and determination to accomplish their goals. They graduate, earn scholarships, win awards, and go to college.

Although Appreciative Intelligence is an individual ability, leaders and innovators have impact on their environment and build organizations and systems that exhibit a culture of Appreciative Intelligence. Often by deliberate design, they embed principles and processes of Appreciative Intelligence into their daily routines and the foundations of their organizations. They help others develop and enhance their own Appreciative Intelligence. So it is with Delaware Valley Friends School. As mentioned previously in this chapter, "the institution is the star—not the individual leader. . . . From its founding, our philosophy and focus have shaped the institution. That focus on the worth of every individual informs everything we do. It lets students see they are capable, valued and important members of the community."

The founders of the school set the tone for the organization through the mission that still exists today, in part to "nurture the unique personal worth and potential good inherent in each individual . . . The school also recognizes that it has a responsibility to share its expertise with teachers and students beyond the school community."

In addition to designing a library that would entice students to make use of its resources, the school reframed the cafeteria as well, naming it "The Café" and redesigning the physical space for added room for circulation. By design, it encouraged students' families and guests to spend more time eating and talking with their children and each other.

Clearly, the founders exhibited Appreciative Intelligence when they founded the school. Likewise, teachers, administration, and staff demonstrate Appreciative Intelligence as they bring out the best in their students, help them see possibilities for the future, and reframe school as a place of hope and learning. Although we cannot jump to conclusions without further knowledge and empirical study, and although we recognize that the idea will seem provocative for some, based on our initial observations we also believe that the students are unconsciously modeling their teachers' behaviors and mindset and developing the Appreciative Intelligence that is within themselves. There is qualitative evidence that students and graduates begin to frame themselves as successful, valued community members with career options and the world as a place of opportunity and where they can spark change. Although we don't know how many students develop their Appreciative Intelligence, to what extent, or how long it takes, we could see its ensuing qualities. We saw the effect of persistence in students who graduated instead of dropping out of school. There was evidence of increased conviction that they could accomplish goals, such as in the student who came back from college with the three-page paper and said she was confident. We could see the quality of dealing with uncertainty in the students who started a hair salon franchise and helped found two schools in Ghana. In short, they seemed to be enhancing their own Appreciative Intelligence.

Building Appreciative Intelligence at DVFS

Delaware Valley Friends School wove its members' Appreciative Intelligence into the fabric of its culture. As faculty, staff, and others reframed, appreciated the positive, and saw the future unfolding from the present, practices emerged that built Appreciative Intelligence throughout the school community. Leaders displayed successful practices for others to model. They used language that reframed reality in a positive, generative way. They took reward and appreciation to new heights. They set high expectations for individuals and the organization, while providing freedom and resources to excel.

45

Modeling Success

At all levels of the school, people consciously and unconsciously exhibited successful behaviors for others to mimic. In the case of the faculty influencing the behaviors and decisions of students, the Adventure Based Learning Experience (ABLE) teacher serves as a role model for students who are considering a career that involves generating creative ideas, taking on physical challenges, working with people, and helping them find their strengths, but does not involve significant amounts of reading or writing.

In the case of the Eye-to-Eye mentoring program, juniors and seniors show younger students from other schools successful behaviors and strategies for coping with learning differences. They don't directly discuss learning differences, but demonstrate ways to deal with them while playing sports or games, eating snacks, or reading books together.[16]

Positive, Generative Language

Members of the community have a particular way of talking about skills, abilities, learning, and school. They reframe situations and challenges for possibilities and potential solutions through their language. They deliberately use terminology that opens the door for new possibilities. They talk about learning differences, not learning disabilities, to indicate that students have abilities and that they can acquire knowledge through alternative teaching styles and methods. By talking about reading as a skill, not an ability, they send the message that reading can be taught, motivated, and learned through mnemonic devices and rules such as "Gentle Cindy," a tool for remembering how to sound out the letters "g" and "c."[17]

Through conversation, faculty and staff reinterpret the concept of school for students with dyslexia, and for their parents, as a place of belonging and success, instead of isolation and failure.

Often, they use stories to reframe situations, inspire values and success, and shape the future. Each year on Alumni Day, DVFS graduates return and speak about their college and career experiences. One year a woman spoke about her remarkable journey after high school graduation—her short stint in college, numerous career changes, and eventually discovery of her talent. She started a hair salon and grew the business to a franchise. Students resonated with the salient theme of seeking a successful career despite difficulties with reading, writing, and math, and they became inspired by her success.

Jonathan Mooney, a Brown University graduate, co-author of *Learning Outside the Lines* and an academic survivor despite learning differences, has also spoken at DVFS. His personal story of overcoming challenge after challenge and dealing with both the joy and depression associated with learning has reached students who have lived through similar experiences. His ultimate success gives them hope and influences the way they think about their own lives and futures. His story of developing the Eye-to-Eye project motivated DVFS to create its own version of the program.

Reward and Appreciation

Similar to other organizations where Appreciative Intelligence is in action, DVFS lets its community members know that their attitudes, attributes, and actions are valuable. The school makes a point of publicly recognizing and rewarding students at an award ceremony at the end of each academic year. A range of awards recognizes a range of talent, accomplishment, and embodiment of the school's values. Honors include the Head's Award for a student who influences quietly and leads by example, the Leadership Award for a team captain or student government representative, the Improvement Award for someone who has shown progress, and others for persistent participation and subject matter improvement.

Ten years ago, art and cooking teacher Norma Gottlieb created a contest and the Golden Rolling Pin award as a distraction and morale booster for students after one of their classmates perished in a car accident. Since the contest's poignant beginnings, the students have risen to the challenge of the competition and vied for the coveted award. Students choose meal themes (such as a spring meal or food from around the world), design menus, find recipes, and prepare the food in a limited time. A few selected teachers judge the meal on taste, theme, and presentation. Outcomes include restaurant-quality meals, experience for students who move on to careers in the culinary arts, recognition and appreciation for the student chefs, and, for the top team, the bragging rights that accompany the Golden Rolling Pin award.

Setting High Expectations

At DVFS, leaders and innovators with high Appreciative Intelligence have created organizational success by setting high expectations for students, themselves, and the school as a whole. The faculty aims for more than one year's worth of reading improvement for each year at the school. For example, if a student enters with a fourth-grade reading level, they set a first-year goal of a sixth-grade reading level, and the goal of an eighth-grade level the following year. "We promise the students that they will see improvement and that this will work," said Keeney. By doing so, the teachers hold themselves responsible for connecting with students and providing them with the best learning tools available. At the same time, they set high standards and indicate high hopes for students. The students rise to the expectations.

Students also set high expectations for themselves. Knowing they're not stupid, they demand higher level tasks and pick up on attempts to "dumb down" the curriculum. According to Keeney, they want to read the same novels that other high school students read and ask for the tools to accomplish their goals. They listen to recordings of the text as they read books and learn new strategies for reading, a process that takes time. Ultimately, they might read fewer books than their peers, but they read the same ones.[18]

Freedom to Excel

At the same time DVFS's leaders set high expectations, they provide freedom to excel and resources to enable success. Shortly after the school's inception, teachers decided that the traditional IEPs (Individual Education Programs) used in public schools had shortcomings. Although the documents were meant to tailor an educational plan to individual children's specific disabilities, the faculty believed that the detailed prescriptions for strategies and desired behaviors often limited what would happen in the classroom. Instead of relying on IEPs, they adopted profiles for individual students' learning styles, including their strengths and difficulties. The profiles serve as a guide to help each student achieve individual goals through personalized attention and teaching methods, but they give faculty and students the freedom to go beyond them.

Like venture capitalists, the school administrators and faculty apply resources to what works, rather than focusing on what doesn't work. For instance, since one-third of students go on to art schools or become art teachers, they recently allocated more classroom space for an expanded arts lab. Because of the increasingly important role of technology in enabling success in the organization and expression of ideas—for reading, writing, and art—each student has his or her own laptop computer.

Successful Results

School leaders have shaped the organization, and the organization has reinforced a culture of appreciation. Together, they have set up a cycle of innovation, creativity, and success so that the individuals (students, teachers, and staff members) and the school thrive.

The results of the culture with Appreciative Intelligence created by Delaware Valley Friends School founders include innovation at all levels of the organization. When students wanted an alternative to the regular cafeteria food, in entrepreneurial fashion they checked out local restaurants, developed new menus, and prices, and restructured the lunch program with fare from local sandwich and pizza shops.

Students also initiated a new student government structure, founded the first high-school-aged Eye-to-Eye program, and started a Frisbee team. With the help of an advisor, they designed the school's most innovative marketing material: a viewbook that is printed so that the right-hand pages read the same way when the booklet is turned upside down and backwards. At the same time such changes create the school programs, food, and sports teams students prefer, the successful experiences build a feeling of empowerment for them.

Teachers too exhibit creativity as they work to reach individual students. For example, the science teacher figured out how to teach engineering and robotics principles through an iconic (pictorial) software program and hands-on experience to high school students who had low-level language skills but high-level interest in mechanics.[19] Others designed awards to recognize and appreciate special talents and efforts. A couple of faculty members have developed and pioneered new methods for teaching students with dyslexia.

Finally, DVFS's 20-year track record of success for individuals and the organization—a rate of 98% of students who go on to college, top-notch retention of teachers, nearly perfect attendance by the elementary-school-aged participants of the Eye-to-Eye mentoring program, awards and recognition including photo and film festival prizes and National Merit Scholars, personal and professional success for graduates including teaching, law, broadcasting, and art degrees, achievements in business, and attainment of healthy and happy family relationships and friend-ships—speaks for itself.

What if more people experienced Appreciative Intelligence in action? What if they enhanced the intelligence that is already within them? What if more schools and families worked to reveal the best in their members? What if more corporations, nonprofit organizations, and government agencies sought to identify people who exhibit high levels of Appreciative Intelligence? By our learning more about reframing, appreciating the positive, and seeing how the future unfolds (discussed in the next three chapters), and by our understanding how Appreciative Intelligence works in organizations and developing it in individuals and groups, the future itself could look very different.

Chapter 4

Reframing Reality for a Great View

*Discovery consists of looking at the same thing as
everyone else and thinking something different.*
—*Albert Szent-Gyorgi (1893–1986)*

Every day, every situation, and every encounter is a crossroad. As though
the present were a landscape, we make decisions consciously or unconsciously each moment to move forward, turn to the right or left, ignore
some possibilities, and partake in others. We make these decisions based
on the way we perceive reality or how we interpret and evaluate the
stimuli in our environment. Some decisions are made deliberately, with
careful thought over a period of several seconds, minutes, or even weeks.
Others are made nearly instantly, and we may not even be aware they
have occurred. This chapter sheds light on some of the mysterious quirks
of perception and insight. We provide more detail about reframing, the
first component of Appreciative Intelligence. We also talk about what
Appreciative Intelligence is not.

Perception

Sometimes it is possible to spot differences in individuals' perception
of reality based on their reactions to certain stimuli. For example, one
afternoon a man and his daughter and young granddaughter discovered a
huge spider in a web that stretched from an eight-foot-high tree branch

to the ground. The man, a retired scientist, approached the situation with technical interest and expounded on the characteristics and benefits of orb weaver spiders. His daughter recoiled in surprise. His granddaughter looked closely at the spider with curiosity, reacted as though she had met a new playmate, and gave the spider a name. The individuals' behaviors—talking, stepping back, or looking closer—reflected different perceptions of the same stimulus—the spider. Their perceptions and ensuing actions were based on their underlying attitudes, conditioning, experience, and expertise.

In other instances, however, we cannot see our different perceptions at work. When objects or situations are not the focus of attention (as was the spider in the aforementioned story), or when we don't discuss our reactions to our environment, significant differences in perceptions go unnoticed. Furthermore, much of the time we are barely aware of parts of our environment. A great deal of our landscape of reality is little more than background scenery.

This point is illustrated by the true story of a high school student who was cleaning up after a National Honor Society ceremony in the library late one evening and took more than a casual glance at the dozen or so paintings on the walls. He noticed that some were prints and others were originals. He wondered aloud to his companion whether anyone ever paid attention to them, knew their value, or cared if they were there. The student removed all the paintings from the library and hid them for 48 hours. Then he snuck back into the library and replaced them. There was no whisper of conversation about the paintings for the two days they were missing. The only question about possible wrongdoing was asked by a security guard, who took the license plate number of the pickup truck that left the school parking lot at a suspiciously late hour. Three days later (when the paintings were back in place), the police tracked down the owner of the vehicle, and the student confessed his prank. But when the officer investigated the situation, he found an odd situation. School administrators said they had not seen any changes in the library. The librarian insisted that the paintings had been in place all week. Even after the facts were presented to the school staff, no one recalled seeing anything out of the ordinary. In this case, individuals' markedly different perceptions of the paintings—objects of curiosity for the mischievous student and nearly invisible background scenery for the librarian and others—would not have been observed or considered without the intervening prank.

With the overwhelming number of stimuli in our surroundings, it would not be possible to notice consciously every aspect of our environment or make deliberate decisions about every situation. In fact, to do so would be downright dangerous. For instance, if we had to take the time to make a conscious choice about moving a hand away from a hot surface, rather than being driven by a reflex, we would suffer a serious burn. In many other cases, however, like the library patrons and staff who didn't see the blank library walls, we miss opportunities, needs, people, or possibilities right under our noses, because we do not perceive them as relevant or significant.

The story about the library paintings illustrates the basic distinction between *sensation* and *perception*. Sensation is the physiological stimulation of sensory receptors in the eyes, ears, nose, tongue, or skin. Perception is the process by which we interpret and organize sensation to produce a meaningful experience. Perception is sensation plus selection and interpretation. In the aforementioned example, the library visitors' sense organs—their eyes—translated light energy from the environment into electrical impulses processed by their brains. The human mind does not merely understand these signals as pure energy. The process of perception allows us to interpret them as objects, events, people, and situations. When the school administrators looked at the wall without the pictures, the sensation would have been that of the light reflected from the blank wall, but the perception that something was missing did not occur.

Perception is highly subjective and selective and is influenced by a person's history, interests, beliefs, attitudes, and values. Perception is subjective because it takes place in the mind of the receiver. It is selective because we are not able to perceive all the stimuli around us and we subconsciously choose the ones deserving of attention or reaction. The school administrators did not pay attention to some of the stimuli around them—specifically, the blank library walls—because they chose to focus their attention elsewhere, possibly on other student actions, interactions with parents or faculty, paperwork, or a multitude of other stimuli.

People who work near those with high levels of Appreciative Intelligence notice differences in their colleague's perceptions. During interviews, they remarked that the leader or innovator appeared to hold a different view of reality from much of the rest of the world. A colleague said of Rotarian Herb Pigman, who was instrumental in seeing the opportunity to conquer polio and to treat the endemic as an organizational, not medical, challenge: "He doesn't see reality like everyone else does." An employee of Shareholder.com, a company that uses technology to help public companies communicate with investors, said that the president and founder Ron Gruner "has a sight." Another concurred: "Ron sees things within the company that others don't see. He's a leading innovator. Given infinite time, [others] wouldn't come up with the ideas he does."

People with Appreciative Intelligence have the ability to see parts of the landscape as more than background scenery. They perceive situations, people, products, and ideas as part of a larger picture, connected or related to other situations or people, and as something valuable waiting to happen. They see qualities of newness, creativity, or innovation. They reframe the current reality to see something positive inside occurrences and people.

In the leaders we studied, the ability to reframe the present to see the positive aspects of the situation, and to act accordingly, showed up in many areas: problems, products, situations, and people. Rotarians addressed the problem of polio as an organizational and political challenge for which they had nearly a million experts. W. L. Gore's associate Dave Myers saw improved puppet cables and guitar strings in coated bicycle gear cables that allowed smoother shifting;[1] an editor with high Appreciative Intelligence said he could see the potential for a good book under a new line of literature in a few short, unpolished chapters of a manuscript. William Coleman, visually challenged founder of the company best known for the Coleman lantern, reframed his business of selling lamps as the service of providing brighter light through rented equipment.[2]

The story of the organization FIRST (For Inspiration and Recognition of Science and Technology) provides a clear example of framing a situation to see its positive aspects, resulting in positive outcomes. In 1989, Dean Kamen, entrepreneur, founder of the DEKA Research and Development Corporation and inventor of a wheelchair that climbs steps and an insulin pump for diabetics, became concerned that the number of U.S. students pursuing a degree or career in engineering, science, or technology was decreasing. A technologist himself, he understood the importance of introducing science and technology to students at an early age. He also knew the educational requirements for such pursuits. Kamen founded FIRST, whose mission is "to create a world where science and technology are celebrated . . . where young people dream of becoming science and technology heroes."[3]

Instead of boosting kids' interest and education through greater numbers of traditional classes or science fairs, Kamen and FIRST's early advocates introduced the world of engineering problems and solutions through a robotics competition and giant Olympics-type event with teams, referee-type judges, balls or other game pieces, robots, bands, and cheering spectators. FIRST garnered financial support for the program by encouraging corporations to sponsor teams as an investment in their companies' future, instead of as a contribution to charity.

Kamen's innovative solution and its resounding successful results are the result of framing a situation in a new way. According to FIRST's founder, the traditional way of perceiving the decline in engineering, technology, analysis, and problem-solving abilities was as either a problem of education or one of supply—a lack of tests, standards, or teachers. Instead, he viewed the challenge as a cultural problem—one in which distractions pulled kids away from important issues in life and their predominant role models came from a limited number of figures from Hollywood and professional sports leagues. Kamen uniquely framed three situations for extraordinary results: (1) He reframed the decline as a cultural problem, not as an educational one; (2) he reframed the way to learn science and technology as a fun, Olympics-type event facilitated by mentors and role models, not a science fair or classroom learning experience led by a solitary teacher; and (3) he reframed financial sponsorship as investment in future assets, not as charity.

Consequently, the leaders of FIRST expanded the organization from 28 high school-aged teams in 1992 to nearly 1,000 teams in 2005. They added a FIRST LEGO league with more than 5,000 teams for middle-school-aged students. The organization has enjoyed financial and mentoring support from 2,500 partnering organizations including corporations (RadioShack, FedEx, and Kimberly-Clark, to name but a few); agencies including NASA and the Central Intelligence Agency; and several universities.[4] Along the way, the program has raised awareness of technology and promoted esteem and enthusiasm in tens of thousands of students. Through reframing, FIRST has experienced innovation, creativity, and phenomenal success.

Solving Problems

According to systems methodology and project consultant Eric Metzker, most projects (such as eradicating polio, increasing the number of engineering graduates, or designing a new product) are a series or long chain of problems and decision points, some consecutive and some simultaneous. Three situations can bring a project to a halt or an unsuccessful ending. First, when evaluating a potential solution to any one of the problem points in the chain, project participants can decide that the potential solution will not work (irrespective of whether it will or not). Second, participants can determine that a solution might work, but they take no action, because they cannot figure out how to move forward. Third, participants can look too far down the chain, feel overwhelmed at the prospects, and prematurely give up looking for solutions.

In our study of leaders, problem solvers, and innovators, those with high Appreciative Intelligence approached situations in such a way that solutions continued to flow along the chain. First, by remaining open to a myriad of possibilities, they created the mindset that allowed the insight of how to frame the situation for success to appear. In an interview for *Smithsonian* magazine, FIRST's Kamen talked about the huge numbers of possibilities and options that he sees before a solution "lightbulb" turns on: "You get this spaghetti bowl of paths and dead ends and changes in perspective and requirements and expectations, and sometimes you're lucky and you end up at the intersection of a technology that's right and works."[5] The Director of NASA's Academy of Program and Project Leadership, Ed Hoffman, said, "My style is intuitive, not analytical. . . . My experience isn't linear."[6] By framing the situation so that a problem can be solved and by holding a strong vision of the future state, they remained open to options and potential solutions along the chain of problems. Second, through the process of framing, they linked existing resources and possibilities within the present to the desired future state. By linking the generative potential of the present state to the future, they set themselves up with a course of action that appeared obvious and accomplishable because it was already part of the system.

In Rotary's case, the polio eradication initiative was framed as an organizational and managerial challenge. It could be addressed by an already existing worldwide network of volunteers whose mission was service to others for humanitarian causes. Rotarians knew how, and held the necessary resources, to solve organizational problems in the chain. They already knew key players in government and had geographic proximity to the children who needed the vaccine. Rotarian Bill Sergeant said they might not have pursued polio eradication as a project if they knew at first how much money, effort, and time it would take.[7] But by remaining open to possibilities along each step of the way and perceiving that the future goal could be accomplished, they raised hundreds of millions of dollars, persuaded national governments and millions of volunteers to join the effort, solved countless logistical puzzles, and immunized hundreds of millions of children. They stuck to their goal, they solved each problem in the 20-year series, and the program continues toward its finish line of worldwide polio eradication.

Building a Frame

Some of the contemporary intellectual discourses, such as postmodernism and social constructionism, are based on framing of issues.[8] Issues can be framed in any way, provided they are based on solid or logical assumptions.

While analyzing social movements, researchers David Snow and Robert Benford identified and labeled three types of framing that appear in many situations: diagnostic, prognostic, and motivational.[9] We can apply their definitions of framing to the story of FIRST. As the name suggests, *diagnostic framing* involves identifying and naming a problem that needs fixing. A statistical research report in the late 1980s might have indicated that a certain number or percentage of American students was graduating with an engineering or technology degree. It might have compared measurements of that decade with those of a previous decade. The conclusion may have been framed as a problem: that the United States would need a certain number of engineering graduates by a certain year, but that there was a decline in the number of graduates. *Prognostic framing* involves proposing a solution to the diagnosed problem and outlining what needs to be done. Prior to Kamen's position, traditional solutions to the decline in engineering graduates involved increased class time, more teachers, or more books on the subject, because the assumption was that the decline was a problem of education. Finally, the most important framing for bringing about change, *motivational framing*, involves "a call to action," according to Snow and Benford, to realize the solution as well as to communicate the reasons it is necessary. In the case of FIRST, Kamen recruited mentors to work with students and called upon corporations and organizations to help with financial support by framing the robotics program as an investment for the future—educated and confident youths, a pipeline of employees with technical expertise, and a special ingredient of a healthy national economy.

In addition to diagnosing problems or mobilizing a response to them, there are other practical uses of framing indicated by Snow and others. Frames are employed for building alliances between competing groups, for clarifying and solidifying group members' beliefs and values, and for extending those values to other groups.[10]

In general, framing reality in a negative light can have the downside of leading to reduced alternatives and opportunities. By contrast, framing reality for a great view of the future has some very positive effects. For example, in a study with significant implications for business and politics, Margaret Neale and Max Bazerman found that negatively framed negotiators resolved fewer contracts and had less successful contracts than positively framed negotiators, while the opposite occurred when negotiators used more positive framing.[11]

To see the difference between negatively and positively framed conversations, consider the questions and answers in the following two scenarios. Both involve a parent who is concerned about a child's midterm evaluation. In one scenario, the dialogue might proceed this way:

Parent: *Why did you get a D on your midterm evaluation?*
Child: *I don't know.*
Parent: *What do you mean you don't know? Were you in class?*
Child: *Yes, I was there every day.*
Parent: *If you were there every day, why did you get a D?*

Child: *I don't know. Maybe I didn't do well on the tests.*

Parent: *Well, why did you get bad grades on your tests?*

Child: *Maybe I didn't do well on my homework assignments.*

Parent: *Then why didn't you do well on homework assignments?*

Most likely, the conversation would continue in the same sort of downward spiral.

The conversation might, however, go something like this:

Parent: *I see you got a D on your midterm evaluation. Is this the grade you were expecting?*

Child: *No. I thought I would get a B.*

Parent: *What happened?*

Child: *I don't know.*

Parent: *Well, let's work backward and see what happened this quarter. What tests and assignments did you have?*

Child: *I had three tests and one project.*

Parent: *How did they go? Did you turn in your project on time?*

Child: *The tests were okay, but I turned in my project late.*

Parent: *The project was late?*

Child: *I thought I could finish it after watching TV, but I felt too sleepy to work on it after the show.*

Parent: *What grade do you think you could have gotten if you had turned the project in on time?*

Child: *I think I would have gotten a B.*

Parent: *How do you think you could get a B in the course?*

Child: *I could see if I could do a make-up assignment.*

Parent: *What else would need to happen to make that possible?*

Child: *I could talk to my teacher.*

Parent: *Would it help if I recorded the TV show to watch after you had finished all your assignments?*

The first and second conversations are different. The first, negative framing of the situation, demonstrates retrospective sense-making with no future outcome in sight. The parent's language focuses on the poor grade, or the opportunity lost for getting a good grade. There is no evidence of what the parent wanted the child to learn or do or of what result would have been preferable. In contrast, the second conversation was an example of positive framing. This dialogue focuses on a goal, a positive generative outcome of changes in study behaviors (watching TV after assignments are completed) and potential for a future higher test grade. Although negatively framed conversations may not always go as badly as narrated here, and positively framed ones may not go this smoothly, it is clear that the two types of framing will produce different outcomes.

Framing is the psychological process inherent in perception whereby a person constructs or puts an object, person, context, action, issue, or scenario into a certain context or sees it in a certain way. It is a critical activity in the construction of social reality because it helps shape the perspectives through which people see the world by providing contextual cues that guide decision making and inferences. Framing involves processes of including, excluding, and emphasizing particular parts of reality. Social scientist Robert Entman summarized the essence of framing processes in the following explanation:

> Framing essentially involves selection and salience. To frame
> is to select some aspects of perceived reality and make them
> more salient in the communicating text, in such a way as to
> promote a particular problem definition, causal interpretation,
> moral evaluation and/or treatment recommendation.[12]

In other words, Entman categorizes framing into two basic components: selection and salience. According to him, selection is basically choosing the reality on which the framer focuses, and salience is what is most important or most visible.

A vivid example of selection and salience in framing comes from a classic study by psychology professor and researcher Harold Kelley. In 1950, Kelley told a class of college students that a substitute teacher would teach a class. He divided the students into two groups and informed one that the substitute teacher would be warm and friendly, while the other group was told that the teacher would be distant and cold. At the end of the class, students were asked to evaluate the teacher. Though both groups listened to the same teacher at the same time, the group that was primed to expect the teacher to be warm and friendly actually rated the teacher as warm and friendly, while the group told to expect the teacher to be cold and distant rated the teacher less friendly and unapproachable.[13]

Kelley created different expectations for the two groups of students, which in turn led them to interpret the actions of the substitute teacher differently. The students selected elements from the context of the class and teacher presentation in such a way that they were able to see warmth and friendliness or indifference and unfriendliness in the substitute teacher's behavior. The reality of the classroom situation was that there was a range of behaviors exhibited by the teacher. But the tipoff by the researcher that the teacher was "friendly" or "unapproachable" created a framing process in such a way that the students selected aspects of the teacher's behavior as belonging to one category or another. For example, a smile by the "friendly" teacher was a salient behavior that was noticed by students in the first group.

Thus, how a person frames a situation—"seeing" a glass as half full or half empty, a teacher as friendly or unapproachable, or engineering education as classroom study or a competitive game—drives further perceptions, expectations, and ensuing behaviors and decisions.

Insight

By framing reality in a new and positive way, people open their minds to seeing new connections between ideas, people, or situations. When they suddenly see connections that previously eluded them, they are said to have a flash of insight, according to researcher John Kounios of Drexel University.[14]

Insight plays a role in successful leaders' solutions to challenges and difficult situations. It helps them address problems, discover hidden talent, and invent new products. According to psychologists Robert Sternberg and Janet Davidson, insight is associated with a range of mental processes including framing, perception, pattern recognition, and evaluation of the environment. These processes occur in puzzle and problem solving, comprehension of a situation, and creativity in business, art, science, and a variety of practical activities.[15]

Most of our interviewees said that solutions came to them through insight, or described instances similar to that of Archimedes, who experienced the original "Eureka" moment when he stepped into the bath and realized in a flash of inspiration how to determine the density and composition of a crown. They reported that nearly instantaneous answers appeared in a flash, after a period of "blanking" or having no answer to their problem.

Charlie Pellerin, who found the solution to the flawed mirrors of the Hubble Telescope, talked about finding answers through insight. "Get clear about the outcome and the path will show up," he said. "This is true. [Solutions] were always there, but now you see them. Focus your mind and the answer will appear."[16]

Yet most of the time, the same leaders could not describe how their thoughts came to them or what mental processes employed when they came up with insightful solutions. When Carol asked Ron Gruner, founder and president of Shareholder.com, how he figured out a response to a recent challenge, he replied, "I don't know how it works. I let my subconscious work. I formulate a problem or write it down. I leave it in the back of my mind. Then a solution pops into my mind—while I'm driving or in the shower. I don't draw a flow chart and create a solution. It jumps right out—intuitively." For these leaders, like most of us, how the mind works and how solutions emerge through insight is a mystery.

At the Drexel University EEG Laboratory, however, John Kounios has had some insights of his own. He and fellow researchers have identified patterns of activity in the brain that further explain how insights are formed.

A Closer Look

Kounios, a professor and researcher who sports a Ph.D. in experimental psychology, greeted one of us (Carol) at the EEG lab with a warm smile and a handshake. He spoke enthusiastically as he gave a tour of the facilities where he and his team conduct experiments with EEGs (electroencephalograms) to measure timing of events in the brain. Kounios talked about his work over the past decade with Mark Jung-Beeman, a researcher at Northwestern University, and explained how their EEG studies relate to experiments at another lab that conducts corresponding fMRI (functional magnetic resonance imaging, a medical diagnostic tool that helps us see areas of the brain at work) studies.

Drexel EEG lab's two small adjoining rooms are similar in size and equipment to typical office cubicles. The first room holds little more than a comfortable chair and a small table with a desktop computer. It is quiet and windowless, with no distracting wall decorations or paraphernalia. In this room, a person who is the subject of a study performs word puzzles and answers questions at the computer while wearing an electrode cap, a close-fitting rubbery head covering that resembles an old-fashioned swimming cap, studded with many tiny metal dots—electrodes. Cables connect the electrode cap to a boxlike electronic device slightly behind and out of sight of the seated subject. As the person thinks, the electrodes pick up the brain's electrical activity, the wires transmit the electrical signals to a recording machine, and the signals are analyzed by computer software and converted to graphs of wavy lines on the screen.

As the subject thinks about puzzle solutions and clicks the mouse, patterns of brain waves and puzzle responses are monitored and recorded in the adjoining room of the lab. In this second room, researchers watch three computer monitors—one to view the subject to see whether he is drowsy or resting his head on his hand and thereby displacing the electrode cap; the second to view the EEG data; and the third (synchronized with the second) to view and track the subject's responses to the puzzles.

While the lab appears nothing like the proverbial futuristic control room operated by a mad scientist, and even the electrode cap is only mildly strange looking, the results of Kounios' and his team's studies at this and the fMRI lab seem like something from an episode from the television show *Star Trek*. Their findings are extraordinary. Their implications for people and organizations looking to increase creativity, innovation, and problem solving are far-reaching.

In their 2004 study,[17] Kounios and Jung-Beeman not only located the portion of the brain in which insight occurs; they learned two other important pieces of information as well. They found that subjects were putting their brains into either a state conducive to solving problems by insight or a state conducive to a noninsight approach, even before they began to solve a problem. They also found that study subjects made fewer incorrect responses with the insight approach to problem solving, but they also more often ran out of time when answering a question with that approach. In the insight mode of processing, problem solvers don't know when or whether a solution will appear. With noninsight processing, the problem solver can work toward a solution and arrive at one that is correct, incorrect, or partial. With insight, however, the solution is all or none, and timing is unpredictable.

What their findings tell us is that people can (and do) deliberately prepare their brains to come up with a creative answer or solution. This suggests that whereas some people, perhaps those with high Appreciative Intelligence, have a predisposition to preparing to find an answer through insight, others can find techniques that may help them do so. Or those who may already put themselves into a state conducive to insight may be able to learn to do so as needed when a problem arises.

A further implication of Kounios and Jung-Beeman's findings is that if insight solutions are more often correct but all-or-none and unpredictable with respect to timing, people and their organizations may need to consider trade-offs between hard-and-fast deadlines and milestones on the one hand and innovative solutions on the other.

In an intriguing follow-up study, Jung-Beeman and fellow researchers added a questionnaire about the subject's emotional state to an otherwise identical study involving word puzzles and insight. Before embarking on the puzzles, subjects rated their moods. What the researchers found was that subjects solved more problems with flashes of insight when they were in a positive mood.[18]

Combined with results of a study in Germany by Annette Bolte et al. that linked positive emotional states and the ability to make intuitive judgments,[19] the findings support the notion of the link between neural functioning and the thought processes that constitute Appreciative Intelligence. A positive perspective makes a difference in flexible and creative problem solving.

What Appreciative Intelligence Isn't

In Chapter 1 we discussed what Appreciative Intelligence is—perceiving the positive inherent generative potential within the present. We also discussed its components of reframing, appreciating the positive, and seeing how the future unfolds from the present. A discussion about Appreciative Intelligence would not be complete without a few words about what it is not.

Appreciative Intelligence is not about seeing the world through rose-colored glasses. People with Appreciative Intelligence reframe a situation to see what is positive, but they do not deny that any negative aspects or destructive possibilities exist. They do not bubble over with happiness all the time; the people we interviewed experienced and expressed a normal range of emotions. They exhibit diverse personalities. Their dreams and expectations are very high, but not completely ungrounded. They do not attempt to create solutions through "pie in the sky" ideas. They see the oak, not a tropical mango, in the acorn.

The July 2003 *Harvard Business Review* article, "Delusions of Success: How Optimism Undermines Executives' Decisions," addresses the hazards of business managers who underestimate their competitors and overestimate their own capabilities. A high percentage of new initiatives, mergers, and acquisitions fail, partially because of leaders' tendency to focus too closely on behaviors, attributions, and previous events within the company rather than combining those observations with comparable examples and results outside the company. According to the article's authors, Dan Lovallo and Daniel Kahneman, "They spin scenarios of success while overlooking the potential for mistakes and miscalculations."[20]

Dean Kamen talked about conflicts between the desire for stability and innovation. Managers, as they aim for knowing what will happen in order to reduce risk and surprises, often avoid failure. "This keeps society stable," Kamen said, "but it is contrary to innovation." As organizations aim for consistency of quality, the price may be reduced innovation.

It isn't that individuals with high Appreciative Intelligence make no mistakes or never experience failures—quite the contrary. They use both positive and negative experiences to move to new solutions or achievements. The leaders we studied were realistic, keenly aware of their environment and what was happening in the present. They did not deny threats, risks, and troublesome situations that could result in serious, damaging consequences. Their perspectives encompassed a larger picture and their solutions were grounded. Charlie Pellerin did not dream up a "supernatural" fix for the telescope but used the knowledge, tools, and resources available to him at that time. Asa Candler did not overoptimistically try to continue selling Coca-Cola as a health tonic; he saw something different—a good-tasting beverage. A Hurricane Katrina victim whose New Orleans business was devastated by the 2005 massive flooding did not deny that he and others felt shock and pain over their evacuation and losses, but he was able to reframe the destruction of homes and offices as a need for someone to help with insurance claims and reconstruction. By the time he was allowed to return to New Orleans to salvage what office equipment was left, he had made plans to start a new company to address those needs.[21]

Appreciative Intelligence is not just the possession of a positive outlook. It is an ability that corresponds to intentional and generative acts. The difference between Appreciative Intelligence and simply a positive outlook is underscored by the comment of architect Greg Radford when he explained how he deals with challenges: "Having a positive attitude isn't like having a magic wand. It's like a canoe paddle. Going upstream, you have to use it and work with it. Just having it isn't good enough."[22]

Appreciative Intelligence is also not about pasting a label of "good" on something that is not good or about unreasonably calling a negative situation positive. It is not about seeing negative aspects of people as positive, or complimenting or rewarding incompetence or lack of talent. Candler did not continue to promote Coca-Cola as a great health remedy. Pellerin did not market the telescope's blurry images as fabulous scientific discoveries. Brownie Wise did not perceive the wardrobe or vehicle possessed by her job candidate as something good; she simply didn't see those possessions as salient in her framing or judgment of character and ability. Likewise, Estee Lauder did not deny that her prospective client was shoeless; she didn't perceive the lack of shoes as salient to the transaction of selling and buying cosmetics. Teachers or business leaders with high Appreciative Intelligence do not mold expert mathematicians or financial analysts from those who have little interest, ability, or talent in algebra; instead they see and develop the language, artistic, physical, or other skills inherent in students or employees. Appreciative Intelligence does not mean pretending that terrible things have not happened to people or erasing tragic events in history. Instead it allows painful memories to be viewed as history, not the present, and as an opportunity to create a different action for a better future.

Appreciative Intelligence is not about denying that part of reality exists. It is about the ability to reframe it for a great view of the future.

Chapter 5

Appreciating the Positive

Leaders have an intuitive sense that things will
work out for the best. I do not see the dark side.
—Howard Schultz, Chairman and
founder of Starbucks[1]

The second component of Appreciative Intelligence is appreciating the positive. Beyond envisioning the future oak tree, those with high levels of Appreciative Intelligence see acorns that become large, healthy oaks with future generations of acorns and trees. Through reframing, leaders and entrepreneurs see and select aspects of the present that are useful, valuable, or desirable. They focus on positive attributes of a current situation that can generate a successful future.

Appreciation has its skeptics and critics as well as its advocates. Like a medical doctor who diagnoses what is sick in a patient in order to determine treatment, many organizational change professionals seek deficiencies in a business or organization to set a course of action.[2] The "Pollyanna" figure, or one who cheerfully looks for the best, is sometimes viewed as one who is unrealistic, naïve, or overly happy. "Real" work is sometimes synonymous with seeking what is wrong or broken in order to bring it back to a steady state. Individuals and organizations are assumed by some people to be full of problems that should be fixed in order to see improvement.

As noticed by Tojo in his university department years ago, however, a culture of appreciatively framing others' ideas into possibilities leads to more original and more rapidly generated concepts and discoveries than does one of pointing out gaps or deficiencies. Although there is less information about appreciation mechanisms and framing in a positive light than there is about critique, gap analysis, or examination of what is wrong in order to change through intervention, historically the concept of appreciation has been explored by philosophers and spiritual and religious leaders. More recently, psychologists, teachers, managers, and other organizational practitioners have looked more closely at how it works and its benefits. According to a small body of work on appreciation, there are different aspects of it and various models for the way it works. There are benefits for people who appreciate as well as for those who are appreciated by others.

Rats, Flatworms, and Bloomers

Studies and findings of bringing out human potential through appreciation is perhaps one of psychology's most fascinating stories. The story began with revealing hidden abilities in animals and ended with astonishing results with children. The most famous of these studies were conducted by Harvard psychologist Robert Rosenthal and his team.

In one set of experiments, Rosenthal and co-researcher R. Lawson gave 12 student experimenters five rats each. All the rats came from a standard laboratory strain, but they were divided at random into two groups labeled "bright" and "dull."[3] Rosenthal and Lawson told the experimenters that some of the rats were the products of generations of selective breeding for top performance in standard mazes. They pointed out the others that were "dull."

The student experimenters then spent five days training their rats to run a maze. From the first day, the rats identified as "bright" ran the maze better than the "dull" ones. Overall, the rats that were supposedly bright made 51 percent more correct responses and learned 29 percent faster than the others that were labeled as dull. Rosenthal and Lawson also observed that the students who worked with the "bright" rats seemed more relaxed and enthusiastic as they worked with the animals, had fewer instances of talking negatively to them (fewer outbursts of "You stupid rat!"), and handled them more.

Another "frame-breaking" study caused further astonishment. In this experiment, researchers Lucien Cordaro and James Ison randomly divided a group of nearly identical flatworms into two groups. They told experimenters that one group was a strain of "low-response-producing" worms that showed few head turns and body contractions and that the other was a "high-response-producing" group of worms that turned and contracted frequently. In the end, the experimenters found, on average, five times more head turns and 20 times more contractions in the allegedly high-response-producing worms than in the others.[4] While the thought of rats performing extraordinarily because of high expectations and extra care seems within the scope of imagination, the thought of a simpler creature doing the same merits serious consideration. If average worms can transform into "superworms" through high expectations and added attention, what are the implications for humans?

Encouraged by the results with rats (and worms!), Rosenthal thought it wouldn't be far-fetched for children to become brighter when expected to become so by their teachers. The resulting study changed the way we understand the power of expectations and has profound implications for the effects of appreciation.

In a classic classroom study a few years later, Rosenthal and co-researcher Lenore Jacobson administered an IQ test to all students in an elementary school in San Francisco.[5] They told the teachers that some of the students scored very high on the test and would "bloom" academically. The researchers then identified the bloomers to the teachers. In reality, the students were picked at random, but the teachers did not know this. Teachers for the other group of students were not given such instructions and hence they believed that their students were just normal.

Rosenthal and Jacobson tested the students' IQs eight months later and found that the "bloomers" actually bloomed! The mean IQ of the "gifted" group was statistically significantly higher than that of the "normal" group. The findings were so consistent in repeat experiments in school environments and other organizational contexts that the phenomenon was eventually called the "Rosenthal effect." As you would imagine, teachers gave the "blooming" students more attention, better feedback, more challenging tasks, and more class time for comments.

In this vivid example of framing, selection, and salience, the teachers selected elements of their situation in such a way that they were able to see "giftedness" in some students while not seeing it in others. The reality of the classroom was that it was more or less homogenous—a regular class of elementary school children. But the "tip-off" by the researchers that some of the students were gifted created a framing process in such a way that the teachers selected specific aspects of the "gifted" student's behavior as examples of higher intelligence. For example, raising of hands by "gifted" students was a salient behavior that brought attention from teachers. When the supposedly gifted students raised their hands, the teachers made the action more salient by encouraging them to ask similar questions or by acknowledging them in front of the rest of the class. By setting high expectations and following through with more challenging tasks and more time for comments, the teachers helped create the "bloomers." Appreciation had a huge impact on the teachers and students.

Aspects and Models of Appreciation

Psychologist Mitchel Adler defined appreciation as "acknowledging the value and meaning of something—an event, a person, a behavior, an object—and feeling a positive emotional connection to it."[6] Together with Nancy Fagley, he identified and defined eight distinct types of appreciation, four of which relate closely to aspects of Appreciative Intelligence: a "have" focus, "present moment" appreciation, "awe," and "ritual."[7]

In a "have" focus, people pay attention to what they have, rather than what they do not. It is "noticing, acknowledging, and feeling good about (i.e., appreciating) what we have in our lives."[8] This aspect of appreciation was evident in the Rotarians who paid attention to their management and logistical abilities to address the challenge of polio eradication, rather than their lack of medical expertise or initial lack of money.

The "present-moment" aspect of appreciation is similar to the concept of *mindfulness*—thoughtfully and deliberately engaging in the experience at hand. When people look at reality around them with an open mind, they become able to see or appreciate parts of the landscape they had not seen before. This type of appreciation is demonstrated in the previous chapter's story of the student who saw the paintings on the library wall and wondered whether they were potentially valuable originals or reproductions.

According to Adler and Fagley, "awe" provides a person with a special experience that stands out in contrast to ordinary experiences. This aspect of appreciation is linked to the concept of curiosity, which allows people to experience the mystery, or awe, of an event, a situation, another person, or a challenge. It is this aspect that relates to the framing that occurs when innovators face a quandary, problem, or need and that leaves them curious and open to solutions, as Dean Kamen was when choosing to follow a "spaghetti bowl of paths"[9] that led to a solution resulting in new technology.

Finally, the "ritual" aspect of appreciation refers to the routines or structures that enhance appreciative faculties by prompting us to stop, reflect, and take notice of what is positive around us. In an example discussed in greater detail in Chapter 7, as part of its annual robotics competition, each year FIRST asks teams to submit information about the ways they showed sportsmanship, respect, gracious attitudes, and behaviors, as part of their event entry. To do so, they must deliberately think about ways to act with professionalism, take action, and record instances of those behaviors.

In addition to various aspects of appreciation, there are also models of appreciation. One of the most important was that of Geoffrey Vickers (1894–1982), an English bureaucrat-turned social scientist. His concept of *appreciative systems* clarified how framing, appreciation, and ensuing behaviors are related in a circular process. According to Vickers, day-to-day life is a continuously changing flow of interacting events and ideas. As people encounter events and ideas, they make judgments about reality and its value, deciding what is good or bad based on previous experiences. He argued that those judgments eventually lead to "action judgments," or decisions to act, which in turn affect future events and ideas. Thus, in an appreciative system, people's judgments of something's value or worth dictate their actions. If they frame perceptions and judgments appreciatively, or as something valuable, they also act in a way that reflects reality's positive value.[10]

Vickers held that the first element of appreciation is the selectivity in perception:

> To account for the appreciated world . . . I postulate that experience, especially the experience of human communication, develops in each of us a readiness to notice particular aspects of our situation, to discriminate them in particular ways and to measure them against particular standards of comparison [11]

For Vickers the model of an appreciative system was a continuous and recurring loop in which people perceive reality, make a value judgment about it based on past experiences and values, and take action based on those judgments. In a continuous cycle, those actions form the basis for future values, judgments, and actions. In the scenario of the art museum described in Chapter 1, the museum visitor creates the loop between the act of visiting the museum (as opposed to the flea market), intentionally looking for aspects of a painting that make it world-class, and judging the artwork to be superior.

In individual appreciative systems, depending on what type of value judgment is made and what corresponding action occurs, different people experience different aspects of reality. While Vickers pointed out the selectivity of the appreciative process, he did not speculate about what makes some people derive stronger value judgments from the same stimuli than others do.

Adler and Fagley responded to that missing explanation by suggesting the notion of an *appreciative disposition*. According to them, the construct of appreciation has both *trait* and *state* qualities. A natural tendency to be more appreciative than others might be called a *disposition* or *trait*. Independent of this disposition, a person can also experience a temporary *state* of appreciation at any time. By weaving together the ideas of Vickers with those of Adler and Fagley, we create the possibility of an appreciative system in which people with a higher level of Appreciative Intelligence (disposition) are able to frame everyday events (using positive value judgments) into great possibilities (action judgments). Such individuals, over a period of time, become more mindful in their behavioral patterns and begin to see more and more opportunities and generative possibilities in everyday encounters.

Along with the benefit of greater ability to see generative possibilities, there are other advantages of appreciation. According to Adler, "Experiences of appreciation enhance one's positive mood and feelings of connection to the appreciated stimulus (i.e., event, person, practice, or object) and/or to oneself and to the nature of existence (as in a feeling of awe or wonder)."[12] He and Fagley further pointed out that being appreciative enhances subjective well-being.[13] Likewise, experimental cognitive psychologist Sandra Schneider argued that the ability to appreciate promotes more satisfying relationships and improved ability to cope with stress.[14]

Seeing the Best in People

People with Appreciative Intelligence don't limit their ability to see what is positive to reframing situations or products. For many, Appreciative Intelligence is exhibited in a capacity to see other people and their talents in a unique way. Their ability to perceive, make connections, and have insights about people around them results in revealing hidden talents or exposing the best in others.

Stories about Tupperware's marketing genius Brownie Wise and cosmetic company founder Estee Lauder exemplify the ability to see past stereotypes or perceive people in a different light. Wise once hired a poorly dressed woman who showed up for a job interview in a coal delivery truck but who had a determined expression in her eyes.[15] Lauder saw a shoeless woman in an upscale department store as a potential customer, a perception that had bearing when she sold two of each of her cosmetics products to her and more to her relatives the next day. Although another sales person deemed the woman's appearance and lack of footwear as an indication that she had little money to spend and, therefore, ignored her, Lauder greeted her and demonstrated products to her as she did for others.[16]

Ed Hoffman, who transformed the small program that addressed the *Challenger* disaster into NASA's Academy of Program and Project Leadership, has been referred to as one who "has an eye for talent."[17] We asked him what was behind that ability. Hoffman described thoughts and feelings similar to those who believe that a unique solution or new invention is possible. "I work toward the future in relationships," he said. "I find out what's working. I believe that everyone has a talent in an area." He said his job at the academy is to help each person find his or her place.[18]

In another interview, Greg Radford—an architect who has worked solo and on teams and on a wide variety of original and renovation projects, ranging from such American icons as the Rainbow Room of Rockefeller Center to ordinary buildings in a small town—explained how he works with his family and professional colleagues to bring out their top skills, ideas, and innovations. "The most important thing is to be open to suggestions—to examine ideas without criticism." He said he encourages diversity and the sharing of ideas and personal interests.[19]

Although Bill Gore, the founder of W. L. Gore & Associates, died in 1986, his ability to reveal the positive potential in people lives on in memories and stories that continue to be told in the company that bears his name. New generations of company associates perpetuate his philosophies and practices. Matt Schreiner, a Gore associate who specializes in footwear development, said he never met Bill Gore, but he is keenly aware of Bill's basic belief that every person has something valuable to offer. Given enough freedom and support, every individual will determine what that is. Schreiner described methods Gore had for helping that happen. "[People who knew Bill Gore] said he was a phenomenal listener," said Schreiner. Gore also answered questions by asking further probing questions. He redirected associates to find answers themselves, thereby stretching their own knowledge and growing their own abilities.[20]

Another Case in Point

When 26-year-old Fleur Frascella founded Philadelphia Tribal Bellydance, she had no physical space, no funding, and only two willing but young and inexperienced student dancers. By choreographing a piece that could be rehearsed at home and that showcased each of their strengths and talents, however, she created a premiere performance for the Philadelphia Fringe Festival that "appealed to the audience and made the students look like amazing dancers," she said.[21] Over the past five years, through appreciation—looking past the convention that dancers in a troupe must have similar body types and must be very thin—she has created an active, healthy, and successful dance company that also dispels the myth that beauty comes in one size and shape.

When an older student worked diligently, attended classes consistently, and practiced with self-motivation, Frascella began paying extra attention. She noted her progress and let the student know each time she was doing something right, all the while inspiring her confidence. The student not only became a dancer in the troupe, but as a confident, reliable, and consistent performer, she usually leads the line of dancers onto the stage. Through an approach of guiding the student in a process of reframing her reluctance toward solo performances, Frascella also helped her push the envelope of her talent.

Similarly, when the company's drummer left, another approached Frascella. He admitted that he might not be as talented as the previous musician, but he wanted to drum. She said that she couldn't teach him to drum, but she trusted the process and invited him to practice with them. He attended and practiced at the rehearsals, becoming a top-notch musician and, eventually, the permanent drummer with the troupe.

"I realized you can audition talent or grow it from within," said the artistic director. "What's most important is the desire to be there." Rather than seeking proficient performers from elsewhere, she helped those around her become stars in their own right.

As with other appreciative leaders, Frascella's ability to bring out the best in others is based on appreciation or framing to focus on the positive. She selects dance steps that each dancer executes well or other salient features, such as stage presence or strength, to highlight in choreography. On the other hand, she does not judge uniform body type as a salient feature of performance ability. As Gore did, she asks students nearly as many questions as they ask her: "What muscles do you feel during that dance step?" or "What makes you feel confident?" Such questions assume that students already have deep knowledge about their bodies and personalities that will help them achieve their personal goals. Simultaneously, the questions stretch their awareness of the technicalities of dancing and help the dancers pinpoint correct movements and find strategies for improvement based on what works with their own musculature and temperament. At the end of most classes, Frascella starts an improvisational exercise in which every class member takes a turn at leading the others in a spontaneously choreographed dance. Each student leader decides how long she will lead and what steps she will take. The exercise assumes that each student has creativity and the ability to demonstrate at least a few dance steps successfully for others to follow. At the same time, it provides an opportunity for choreographic and leadership skills to flourish. It highlights and helps strengthen steps a student knows. The exercise helps develop sensitivity to what the student followers can do and what helps the group stay together in an artful dance.

Also characteristic of people with high levels of Appreciative Intelligence, and an example of a "have" focus described by Snow and Benford, is a belief that accomplishing a task is less dependent on the extent of abilities or resources available than on how the abilities and resources already available can be utilized. Frascella demonstrates that belief: "I can coach a show into being a better show. I can coach dancers into being better dancers," she asserted. Like Frascella and the computer company founder Michael Dell, who learned that hiring a job candidate based on "potential to grow and develop" rather than on the "company's immediate job needs,"[22] the leaders we interviewed paid little attention to the proverbial greener grass on the other side of the fence. They appreciated and fertilized the grass on their own side.

As shown by real-life leaders Hoffman, Gore, and Frascella, it is possible to help adults bloom in the same way that the students in Rosenthal's studies bloomed. The capacity to bring out the best in others is rooted in one's belief in others through a concept known as the *behavioral confirmation process.*[23] This is shown in the following business example. In an interactive process, a manager adopts positive expectations about her employees and treats them differently. She sees positive qualities in them because she is looking for them. The employees are then more likely to respond by fulfilling those expectations, thus leading to behavioral confirmation.

Recent studies such as those by psychologist Darcy Reich also show that such expectations allow managers or perceivers to overlook or underplay negative information and selectively seek positive actions. Such managers make concerted and deliberate efforts to see the good in their staff, leading to consistent behavioral confirmation.[24]

Ultimately, leaders with high Appreciative Intelligence are able to bring out the best in people, because that's what they see. Such leaders expose hidden talent and excellence by appreciating individuals and their ideas, by providing resources, and by setting up an environment that allows individuals to accomplish things that they themselves, or others, may not know that they can do.

Appreciative Inquiry

The aforementioned study by Reich is one example from a relatively recent and growing field called *positive psychology*. Described in more depth in Chapter 9, positive psychology is focused on understanding optimal individual human psychological states rather than pathological ones. Its counterpart for understanding organizations, positive organizational behavior, is geared to understanding optimal organizational states.[25] Both positive psychology and positive organizational behavior open the way for new, positive, and appreciative approaches for making changes.

One of the most innovative approaches for strengthening organizations is *Appreciative Inquiry (AI)*. First developed by David Cooperrider and Suresh Srivastva, professors of organizational behavior at Case Western Reserve University, it is a technique for sparking organizational change as well as a theory of how organizational realities evolve. It is based on the belief that reality is a product of human imagination[26] and that there is more to organizations than recurring problems that must be solved. In contrast to a traditional deficit or problem-finding focus, Appreciative Inquiry provides an alternative of focusing on what is already working and what is possible in an organization.

Cooperrider and his co-author Diana Whitney describe Appreciative Inquiry as follows:

> Appreciative Inquiry is the cooperative search for the best in people, their organizations, and the world around them. It involves systematic discovery of what gives a system "life" when it is most effective and capable in economic, ecological, and human terms. AI involves the art and practice of asking questions that strengthen a system's capacity to heighten positive potential. It mobilizes inquiry through crafting an "unconditional positive question" often involving hundreds and sometimes thousands of people. In AI, intervention gives way to imagination and innovation; instead of negativity, criticism, and spiraling diagnosis there is discovery, dream, and design. AI assumes that every living system has untapped, rich, and inspiring accounts of the positive. Link this "positive change core" directly to any change agenda, and changes never thought possible are suddenly and democratically mobilized.[27]

The process of Appreciative Inquiry involves asking members of a group questions such as "What was a recent positive experience that made you feel most valued or alive, and what about the experience made you feel that way?" Each member has a voice, and each answer becomes part of a larger picture. Through the answers, Appreciative Inquiry identifies the underlying values of an organization. The values vary between organizations—such as trust, financial reward, flexibility, or stability—because they are specific to the members and their organizational culture. The answers to the questions also point out the capabilities of an organization. By understanding what works—not focusing on deficits, which often results in finger-pointing and blame—an organization can transform from the best of "what is" to a collective image of "what might be." It helps group members create possible strategies for the future and map out specific plans for change by stretching their talents and capabilities, by working within their value system, and by building on their beliefs about what would make a great future.

Appreciative Inquiry and Appreciative Intelligence are not the same things. Appreciative Inquiry is an organizational analysis approach and methodology, whereas Appreciative Intelligence is a mental ability found in an individual. The two share a common element, however, in that they both focus on what is valuable or positive. Appreciative Inquiry seeks to locate the core values or "life-giving forces" of an organization and strives to create processes to enhance what is already working right in such settings. The presence of people with high Appreciative Intelligence can accelerate that process of identifying the core values, and the subsequent steps of designing and constructing concrete actions to help lead the organization in a desired direction. In short, Appreciative Intelligence in leaders and stakeholders of an organization engaged in Appreciative Inquiry will help generate better outcomes that are sustaining and significant.

Appreciating the positive—focusing on the aspect of the oak that is healthy and thriving, not what is withering or unable to grow—is a vital component of Appreciative Intelligence. It clarifies that Appreciative Intelligence does not mean reframing to see what is negative, or to move backward through destruction. By seeing what is valuable, constructive, or wonderful in the present, the door opens wide for a positive future.

Chapter 6

Seeing How the Future Unfolds from the Present

"The Ancient Greeks," I say, ". . . listened to the
wind and predicted the future from that."
DeWeese squints. "How could they tell the future
from the wind?"
"I don't know, maybe the same way a painter can tell
the future of his painting by staring at the canvas."
—Robert M. Pirsig,
Zen and the Art of Motorcycle Maintenance

What if, however unlikely, Rotarians reframed the challenge of polio eradication as an organizational challenge but didn't perceive that the leadership skills, business expertise, and resources of their fellow Rotary members could be applied to it? Or what if Bill Gore reframed Gore-Tex as a valuable new kind of dental floss, but no one could see how to get the product to consumers? Polio might still be epidemic in parts of the world, and Glide-Floss might not exist except on the end of Bill Gore's toothbrush. Appreciative Intelligence would not have been at work in these situations, because the third component—seeing how the future unfolds from the present—was missing.

There are thousands of talented artists, business people, and creative individuals in the world. Many of them are able to reframe reality and appreciate the positive. But many of their projects or products do not succeed or survive in the marketplace because the crucial last component of Appreciative Intelligence is not present.

People with high Appreciative Intelligence are able to realize that unfolding the future from the present is a critical final step. They are able to recognize the role of environment or external factors in this process, and they have a unique ability to see how the generative potential of the present connects directly to the future. They can see how positive aspects of the current state could be directly applied to achieve goals. One of us (Tojo) has used the term "future-present"[1] to describe the mindset in which a person is able to see the future in the present, as if bringing the concrete experience anticipated in the future to the domain of the present. People with high Appreciative Intelligence are able to visualize and create the sequential small steps that build on one another, thus creating the momentum for change in individuals and their environments that leads to positive outcomes.

In each case we studied, those with Appreciative Intelligence reframed the present—the current state—such that a positive future state could be reached through resources, tools, and concepts that already existed. Pellerin reallocated money and capabilities already within the NASA system. Kamen's breakthrough inventions were based on recognition of culture, knowledge, and principles that already exist. By linking the future to the present, their innovative and creative solutions were grounded, led to action, and were accomplished over time.

Several years ago, the polio eradication program ran into a hitch. In India, for cultural reasons, many fathers resisted immunization of their children. Rotarians and their program partners held National Immunization Days, but few families visited the immunization sites to receive the vaccine, a situation that threatened to leave children vulnerable to the crippling or fatal effects of the disease. Using Appreciative Intelligence, Rotarians yet again switched frames, from a medical or organizational frame to a cultural frame. They also saw and appreciated that a beautiful and talented movie actress named Manorama was popular among men. They saw how the celebrity could apply her talents and charisma to educating and persuading fathers to take their children to immunization sites. By understanding the role of the environment and culture (the men's discomfort with having their children immunized and their enjoyment of Manorama's films), polio eradication coordinators were able to see how to address the issue. They saw how change was possible through the concrete action of filming Manorama in an appeal to immunize children against the disease. The short film helped overcome paternal resistance. Crowds gathered at the immunization sites, and in some areas the oral vaccine drops were dubbed "Manorama drops."[2]

Although we separate Appreciative Intelligence into three components for the sake of explanation and discussion, many of the leaders we interviewed described solutions as coming to them in one mental process. They did not reframe one day, see what was valuable the next, and determine a week later what aspects of the present could set the course for a desired future. Their answers came in one "piece," and all three components were interwoven. They were able to identify proactive action steps at the beginning. In the instance of Manorama's film for the polio eradication campaign, the positive generative present and future aspects were integrated: Rotarians' reframing of polio eradication as a cultural challenge specific to a portion of the male population, appreciation of the actress's appeal and ability to influence that audience, and concrete plans to create a film to encourage fathers to have their children immunized.

George Shaw, a sales associate at W. L. Gore, described his flashes of insight, including one that led to a new oil and gas exploration subsidiary for his company. "The idea comes all at once," he said. "You can see the idea from beginning to end all at the same time."[3] Analogously, he could see the thriving oak tree as he looked at the acorn in hand. Shaw's descriptions of his mental images concurred with others' accounts of understanding and envisioning the future outcomes and a few specific steps to get there in the present. In many cases, projects progressed over long periods of time by forming a chain of insights and answers each time a new question arose.

Creating (Not Just Predicting) the Future

Business success stories, management researchers, and psychologists provide us with insights about the ways leaders and entrepreneurs see and realize the future unfolding from the present. They offer theories and examples of enactment and generative language. Rather than hand us a crystal ball that conjures images of the future based on notions from an isolated tower, they provide clues as to how people create and shape the future by interacting with others.

One of the key challenges of having the ability to see the future unfold from the present is figuring out what is going on in the environment or market. An idea is perceived as brilliant when opinion leaders or the professional community judge it to be so. Similarly, something is perceived as innovative when the leaders behind the concept succeed in getting the market to judge and value the idea, product, or process as innovative.

Consider the case of BlackBerry™, the wireless device that acts as an e-mailer, Web surfer, phone, and personal digital assistant, all in one. Due to its substantial use and popularity among celebrities as well as the general public, BlackBerry has entered colloquial speech as a verb. People Blackberry (send messages back and forth) their friends while waiting at the airport, similar to the way consumers Fedex (send via overnight service) packages and Xerox (photocopy) documents. The story of Research in Motion (RIM), the Canadian company that makes BlackBerry, is a good example of the ability of its 45-year-old founder, Mike Lazaridis, to see the future unfolding from the present.

In 1997 Lazaridis began thinking about combining e-mail with wireless networks used by pagers at that time and developed a gadget he called Inter@ctive Pager. Lazaridis could not get the mobile phone companies to buy into his idea, because they were focused on earning revenue from voice calls on their analog networks. To create his vision of the future of everyone sporting a BlackBerry, RIM bought airtime on pager networks and offered the mobile e-mail service itself. The company marketed and sold its services to investment banks and law firms. By 2002, RIM had signed up half a million BlackBerry subscribers.[4] That number is projected to reach 4.5 million by the end of 2005 with 200 carriers.[5]

It is evident how Mike Lazaridis reframed pagers as a two-way, instead of one-way, communication device along the lines of e-mail. He appreciated certain aspects of communication technology available at the time and people's natural desire for back-and-forth dialog. Above all, he was able to envision the early steps necessary to get to the future from the present, inventing "a back channel so messages could go both ways" and, later with members of RIM, designing a system that would work on limited battery power, raising capital to fund research and development, and licensing some BlackBerry features to earn more money and take the product to a larger market.[6]

People with Appreciative Intelligence knowingly incorporate a view of the environment or the landscape of reality into their daily lives, much the way the student in the story in Chapter 4 perceived the library's paintings as more than background scenery and Lazaridis noticed people's desire to communicate time-sensitive information two-way. At the same time they respond to the environment, they also, in turn, invent it. For them, environment is not only something that is "out there"; it is also created by their imagination and actions. People with Appreciative Intelligence believe that they have a great deal of control in determining what environment they are in or will deal with (conviction that actions matter).

Management researchers Lloyd Sandelands and Robert Drazin expressed this notion at the organizational level in a way that, we believe, can be applied at the individual level. According to Sandelands and Drazin, "Environment is the idea that there is something outside the organization that somehow explains what is inside. As a point of logic, environment could not determine organization because it is defined by organization. By definition there is no organizational environment until there is an organization to have it."[7] Likewise, a person's environment exists when there is a person to have it and define it.

Such interpretations allow people with high Appreciative Intelligence to recognize that they are part of the environment or the world around them as opposed to being an entity independent of it. They understand connections between themselves and the world around them. They see the circular process of their actions affecting people and situations around them and, in turn, their surroundings driving their actions also. The Nobel laureate Herbert Simon (1916–2001) clarified this process: "The first step in rational action is to focus attention on some specific (strategic) aspects of the total situation, and to form a model of the situation in terms of the aspects that lie in that focus of attention. Rational computation takes place in the context of this model, rather than in the response to the whole external reality."[8]

Based on a framework provided by noted management thinkers Karl Weick and Richard Daft,[9] we conceptualize a model for unfolding the future from the present by extrapolating their organizational level analysis to the individual level. Two key dimensions of this framework after our adaptation are (1) an individual's beliefs about whether or not his or her environment can be understood or analyzed and (2) the extent to which the individual engages with the environment to have an impact on it. When an individual believes that the environment is relatively simple to understand or views it passively, rather than actively engaging it, he or she is more likely to accept information about the environment by chance, routine data analysis, or discovery. An individual with high Appreciative Intelligence, on the other hand, aware of the complexities of the environment and believing that his or her actions matter, is more likely to see that the world is not static and simple to analyze and that active interaction can have an impact on the world and the future. In the mode Daft and Weick call "enactment," the individual interacts with his or her surroundings by experimenting, learning by doing, creating opportunities, and inventing pieces of the environment. Such individuals create an environment or market for new ideas, products, or services instead of waiting to find out to what extent a need or desire already exists.[10]

A term that captures the sense of physically taking action or "doing something," enactment can be viewed as bracketing some experiences from the stream of events and swarm of experiences.[11] The product of enactment is the transformed environment that has been acted upon by the person who has selected salient aspects of the events and experiences.

In a vivid example of inventors and inventions taking action and changing the market rather than waiting for the market to call for an invention first, Sony and JVC engineers once looked at a $50,000 tape recorder produced by Ampex in the late 1950s and imagined a market where a similar product could be sold for $500.[12] The affordable personal tape recorder, like some of Sony's other successful products, was once seen by others as an unattainable dream. Yet the company gave its engineers and designers the freedom to imagine and create the technology necessary for transforming their visions into reality.[13] By inventing and offering people the chance to try smaller and less expensive tape recorders, radios, and tape players like the Sony Walkman, they created a market that demanded affordable portable devices for recording and listening to music,[14] as well as other gadgets for entertainment.

Similarly, no market research would have predicted the need for microwave ovens, instant cameras, cellular telephones, compact disc players, fax machines, the BlackBerry, and the Internet. Instead, by introducing the product, the market was created.

As the stories of Manorama's film about immunization and RIM's Blackberry illustrate, the key step of unfolding the future from the present entails the "enactment of possibilities" as opposed to "enactment of limitations," a distinction first articulated by Karl Weick. What Weick referred to as the enactment of limitations is a process wherein "inaction is justified by the implantation, in fantasy, of constraints and barriers that make action impossible. These constraints, barriers, prohibitions then become prominent 'things' in the environment. They also become self-imposed restrictions on the options that managers consider and exercise when confronted with problems."[15] The result is a "failure to act rather than a failure while acting."[16] By avoiding testing possible ideas, which precludes testing their skills, individuals may come to the conclusion that constraints exist in the environment limiting their potential responses.[17] In other words, in behaviors and mindset that can be recognized in consistent "nay-sayers" in a group or an individual who gets stuck in recurring problems, people mired in enactment of limitations quit solving a challenge before they even get started.

In contrast, the enactment of possibilities is the mindset that leaves the door open for potential action and solutions. A strong image of "anticipatory reality"[18]—that is, seeing the detail of the future as if it has already happened—helps in diverting attention from what is not possible to what is achievable for the enactment of possibilities. What is also important for creating enactment of possibilities is action. People can "construct, rearrange, single-out, and demolish many . . . features of their surroundings."[19]

One of the basic tenets of enactment of possibilities is the notion that action precedes and determines cognition.[20] Action is the source of knowledge about the environment, and it helps the person who is thinking and acting in the environment make sense of the events taking place. As we mentioned in our previous discussion of perspective and framing, people select an aspect of the environment on which to focus and then take action. Essentially, what this notion describes is that we find what we seek, we act on what we find, and we change and learn about our world by acting on it. That is, possibilities are realized through behaviors that create a self-fulfilling prophecy.

In an example of enactment, or realizing possibilities through actions that create self-fulfilling prophecies, teachers at Delaware Valley Friends School select talents of a particular student to focus on. Once that selection occurs, teachers work to reframe the talents of the student to bring out her best, show her the various steps she needs to take (such as attending specific classes and accomplishing certain types of projects), and finally believing strongly in the student's capacity to realize her potential. The teachers see the anticipatory reality. They see the future in the present and share it with the student so that she can "see" it for herself. Encouraged by the support of teachers and other members of the school community (an important validation for the student who previously was plagued by self-doubt, developed from double messages she had received from traditional schools or society at large), the student enacts by engaging in a series of focused activities to achieve the end state of success in learning.

Creating the Future through Language

Our framing of situations, interactions, and relationships influences what happens in our future. The way we speak—the language we use to frame our conversations—also shapes the results of projects and problems. Language is generative, meaning that the words we use actually construct our reality, as shown in the following true story.

A friend (let's call her Ellen) grew up in a foreign country. Some of her childhood experiences—such as singing in the bathtub and putting on plays for her parents—were similar to the author's. Other things were different. For instance, she had never seen an electric garage door opener before she came to the United States.

She and her husband bought a home with an electric garage door opener. There was only one remote control, and my friend kept it in her car.

Every evening after work Ellen pushed the remote button to open the garage door automatically. She drove the car into the garage, and flipped the wall switch to close the door as she walked from the garage into the house.

Each morning before work, Ellen performed a different routine. She walked from the house into the garage, flipped the wall switch to open the garage door, and drove the car out of the garage. Then she got out of the car, walked back into the garage, flipped the wall switch to close the door, and dashed out—in high heels and suit—under the slowly closing garage door. This routine continued for several months until her husband made an unexpected morning trip back home to pick up a forgotten item and witnessed her exit from the garage.

"What are you doing?" he asked in amazement.

"Closing the garage door," she replied. "What does it look like?"

"Why don't you use the garage door opener?" he asked incredulously.

"Oh." Ellen broke into a grin. "It closes it, too, doesn't it?!"

Ellen's thinking and behavior—use of the remote control as solely an "opener"—had been limited by the word she used to label the product. Similar processes are at work as leaders and innovators frame employees as friends instead of as parts of a system or as talented practitioners instead of as cogs in a wheel, and situations as challenges or mysteries instead of problems or showstoppers. Such language is called "generative" because by virtue of its use, it creates or generates a particular reality, path, or outcome.

Psychologist Kenneth Gergen has written extensively about generative theory and generative language. He indicated that generative theories are "accounts of our world that challenge the taken-for-granted conventions of understanding and simultaneously invite us into new worlds of meaning and action."[21] For example, psychoanalyst Sigmund Freud's theories included the concept of repression, which allowed him to see suppressed memories in his patients. His generative language of superego provided an alternative explanation for morality and conscience. Freud's terminology opened the door for new fields, including psychiatry. The terminology became accepted in the medical and mental health professions and eventually became part of our popular culture and language. Thus, today when we hear terms like unconscious, conscious, repressed sexuality, and defense mechanisms, we no longer think of Freud. We simply think of these terms as something real.

Similarly, Karl Marx's notion of class separatism is an example of generative language that changed how people perceived reality and attitudes toward social change. Terms such as "class struggle" and "capitalism" and names for the working and ruling classes ("proletariat" and "bourgeois")—new at that time, but now part of our history and vocabulary—were generative because they caused people to question the assumption that class differences were natural. The language recast workers as revolutionaries and led to huge political, economic, and societal changes.[22]

According to Gergen, a generative theory "invites us to suspend the traditions, and to experiment with new ways of inventorying the world, describing and explaining. . . . it asks us to take a risk with words, shake up the conventions, generate new formations of intelligibility, new images, and sensitivities."[23] Generative language can create new paradigms[24]—or shifts in what we know or believe or how we see the world—by allowing users to perceive new opportunities when conventional language limits them, the way Ellen was limited by the word "opener."[25]

Another example is that of Swiss watch makers, who once dominated the timepiece industry. The traditional language of watch making—"spring movement"—kept them from perceiving the opportunities afforded by the new quartz movement technology, invented by the Swiss themselves. In their perception, if a watch did not have springs, it was not a watch. The Japanese Seiko Company was open to the generative language of "quartz movement." History tells us that a few decades later the Japanese dominated the watch-making industry, and the Swiss lost control of it.[26]

Leaders' storytelling in their organizations also shapes the future. As with those we studied, their narratives share more than the context and details of an event—who was involved, what action happened, and the outcome or direct lessons from the story. They share emotions, judgments, values, beliefs, and attitudes. Using the process of story framing (described in Chapter 2 of this book), they inspire and build the confidence of others and demonstrate the value of certain behaviors. Storytelling is an engaging or entertaining form of communication because listeners identify with characters or recognize salient themes, thus entering into and connecting with the story as a participant or cocreator.

According to Stephen Denning in *The Springboard: How Storytelling Ignites Action in Knowledge-Era Organizations*, "When the story rings true, it enables the listeners to generate a new gestalt in their minds, which embraces the main point of the change [in the story]. For beyond the obvious transmittal of information, the immersion of the self in the events that constitute the story can have an impact. To follow a story as a listener is to give a kind of implicit consent to exhibit a willingness to participate in a journey leading to a mental destination that at the outset is unknown to the listener."[27]

The result of such willingness to enter a story is often the ability to try out and accept a new frame of reality. According to W. L. Gore associate George Shaw, people in his company share all sorts of stories of their distant and recent business history. "We all know different ones," he said, referring to stories about people flossing their teeth, bike cables, breaking Vieve's stove when the business was run from the Gores' home, and others. Some have changed over time, and others have practically become legends. The real importance of the stories, said Shaw, is that "they let new associates see that everyone has ideas that matter."[28] The moral of these stories is paramount to a company that needs numerous innovative ideas in order to bring a few blockbusters to the market. The moral of the story is also proof for associates that the company as a whole "walks the talk" that "everyone can quickly earn the credibility to define and drive projects."[29]

Similarly, at robotics competitions, work sessions with allies, and other events or in publications, FIRST participants read or hear the true tale of the robot that was once shipped upside down to a competition. As the story goes, members of other teams gathered around the pile of parts and rebuilt the robot with the team that originally designed and built it.[30] As FIRST students hear the legend and pass it along to newcomers to the organization, they identify with the team members who, like themselves, spent time and effort on building a robot. They recognize the plight and disappointment of a mistake beyond their control. Through the story's successful ending, they learn the positive results of respect and professionalism, attitudes behind irrepressible resilience and the power of persistence. As students and mentors retell the story with a tone of pride, the cycles of building conviction that one's actions matter, identification with the students who helped rebuild the broken robot, and an openness to a positive future continue.

One final ingredient important to seeing how the future unfolds from the present seems to be imagination. By applying the imagination of a child to the knowledge and awareness of an adult, innovation can result. One individual described the process as "zooming around mentally," or seeing something new in one place and pretending that the trend or product were fully adopted in another place. He described the hypothetical example of learning about a new software application while watching a business television program and imagining it in use at an airport, an office, and a home. Envisioning who would benefit from it, what the location would look like as a result of the change, and who would have fun was simply the grownup version of pretending forty years earlier that an action figure could run across the floor and figuring out what could be used to approximate human movement—swivels, levers, wheels, and, later, electronics.

By weaving together knowledge about the environment and imagination, people with Appreciative Intelligence see a different future than others do. Through enactment—actively experimenting and interacting with the environment—and generative language, they create new possibilities. They connect capabilities of today and the dreams of tomorrow by seeing the steps that make the former become the latter. People with Appreciative Intelligence see how the future unfolds from the present.

Chapter 7

Appreciative Intelligence at Work

None of us is as smart as all of us.
—Japanese proverb

Talk to any member of a FIRST team the day before the goals and rules of a new robotics competition are announced and the corresponding box of robot parts and game pieces arrive, and you'll catch a contagious feeling of intense anticipation and excitement. Like the starting gun at a track event, receiving the rules and the kit of parts signals the beginning of a thrilling six-week race against time, resources, and budget constraints. Every day counts as teams of high school students and their mentors design and build a complicated robot that fits specified criteria and accomplishes feats like scooping up a ball, stacking objects, climbing steps, or hanging from a chin-up bar. What happens, however, if one team's parts kit doesn't arrive at the start of the game?

That was a challenge that students of Westtown School's FIRST Team 1391 faced during the competition of 2004. Because of snowstorms and icy road conditions in southeastern Pennsylvania shortly after the competition kick-off, a shipment of metal extrusions—parts to build the robot's frame—didn't arrive when expected. A competing team learned of the predicament and loaned the Westtown team enough material to get started. Days later, when the delayed package finally arrived, the students replaced their competitor-turned-ally's parts with their own.

This example of goodwill and sportsmanship is no anomaly among FIRST teams. Similar stories of opponents becoming partners, forming alliances, and helping each other with parts, labor, tools, and ideas abound. In one legendary case, a completed robot—the culmination of the weeks-long project of organization, education and preparation—was shipped upside down to a robotics competition event, causing it to arrive in a heap of jumbled pieces. Members of every team at the event showed up to put it back together again.[1] These stories of what FIRST calls "gracious professionalism" circulate from team to team and get passed down from year to year. They stem from FIRST leaders' philosophy and deliberate efforts to spread it.

Each year, the introduction of the FIRST competition manual includes a discussion about gracious professionalism by Dr. Woodie Flowers, a FIRST National Advisor:

> It is . . . completely consistent with the FIRST spirit to encourage doing high quality, well informed work in a manner that leaves everyone feeling valued. . . .
>
> Gracious professionalism has purposefully been left somewhat undefined because it can and should mean different things to each of us. We can, however, outline some of its possible meanings. Gracious attitudes and behaviors are win-win. Gracious folks respect each other and let that respect show in their actions. Professionals possess special knowledge and are trusted by society to use that knowledge responsibly. Thus gracious professionals make a valued contribution in a manner pleasing to others and to themselves.
>
> In FIRST, one of the most straightforward interpretations of gracious professionalism is that we learn and compete like crazy, but treat one another with respect and kindness in the process. We try to avoid leaving anyone feeling like they are losers. No chest thumping barbarian tough talk, but no sticky sweet platitudes either. Knowledge, pride and empathy comfortably blended.[2]

Gracious professionalism is a vivid example of how leaders with high levels of Appreciative Intelligence deliberately put their ability into action in their organizations. Flowers and FIRST founder Dean Kamen help individuals and teams experience the abilities and attributes that form the three components of Appreciative Intelligence and its four ensuing qualities. For example, they articulate the importance of seeing the positive or working appreciatively: "in a manner that leaves everyone feeling valued." They encourage group actions that allow others to experience irrepressible resilience, as in the teams that were given a boost to overcome missing parts or a broken robot. They set up individuals and teams to find successful outcomes—"to avoid leaving anyone feeling like they are losers." They communicate positively, but realistically, to see the oak, but not a tropical mango—"No chest thumping barbarian tough talk, but no sticky sweet platitudes either." By not fully defining the term or specifying a list of behaviors, they give participants the freedom to excel and to develop their own methods of extending gracious professionalism. Hence, they frame the way teams work with each other such that possibilities are left open for finding their own routes to success.

The program is far greater than the robotics competition itself. FIRST is ultimately about learning, growing, working with others, and learning to succeed in life. Kamen succinctly underscored the nature of his organization and members' Appreciative Intelligence at work when he said, "Let the robots lose, but the people win."[3] As students earn college scholarships through the program, graduate to successful careers, develop relationships with accomplished adults, and learn engineering principles and life skills, winning is just what is happening.

While the preceding example of FIRST is about working with students through a nonprofit organization, Appreciative Intelligence is at work in all kinds of organizations with all kinds of people. The principles also apply to efforts with adults in for-profit corporations such as W. L. Gore & Associates, government agencies such as NASA, and educational institutions for children (such as Delaware Valley Friends School) or adults.

Appreciative Intelligence is an individual ability, but it has a significant impact on larger systems. The most successful leaders and innovators extend their Appreciative Intelligence beyond their personal lives and into the very fabric of their organizations. They build an environment, infrastructure, corporate culture, or system that generates success and helps appreciation perpetuate.

In addition to that of Dean Kamen and FIRST, consider the impact of Bill Gore on the company he founded. His belief in the importance of one-on-one communication without constraints of hierarchy is captured in the writings that guide the company today. That belief is still manifested in a practical way by furnishing conference rooms with round tables.[4] Like the legendary table of King Arthur and his knights, the round tables privilege no individual by their proximity to the head.

In other examples of building mechanisms for enduring success into an organizational culture, Starbucks chairman Howard Schultz once bought hundreds of copies of an inspiring book to give to company employees.[5] Philadelphia Tribal Bellydance founder Fleur Frascella's students now teach and appreciate a new generation of students who are learning that the joy and beauty of dancing are not only for a select, skinny few women.

Individuals and organizations affect each other in a circular fashion. Through their behaviors, leaders create an organizational climate that, in turn, encourages others to consider similar actions and initiatives. Such repeated behaviors, over a period of time, become norms—the group's shared beliefs regarding behavior, values, and attitudes. Norms are "the prescribed modes of conduct and belief that not only guide the behavior of group members but also help group interaction by specifying the kinds of responses that are expected and acceptable in particular situations."[6] Once norms are developed and individuals engage in behavior conforming to them, the resulting patterns or styles of interactions become the culture of the organization.

Just as leaders' initial behaviors help shape the organizations' culture, organizations influence their leaders. The organization as a whole— through individuals' reactions, group responses, and even articulated policies that stem from norms—will reinforce what seems acceptable. It will also put pressure on leaders or other individuals to stop behaviors that extend beyond those limits. Norms extend to all types of behaviors (when or where to take a coffee break, what to wear, how many hours of overtime to work) and cultural style (entrepreneurial or traditional, ethical or free-wheeling, knowledge sharing or hoarding). As individuals and groups live or work together over the long term, the behavior patterns or culture become very strong because each one reinforces the other.

Through this circular process, intentionally and unintentionally, leaders build an environment or culture that spreads their own Appreciative Intelligence to others. And as it seeps into an organization's culture, a cycle of innovation, appreciation, and success repeats over time. Shareholder.com, for instance, a small technology company, has enjoyed a history of successful innovation since its beginnings fifteen years ago. As an early builder of public company Web sites, it was the first to create e-mail subscription lists, to include stock price quotes, and to build an investor relations Web site for its client Campbell Soup. The company invented OpenChannel, a web-based resource for education and idea exchange, and OpenCompany, a network to help public companies communicate with investors, which led to a *Fast Company* Fast 50 award.[7] Its creativity repeats over time.

Appreciative by Design

During FIRST's first season, Kamen said, an unsettling thought occurred to him. What if, along with the thrill and fun of a competition, the program ended up with the whole sports model, including aggressive behavior, cheating, and "the dark side we almost come to expect now with sports," he wondered. So, as he put the robotic parts kits together, he decided to define the winning team as one that exemplified the organization's name: For Inspiration and Recognition of Science and Technology. He announced that the team that inspired others, showed good judgment, and a positive impact, rather than the team whose robot scored the most points, would win the Chairman's Award and, that year, a trip to the White House. That decision was the beginning of FIRST's pursuit of gracious professionalism, now one of the guiding principles of the organization and its yearly event.

Like Kamen, nearly every leader we studied and talked to indicated that influencing others—helping them reframe, appreciate the positive, connect the future with the present, innovate, grow their talents, and develop their persistence, conviction that their actions matter, tolerance for uncertainty, and resilience—was intentional. They articulated and disseminated their ideas—Starbucks chairman Howard Schultz via a book ("My ultimate aim in writing *Pour Your Heart into It* is to reassure people to have the courage to persevere"[8]) and Kamen via a webcast FIRST competition kick-off speech each year. They embedded principles and processes of Appreciative Intelligence into their daily routines and the foundations of their organizations. They accomplished this by displaying successful practices for others to model, using positive generative language, formalizing reward and appreciation, and setting high expectations for individuals and the organization.

Modeling Success

Hand a diaper and a doll to a toddler who has an infant sibling, and often you will see an expert imitation of a caregiver's behavior. For better or worse, parents' mannerisms and words are repeated back to them when they least expect it. How many times, as adults, do we observe our own behavior and remark, "I have just become my mother (or father)."

One of the simplest and earliest ways humans learn is through modeling behavior, as was pointed out by psychologist Albert Bandura in his well-known social learning theory. Also called observational learning or social modeling, the theory became widely accepted as a result of the "Bobo doll" studies. Bandura and his team made a film of a young woman punching and kicking a Bobo doll (an inflatable doll that was weighted at the bottom so that it popped back up after being knocked down) and shouting "Sockeroo!" A group of kindergartners watched the film and did exactly what happened in the film when given a Bobo doll and a chance to play later.[9]

According to Bandura, "Learning would be exceedingly laborious, not to mention hazardous, if people had to rely solely on the effects of their own actions to inform them what to do. Fortunately, most human behavior is learned observationally through modeling: from observing others one forms an idea of how new behaviors are performed, and on later occasions this coded information serves as a guide for action."[10] Bandura identified four parts of the modeling process:[11]

1. *Attention:* The person sees a behavior occurring. How distinctive or novel and how complex it is, how often it occurs, how valuable it would be to learn, and a person's mood when focusing on a behavior all contribute to how much attention is given. In the case of the "Bobo" study, the children paid attention to

the movie and were probably highly focused because of the distinctive language ("Sockeroo") and simplicity of the actions.

2. *Retention:* The person retains and remembers what he or she paid attention to.

3. *Reproduction:* In this step, the person watching the behavior must be able to understand the images or descriptions and copy them. The children who watched the young woman in the Bobo film were able to translate the images they saw on film into actual behavior of their own.

4. *Motivation:* Finally, whether or not modeled behaviors are practiced or repeated depends on benefits to the behavior—for example, personal desire or external rewards.

There are famous examples of such modeling success. Venus and Serena Williams, top-ranked tennis players, started playing the game when they were four years old, thanks to their father, who methodically modeled complex playing tactics for them. Similarly, after observing the generosity of Osceola McCarty, a poor laundry worker who donated her entire life savings to a Mississippi university, media mogul Ted Turner made the largest single donation of $1 billion to the United Nations.[12]

The leaders we observed and interviewed also served as examples for their employees, students, coworkers, and colleagues. In some cases, such as dance students deliberately copying a teacher's arm movements or a teen modeling a FIRST mentor's welding or soldering technique, the connection between leader and follower was obvious and direct. In other cases, the links between leaders' behaviors and the attitudes behind them—recognizing and appreciating talent or diversity, remaining calm and open to new avenues after a setback, and talking about what is possible—and those modeled by students, employees, or colleagues were more subtle, indirect, or delayed.

For the dance students, FIRST team members, and millions of Rotarians who watched and learned the simple process of administering the oral polio vaccine, the modeling process—attention, retention, repro-duction, and motivation—was at work. In these cases, the motivation was also unusually high because of the appreciative and generative aspects of the projects. The focus on positive value and the future were factors in ensuring that the behaviors were repeated to complete the goals.

Positive Generative Language

As we have discussed throughout this book, the way people frame situations, interactions, and views of people affects their expectations, actions, decisions, and further perceptions. The way they speak—the language they use to frame conversations—also shapes thoughts, experiences, and behaviors. In their jobs, the leaders we studied and interviewed used positive and generative language that affected their corporate culture, work productivity, and quality of relationships.

For instance, at Gore the company refers to workers as associates. Titles include "human resources associate," "product associate," and "sales associate" instead of "manager" of a certain group or "director" of a particular project. They don't have "bosses" who help new associates learn the ropes, but "sponsors" who act as mentors. Company members are not just using different words to communicate and replicate the traditional concepts of employees and bosses. Their language generates different relationships and lines of communication.

Researchers have shown how other uses of language can change frames, thus changing work situations. For example, in the context of bargaining and negotiation, Harvard University Business School professor Max Bazerman showed how two different frames of a similar situation evoke different responses from individuals.[13] Research on framing bias has shown that, during negotiations, often whether the decision maker is evaluating the prospect of gains or losses is only a matter of the way a question is presented or worded (e.g., "Is the glass half full?" or "Is the glass half empty?"). Thus the way a decision is framed—that is, positively in terms of gains or negatively in terms of losses—can influence a decision maker's risk propensity and thereby his or her decisions.

The following simple examples show positive and negative frames, or "blame" and "aim" frames,[14] in business negotiations. In both cases, a business unit leader wants money to purchase new tools or equipment for his or her group. Their contrasting frames and language, however, set them up for different results. In a negatively framed negotiation, a unit leader might talk about how he or she hasn't received new equipment for three years or how his or her unit has received less seed money than any other in the company. The language does not lay out concrete steps to proceed with a purchase or specify what the likely outcome of such a purchase would be. Instead, the conversation points a blaming finger at someone real or hypothetical who has denied resources in the past. The result may be to provoke defensive reactions in the other party of the negotiation. A positively framed negotiation, on the other hand, would focus on the financial gains that might be possible from such an investment. It might mention who would use the tools or how the expenditure might make the unit more productive. The unit leader might talk about putting together a budget or how easily the tool could be ordered. The conversation moves to the *aim*—the end goal of getting new equipment—and offers suggestions for what could work.

Another way to create frames through language is through analogies or metaphors. Architect Greg Radford used an architectural metaphor to show those around him how to see things from a different perspective. "My job when doing a building is to take my idea and construct a plan, an elevation, and a section [three types of architectural drawings to show a building from different angles]," he said. "It's three ways of looking at the same things so people can see parts and relationships. That's what people need to do all the time in all things—see parts and relationships."[15]

The leaders we studied also provided or interpreted data that others already had so that they could see possibilities for action in situations that appeared difficult. In the case of Rotary's polio eradication program, local business leaders knew that they could organize large groups of people and complex projects, communicate through technology and the media, arrange transportation, and earn money. Yet, according to Herb Pigman, who was a driving force behind the program, typically business leaders wouldn't understand that they had the overview of the ways they could assist a nation's health officials in a large-scale immunization project.

"I had to convey to them, 'Your knowledge can be applied to the problems of health ministers,'" said Pigman. He worked in-person with Rotarians worldwide to help them realize their value to the project, and he wrote a booklet about the ways business people could help. His efforts paid off in Peru, for instance, where an insurance specialist became the leader of Rotarians who helped the country pull off its National Immunization Day. Rotarians, working with health workers, provided ice to keep the vaccine cold, lunches for workers, and transportation for vaccine and health workers. Pigman told the volunteers, "This is not rocket science to Rotarians—we can do this."[16]

Appreciative Intelligence is also expressed through positively oriented persuasion, beyond the "can-do" hype, to fill in gaps or recognize progress, especially when people begin to struggle or doubt themselves. For example, when Shareholder.com faced a major challenge last year, "we talked about what we're good at," said company president Ron Gruner.[17] Through the discussion, the company harnessed the strengths of its individuals, as well as its unique strengths in the market, to create a competitive advantage. The ability to encourage others verbally or articulate their potential for growth is certainly another instance of Appreciative Intelligence.

There are even stronger expressions of it in exceptionally challenging circumstances. The 2004 film *Hotel Rwanda* unearthed a powerful story of Appreciative Intelligence. The film depicts the heroic actions of Paul Rusesabagina during the 1994 Rwandan massacre, which claimed the lives of about one million people and created three million refugees. Paul was the manager of the Mille Collines, a luxury hotel in the Rwandan capital. Over the years, he had sustained good relationships with the military and government officials who visited his hotel to drink and socialize. When the genocide broke out (which at its peak claimed 8000 lives per day), Paul was quick to reframe reality to save the lives of 1200 people who were staying in his hotel. He reframed guests as refugees, the luxury hotel as a refugee camp, and the hotel's pool as a source of water after their supply was cut off. Instead of feeling helpless and giving up after the international peacekeepers deserted him, he saw an opportunity to cash in on his social capital he had built with the military and police. Using his positive attitude, exceptional capacity to see possibilities amidst the violence and darkness around him, and positive language, he worked the system and began cashing in every favor he had ever earned, bribing the Rwandan Hutu soldiers and keeping the militia away from the refugees for one hundred days. In the end he managed to save the lives of over a thousand people.

Reward and Appreciation

After a technology team at Shareholder.com completed a major, time-consuming project, the chief technology officer expressed appreciation to them by renting an expensive sports car. Each team member was given the keys for a few days—and the time off to make use of them—and was photographed with the vehicle. While the rental car fitted the budget better than employee bonuses during the country's economic downturn, it also fitted the bill as a valued and memorable reward for team members.

Associates at Gore once nominated and presented Matt Schreiner with a unique honor his group calls the Water Carrier Award. Reminiscent of the member of a primitive society who ensured that traditions of the culture were passed to newer generations, the pin, shaped like a person carrying a water jug, signified Matt's overall commitment to sharing knowledge of Gore's culture to other people. He said that the award made him feel appreciated and further demonstrated the company's commitment to practicing fairness to people inside and outside of Gore.[18]

Like those at Shareholder.com and W. L. Gore & Associates, other leaders with high Appreciative Intelligence made a point of rewarding employees and expressing appreciation to those around them, often in creative ways. While this sounds obvious or commonplace, contrast the story of another company president who once told his employees, "We're all grown-ups—we don't need to be thanked," and the all-too-common media article theme of the corporate CEO who boasts of a million-dollar bonus as employee salaries are cut and layoffs are occurring.

FIRST's well-developed recognition structure is an example of formalized appreciation to coach teams and individuals and coax a range of diverse talents out of them. With more than 20 awards, in addition to scholarships for individual students from colleges and universities, FIRST recognizes and celebrates different aspects of excellence: engineering elegance, team spirit and enthusiasm, strength of partnerships, visual appeal of robot, entrepreneurial enthusiasm and skills, a well-designed Web site, safety, and other areas. Through the large number and variety of awards, in a deliberate manner the organization sends the message that there are numerous ways to win and many paths to success. Patricia Spackman, FIRST team 1391's advisor, summed up the program's philosophy on awards: "Each kid could be a star."[19]

Celebrated psychologist B. F. Skinner's initial proposition that human beings can be "conditioned" or shaped to engage in predictable forms of behavior in response to carefully administered incentive-schemes was provocative and unsettling in the 1930s. His ideas are widely accepted today, however. Applying his principle of positive reinforcement—the concept that rewarding a behavior leads to an increase in its frequency—to organizations suggests that if an organization's members exhibit high levels of Appreciative Intelligence by appreciating or rewarding positive aspects of a person's behavior (such as persistence, positive language, or risk-taking), the person will exhibit that behavior more often. When a leader sees a hidden talent or ability in an employee or student, by rewarding instances when the employee uses the talent or demonstrates the ability, the leader helps that employee show it more often. Thus the leader helps reveal behaviors that already existed within the employee.

Setting Expectations

People with high Appreciative Intelligence create self-fulfilling prophecies that result in personal success. They also create organizational success by appreciating and setting high expectations for other individuals and their organizations as a whole.

In Chapter 5 we discussed the Rosenthal effect or Pygmalion effect: the phenomenon in which people live up to the positive expectations others hold for them. In frame-breaking studies that showed the power of such expectations, student researchers and teachers brought about unexpected and positive results in flatworms, rats, and, later, "blooming students." They helped create successful animals and people because they believed those beings had inherent special abilities and were able to meet high expectations. This principle works in business and organizational contexts, too.

The goal of Rotary's polio program—arresting and eradicating a disease—provides a clear example of holding high expectations for individuals and the group. Not only did the originators of the program expect Rotarians to solve each challenge along the way, but two decades later new generations of Rotarians have those expectations and continue to hold themselves and the organization responsible to the goal.

At the same time they set high expectations, leaders with Appreciative Intelligence give others freedom to excel. A manager in one organization we studied said that, within reasonable boundaries, he and others were given freedom to manage with their own styles and to give credit as they felt was right. Philadelphia Tribal Bellydance Artistic Director Fleur

Frascella said that over time she gives a dancer more and more artistic license. In the FIRST program, the leadership team does not fully define gracious professionalism, specify a list of appropriate behaviors, or dictate the design of a robot. In doing so, they provide the freedom for teams to develop their own ways to extend gracious professionalism and find their own creative solutions to design and build a robot.

Another way leaders facilitate others' success is to remove the barriers that keep them from excelling. That sentiment was reflected in the comment, "We try to provide a work atmosphere that when people are working on their jobs, they aren't worrying about their jobs."[20]

Organizational Results

Creatively appreciating and rewarding group members, setting high expectations, and respecting diverse strengths and competencies are more than just good ideas. They lead to innovation, invention, resilience, and entrepreneurship. They are linked with high rates of innovation and member retention.

During the FIRST robotics competition of 2004, Westtown's Team 1391 found a way to benefit from a mishap and, simultaneously, find a creative solution to a budget limitation. One day, a large bouncy ball—a game piece in the season's competition—rolled over a metal shaving and sprang a leak. As team members tried to seal the hole, the ball split wide open. For a moment, the group watched silently. But as they examined the material of the popped ball, they discovered that the inside surface was the perfect rubbery substance to cover their robot's roller, a part that grabbed a ball and pulled it inside the machine in order to be carried. The material provided the perfect grip, and the team had one fewer item to buy. Just one creative solution in a long chain of questions and challenges, the team's final product was an innovative robot that could grab and carry a ball, climb steps, hang from a chin-up bar, and compete with hundreds of other robots with unique designs but similar capabilities. The outcome of FIRST's system, designed by leaders with Appreciative Intelligence, was ultimately innovation.

Dean Kamen said that he applies the same principles with FIRST as he does in business. He described an approach, similar to "Let the robots lose, but the people win," to business competition: One company might be developing an improved pump or a new delivery system for insulin, while its competitor might be working on a pill. The companies can't damage each others' buildings for a competitive advantage. Instead, they need to develop a better product. The competitor with the pill might win the round of competition. As a result, diabetes therapy might progress from using a pump to swallowing a pill. Later, however, a competing company might develop a vaccine. Beyond that, one might eliminate diabetes through genomics. Better innovation leads to a competitive advantage. In the end, the public gets the best solution, he said.[21]

Like FIRST, his company, DEKA Research and Development Corporation, reaps the rewards of a system whose members weave their Appreciative Intelligence into the culture. They experience unparalleled strides in innovation. DEKA's list of achievements includes a stair-climbing wheelchair, a compact dialysis machine that enables people with chronic kidney failure to travel, and other medical devices.

With the intrinsic reward of accomplishment and external awards for talent, expertise, and jobs well done, it is no wonder that many groups with cultures with Appreciative Intelligence enjoy high retention rates or low turnover. The retention rate of FIRST teams from 2004 to 2005 was 87%, and the previous years' rates hovered similarly around 90%. A member of another organization described the effect on his company: "We were willing to work together, there was give and take in problem-solving, loyalty, no backbiting, and [team members] stuck around for a long time."

Finally, we can't dismiss the benefits of innovative products and culture to a company's bottom line. Among the leaders we observed and interviewed, the most consistent and dramatic results were shown at W. L. Gore & Associates. It posted a profit each year for more than 45 years[22] and saw annual sales revenue of over $1 billion for the last several years.

Leaders with Appreciative Intelligence set a tone and example that is followed by the group. They do so by using language that brings out talents and creativity of those around them and elicits innovative solutions to challenging situations. They demonstrate practices and principles for others to model, set high expectations, and give them freedom to excel. As a leader perceives the positive inherent generative potential within the present, so do those around her. When their successful outcomes and accomplishments are rewarded—through appreciation, recognition, financial compensation, or the thrill of a job well done—the culture is further reinforced, thus leading to subsequent innovation, high member retention, loyalty, and organizational excellence and longevity.

Applying Appreciative Intelligence at the Organizational Level

As mentioned previously, Appreciative Intelligence is an individual ability, but it has a significant impact on larger systems. Because individuals and organizations shape each other in a continuous and dynamic circular fashion, organizations are affected by people who have a high degree of Appreciative Intelligence. There is a debate among organizational psychologists, practitioners, and others as to whether or not an organization as a whole can be intelligent. We take the position that only individuals are intelligent and that to say that an organization is "smart" or "intelligent" is to ascribe human attributes to a larger body.[23]

But since organizations as a whole can adapt and survive, and individuals with Appreciative Intelligence have a positive impact on their organizations, we refer to organizations whose leaders and employees have extended their Appreciative Intelligence into their organizational culture as "organizations with Appreciative Intelligence." Individuals can determine who in their organization is exhibiting Appreciative Intelligence, see where their interactions are leading to an overall climate of Appreciative Intelligence, and build on that success to emerge as a more competitive and resilient organization in the future.

Organizational Appreciative Intelligence Profile

To determine where pockets of high Appreciative Intelligent leaders are and what characteristics your organization shares with other organizations with Appreciative Intelligence, please answer the following questions. Focus on what exists or what works, not on what is missing or broken.

1. Write (or speak into a voice recorder) the story of a time in your organization when you, someone else, a group, or the organization as a whole was most successful. (This can be from any aspect or time of your organization—from any

division, at startup or at any other phase. Please answer from an organizational perspective—when *the people in your organization* felt most successful, not necessarily when outsiders thought the organization was most successful.) Use the following questions to help you jog your memory or capture details.

a. Where were you?

b. When did this take place?

c. Who was involved?

d. What were the circumstances or context?

e. What happened?

f. What were the reactions of individuals in the group? If they were mixed, how? Who reacted in what ways?

g. In general, what were people's emotions at the beginning and end? If they were mixed, please specify.

h. How and what did the leader communicate to others?

i. How did the story end?

j. What made this feel successful?

---

2. Describe a time you, someone in your organization, or a group reframed a situation or product in a positive way or generated new possibilities for a challenge.

a. What was the context? (Where were you/they? When?)

b. Who, if anyone, was involved?

c. If you can articulate it, what led you or them to see something different?

d. What part of the future desirable state was already present?

e. What, if anything, was the result?

---

3. Which qualities of Appreciative Intelligence appeared in the story from question 1 or 2? Who in your organization exhibited them? Describe the example.

a. Persistence of thought or behavior _____

b. Communication of confidence or conviction that you could solve a challenge or that actions mattered _____

c. Tolerance or management of risk, ambiguity (ideas that conflicted with the organization's previous beliefs or knowledge), or uncertainty _____

_____

d. Irrepressible resilience (the ability to bounce back from a difficult time or to overcome an obstacle) _____

_____

4. What does your organization do to bring out the best in employees, students, colleagues, partners, and others? Are there deliberate practices or programs in place to help reveal hidden talent or skills in people? Who, if anyone specific, has a knack for revealing or bringing out the best in others? Give examples.

_____

_____

_____

5. Describe a situation in which you, someone else, or a group within your organization came up with a creative or innovative solution, invented something, or solved a problem that you believe has something to do with Appreciative Intelligence.

a. Where were you/they? What were the conditions of the environment? What is/was the culture of the organization or smaller group within the organization?

b. Who was involved? What were you/they doing at the time?

c. What were you/they trying to solve?

d. How long did it take to solve?

e. What were the results of the creativity or innovation?

f. What tools, resources, or help did you/they use or employ in the process?

_____

_____

_____

6. What does your organization do to reward, recognize, and appreciate people and their actions? How often? Who, if anyone, in your organization tends to do this most often, most sincerely, or most effectively? In what sorts of creative ways does your organization appreciate its employees, students, partners, customers, investors, vendors/supply chain, service providers, or any other stakeholders? Provide examples.

_____

_____

_____

7. Who are the individuals in your organization who set a climate of Appreciative Intelligence for others? (Do these people tend to come from the same business unit, department, or division, and if so, which one? Or do they exist in numerous units?)
   a. Who models the behaviors set by others?
   b. Who sets high standards and expectations for herself, others, and the organization as a whole?
   c. Who provides others with the freedom to excel?
   d. Who acts as the venture capitalist (for finances, supplies, human resources, or other resources) and applies resources to what works or comes up with creative solutions to needs for resources?

_____

_____

_____

8. What behaviors associated with a climate of Appreciative Intelligence does your organization perform deliberately? Through what policies, mission statements, articulated goals, training sessions, or communication vehicles does your organization provide a positive view of the environment? Please give examples.

_____

_____

_____

9. What groups have high employee or member retention or low rates of absenteeism? Where are human relationships healthiest? What behaviors related to Appreciative Intelligence are reinforced by leaders and followers and have become part of the organizational culture? Please describe examples.

_____

_____

_____

10. Reflect on your responses so far. Who is most likely to reframe, appreciate the positive, and see how the future unfolds from the present? When? In what business or domain area? What people, units, departments, or stakeholder groups of the organization have specific strengths associated with Appreciative Intelligence? Under what conditions is the organization the most effective, innovative, creative, or successful? Which qualities are your organization's strongest, or which occur most often?

_____

_____

_____

11. Describe or paint a picture of a future scenario in which your organization is thriving or effective in a new domain, or more successful or innovative in a current area. What qualities are stronger or show up more often? What are the stories that are spreading through the organization? Are you generating more possibilities or framing to see a more positive future? How are individuals, different stakeholder groups, and the organization as a whole more successful? (Have talents been revealed? How are they benefiting from creativity, innovation, or inventions? What are the rewards—financial, personal satisfaction, recognition, or other— that others are experiencing? Are they benefiting from framing of situations for a better future?) How can you expand the profile you described in question 10 above to realize this scenario?

_____

_____

_____

Facilitating Organizational Change

Once you understand what your organizational profile looks like (answer to question 10) and have a general sense of what you want it to look like in the future (answer to question 11), you can spark change within your organization by helping others enhance their Appreciative Intelligence and by changing the culture in the organization. While leaders or senior managers of an organization may be in a more comfortable place to help enhance others' Appreciative Intelligence, anyone with a good understanding of the three components and four qualities of Appreciative Intelligence can help create this culture.

How do you do this? This is the million-dollar question. It takes alignment of individuals' goals and abilities and organizational mission, goals, strategy, and tactics.

It also takes time. Appreciative Intelligence, like other intelligences—general or multiple—is not developed overnight, and weaving a leader's Appreciative Intelligence and related behaviors into a culture of an organization takes integrated efforts and mindset. It is easier to build a culture with significant Appreciative Intelligence from the ground up than it is to change an existing culture. It can be developed, however, once you have decided to do it. Leaders must act as facilitators, not barriers, in helping others develop their own Appreciative Intelligence. Completing the Organizational Appreciative Intelligent Profile, talking about it with others in the organization, and reinforcing the areas where it is strong help create a new culture. Furthermore, a leader may create self-expectation in others partly because she communicates her own positive expectations by identifying the inherent potential in others.

Now that we have introduced the construct of Appreciative Intelligence with this book, there is room to grow and refine our understanding of it in the future. We expect that practitioners, researchers, and consultants will develop techniques and approaches for enhancing it and applying it in organizations.

By using Appreciative Intelligence at work, organizations can build a culture that increases and perpetuates the incidence of success and innovation.

Chapter 8

Developing Your Appreciative Intelligence

Genius is 5% inspiration and 95% perspiration.
—Thomas Edison

Some leaders and innovators seem to be born with high Appreciative Intelligence. Many people we interviewed perceived the positive inherent general potential in the present early on in their lives. They seemed to reframe, appreciate the positive, and see how the future unfolds from the present effortlessly. They exhibited the ensuing qualities of Appreciative Intelligence—persistence, conviction that their actions matter, tolerance for uncertainty, and irrepressible resilience—and reaped the benefits of invention, innovation, creativity, and success at a young age.

Ed Hoffman, who reframed the program that addressed the *Challenger* tragedy as the beginnings of a larger initiative to cultivate NASA's leadership skills, showed evidence of the ability to frame situations positively and uniquely as a child. "I grew up in Brooklyn," he said, "an interesting place." In an area where being at the wrong place at the wrong time could have serious ramifications or a seemingly simple conflict had the potential to escalate, "I'd deal with the possibility of getting beaten up or something scary." Many times, he reframed a confrontation as something positive, a moment for humor, rather than aggression. He saw how to realize an outcome that had more helpful results for all involved, not just for kids who were smaller and physically less capable—those without "muscular forte,"[1] Hoffman related.

At the age of 13, when many kids in the U.S. are spending money on hobbies, Michael Dell framed one of his as a moneymaker and ended up operating a mail order stamp business. He started the giant computer corporation bearing his name in his dorm room and paid cash for a BMW at age 17.[2] Thus, he showed early evidence of reframing reality as opportunities. He demonstrated persistence and irrepressible resilience—patterns consistent with that of a leader and innovator with high Appreciative Intelligence—at a young age that has continued throughout his leadership of Dell, including through the downturn in the technology industry and overall economy in the early 2000s.

Everyone has Appreciative Intelligence. While some people such as Hoffman and Dell appear to have a predisposition or seem to be born with a high degree of Appreciative Intelligence, others slowly develop it through unconscious practice. Yet others proactively and mindfully cultivate it.

Identifying, developing, and enhancing Appreciative Intelligence in yourself or other individuals, and applying it for personal or organizational success, can lead to great advantage and reward. At the same time, a few challenges come with the territory of dealing with an invisible entity and trying to approach the complex mental processes directly.

Grasping Intangibles

How much creativity do you possess? How much integrity or hope do you have? Can you assign a numerical figure to the amount of those attributes? Could you quantify how much of them you have today compared to yesterday? Or could you say that you are 20 or 50 percent more trustworthy, open-minded, collaborative, or brave than another person? Likewise, how much innovation or knowledge does your organization have? Can you assign a number or dollar figure to the value of the quality of its leadership, reputation, or credibility?

Characteristics, values, and concepts such as creativity, knowledge, and credibility are intangible. They silently, invisibly influence our lives, organizations, and environment. But because we can't see, hear, or touch them, they're difficult and subjective to define and even more elusive to measure. We can't use a traditional yardstick to measure concepts like trust, talent, and loyalty or set them on a scale to determine their weight.

The importance of the scientific approach and quantified measurement took on new significance in our culture as people moved from an agrarian to a technological society during the Industrial Revolution. Methods for measuring and improving productivity, uniformity, consistency, and efficiency became important as modern automation and factory-produced items replaced physical labor and artisans' hand-made goods. As application of numbers and metrics (speed, quantity of output, and so forth—therefore, observable, measurable objects and processes) became more important to manufacturing, their significance seeped into other aspects of business and life. Other concepts—employee satisfaction, individual creativity, diversity of personalities—moved into a position of less importance or into the periphery of the modern factory mentality. Subjective knowledge and anecdotal evidence moved into the realm of the arts. Later, other concepts such as quality of management and brand reputation became less "trustworthy" if they were not supported by quantifiable metrics that would fit on a corporate spreadsheet. The bottom-line orientation brought most organizational processes to a number game.

Even though numerical representation or measurement of an abstract concept is nearly impossible, and it may not be the best approach to dealing with it, quantifying a concept sometimes affords certain advantages: recognition, measurement, and possibly an enhancement of the concept.

In the field of social sciences, researchers have been making efforts to examine intangible concepts both quantitatively and qualitatively. By attributing specific behaviors to abstract concepts and turning them into constructs, we can assign numbers and make judgments, comparisons, or correlations, such as with scores of resilience or the traditional measure of IQ. New imaging techniques and technological advances help us observe and measure the brain and its electrical activity, as in the identification of the location where insight takes place and how quickly a flash occurs.

Even qualitatively we can define, describe, narrate, and make relative comparisons of invisible concepts among people or organizations (such as "Anika is a stronger leader than Chris is" or "Company X has a better reputation than Company Y") or between different concepts in the same person (such as "Kim is more knowledgeable than she is creative"). Ultimately, we can also know about an intangible and hold knowledge about it, even if it is tacit, unarticulated, or difficult to define.

In the same way, underlying your ability to identify, develop, and enhance Appreciative Intelligence in yourself or others in your organization is the understanding that, for now, you may not be able to approach or measure it directly. You can, however, understand instinctively what it is and spot evidence of it through the qualities that accompany Appreciative Intelligence.

More on Intelligence

In addition to accepting that it is possible to recognize and change your Appreciative Intelligence, although you cannot see it directly, you may also need to learn and accept that intelligence is neither entirely innate nor static. For quite some time, there has been a debate about the origin of a person's intelligence: whether it is determined by nurture (environment) or nature (heredity), or in other words, whether it is shaped by a stimulating and healthy environment or it is a trait programmed by genetic code.

The nurture-nature controversy has continued despite better understanding of the impact of both through research. While there have been hundreds of studies published on the controversy, their findings do not support either position solely, but instead underscore the importance of both. The most commonly cited studies on identical twins (who have the same genetic make-up) show that as they grow up, they have similarities and differences, implying that both genetics and environmental factors play a role in the development of intelligence. Furthermore, irrespective of the scientific evidence, there is an emotional component to the debate. Moral, religious, and political beliefs play a strong role in people's stance on the debate.[3] Yet even if we were to suspend all our personal values and beliefs and look at the evidence, the emerging picture does not point us either to environment or hereditary factors.

The lack of consensus on the relative importance of genetics or environmental factors on the development of intelligence does not diminish the importance of either. Ultimately, however, we need only revisit Rosenthal and Jacobson's classroom with its "bloomers" (as discussed in

Chapter 5) to remind ourselves that even environmental factors such as appreciation and expectation of teachers regarding students' intelligence-related performance can actually improve IQ as measured by standard instruments.

"We don't know to what extent intelligence is hard-wired," said John Kounios, professor and researcher at Drexel University's EEG Laboratory. "It's determined by who your parents were and by environmental differences. We do know that the brain is very plastic." In other words, it can change, he added. He pointed to two pieces of evidence: first, that human neural connections can change during a 20-minute conversation, and second, that rats in an impoverished environment sprout new connections after being placed in a stimulating environment with toys. He also pointed to findings from his own research that show that people put their brains into a pre-creative state before insight occurs. "[The brain] is not a static piece of hardware," Kounios asserted.[4]

Such information is good news for those who want to expand their intelligence. Even if they may not be genetically endowed with high levels of Appreciative Intelligence, people can nurture or train themselves to become more intelligent.

With the right discipline, motivation, determination, and tools, you can enhance your Appreciative Intelligence.

A Model for Appreciative Intelligence

If possible, recall your early childhood experiences of drawing a picture (or a more recent observation of another child's first attempts in art). Most likely, you (or the other child) created colorful but indistinguishable scribbles. You were pleased with your final product regardless of its lack of artistic proficiency. Not too long afterward, when drawing with other young artists, you may have realized that another child couldn't make sense of your drawing or mistook the subject in your picture for something else. The realization that the drawing wasn't as perfect as you once thought may have led to disappointment or confusion. But the knowledge that your drawing had room for improvement may have spurred you to copy others' drawing techniques, trace an object, or make changes. Over time, with practice or art lessons, you became more accomplished at drawing until most people recognized your picture the way you had intended. You probably felt happy with the outcome, a product of relative artistic ability. If you learned more about art and technique, the process repeated as you grew into a better artist.

This example of a learning cycle occurs for sports, playing music, and a multitude of other skills. It is known as the *conscious competence model* of learning.

The conscious competence model—applied and discussed by many practitioners and authors, but from seemingly unknown origins— describes a four-stage learning process: unconscious incompetence, conscious incompetence, conscious competence, and unconscious competence.[5] In the stage of unconscious incompetence, the learner is unaware that she is not an expert, like the young child who does not know that his or her drawings are unintelligible marks. An unexpected occurrence—a fall, failure, loss, or comment from another person—awakens the learner's awareness of ineptitude or low level of skill, thus sending him or her into the second phase: conscious incompetence. To alleviate the discomfort that accompanies knowledge of incompetence, the learner can choose to either deny or ignore the surprise occurrence and resulting awareness (and thus move back into the phase of unconscious incompetence) or go to work. Through deliberate effort the learner practices conscious competence. In this stage, the child in our example intentionally focuses on controlling lines or color in order to produce an acceptable drawing. Through hard work and behavior repetition, the learner progresses to stage four: unconscious competence, in which she is proficient enough that she no longer thinks intentionally about each movement toward the target behavior. In the fourth stage, the child has become an artist who joyfully and unconsciously creates beautiful lines and colors, art that is pleasing to her and others. This model of learning assumes that it takes an outside stimulus to bring about awareness and that learning is continuous.

There are numerous ways to learn, including discovery, resolution of ambiguity, intervention or gap analysis, modeling, and conditioning, to name but a few. Although many have the potential to help you stretch your Appreciative Intelligence, we suggest taking an appreciative approach, a conscious/unconscious model that is adapted to find possibilities and what is positive and that builds on what already exists within you.

A Model of Appreciative Intelligence Development

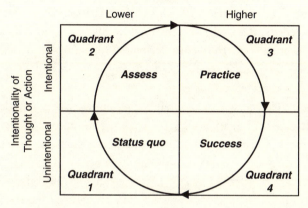

Figure 8.1   A model of Appreciative Intelligence development.

Figure 8.1 describes and walks you through the process of enhancing your own Appreciative Intelligence. In the lower left quadrant 1 (unintentional, lower appreciation), a person unconsciously or unintentionally frames reality in a positive light to see the inherent potential only occasionally or in limited domains (at home, work, with friends, or under other specific conditions). Unconsciously, he may exhibit only some of the qualities accompanying Appreciative Intelligence—persistence, conviction that his actions matter, tolerance for uncertainty, or irrepressible resilience—or he may exhibit all qualities, but to a minimal extent.

Chances are, by reading this book, you no longer live in this quadrant of the status quo. You are now aware of the existence of Appreciative Intelligence and its components, know the qualities that accompany the ability, and have probably considered your own abilities and behaviors by comparing your actions to those of the leaders of our stories and examples. You have already awakened to the presence of Appreciative Intelligence within yourself.

Once you have become aware of its presence, you have entered the second quadrant. By using the Personal Appreciative Intelligence Profile provided later in this chapter, you can assess your current Appreciative Intelligence. In this stage you determine under what conditions you reframe the present for a great view of the future, when or where you see oaks in acorns, and to what extent or how many ensuing qualities you already exhibit. By carefully considering, or reflecting on, what you already do well and what you would like to do in the future, you are ready to move to the next stage.

In the third quadrant of intentional higher appreciation, you deliberately practice reframing, appreciating the positive, exploring how the future could unfold from the present, and practicing the behaviors associated with the qualities of Appreciative Intelligence. You actively look for, metaphorically, mighty oaks in acorns. You transfer the abilities and qualities you found in the previous phase to new domains, such that you reframe in additional areas—seeing possibilities in products, situations, or people. Through discipline, effort, and techniques suggested later in this chapter, you can stretch what works well and enhance your personal profile of Appreciative Intelligence. With continued practice, the process of reframing, appreciating the positive, and seeing connections between the present and future begins to feel more natural. Creativity and possibilities start to flow. Without noticing it, you may slip into the final quadrant.

In the fourth phase of unintentional higher Appreciative Intelligence, your thought processes are often automatic; you simply live and breathe your higher Appreciative Intelligence. You see the mighty oak in the acorn spontaneously and effortlessly; possibilities appear to you before you become aware that you are looking for them. As your qualities of persistence, conviction in your actions, tolerance for uncertainty, and resilience grow, you begin to reap the rewards of success. You reveal your own great view of the future.

Assessing Your Personal Appreciative Intelligence

In the second phase of the model of Appreciative Intelligence development, when you assess your current degree of Appreciative Intelligence and strength of ensuing qualities, it's important to remember two things. First, the same way everyone has general intelligence, everyone has Appreciative Intelligence. It exists to different degrees and in different domains, but it is present in everyone.

Second, when aiming to enhance your Appreciative Intelligence, the best way to go about it is appreciatively. Determine what your abilities and qualities are, where they are strongest, and build on them. Stretch them, strengthen them, and use them in new areas of your life. For many people, this approach will be contrary to what they have learned and the way they may go about business. As indicated by Martin Seligman, leader of the Positive Psychology Movement, the trend in psychology for years was to focus on deficits, problems, and, therefore, interventions.[6] In corporations and elsewhere, consultants and management look for the holes or what's broken and try to fix them. The sticky point about this gap analysis approach is that, often, filling a hole only brings the situation back to a minimal level of what's working right—not to an optimal level or desirable end state. And by pointing out what is wrong, the subsequent finger pointing and blame can cause additional problems. Rarely does such an approach bring about a superlative future.

Therefore, we suggest that as you complete the following profile of your personal Appreciative Intelligence, you focus on what exists (*not* what doesn't), what has been successful (*not* what has failed), and how and where you'd like to expand what is already within you. Your responses to the questions will not lead to a numerical score, but they will prompt you to think about and reflect on areas and conditions where you reframe situations or products, see the best in others, and exhibit persistence or irrepressible resilience—that is, what your Appreciative Intelligence looks like.

Personal Appreciative Intelligence Profile

To determine your personal or individual Appreciative Intelligence profile, please answer the following questions.

1. Think about a success story that you believe has something to do with your Appreciative Intelligence. Write it below (or speak into a voice recorder, if you prefer) so that you can refer

back to it to answer further questions. (This story can be from any aspect or time of your life—a work, family, volunteer, or social situation, during childhood or adulthood. Please answer from your perspective—when *you* felt successful, not necessarily when others thought you were most successful.) Use the following questions to help you jog your memory or capture details.

a. Where were you?

b. When did this take place?

c. Who, if anyone, was with you?

d. What were the circumstances?

e. What happened?

f. What was your reaction?

g. What were your emotions at the beginning and end?

h. If possible, describe your thought processes. (Did you use insight? Did you talk to yourself, aloud or mentally?)

i. How did the story end?

j. What made this feel successful for you?

_____

_____

_____

_____

_____

2. Describe a time you perceived something differently than others did, reframed a situation or product in a positive way, revealed hidden talent or skills in another person, or generated new possibilities for a challenge.

a. What was the context? (Where were you? When?)

b. Who, if anyone, was involved?

c. If you can articulate it, what led you to see something different?

d. What aspects in the present moment did you see as positive or appreciate?

e. What part of the future desirable state was already present?

f. What concrete steps could you see that would create the desirable end result?

g. What, if anything, was the result?

_____

_____

_____

_____

_____

3. Think about a time you came up with a creative or innovative solution that you believe has something to do with your Appreciative Intelligence. Write it below (or speak into a voice recorder, if you prefer) so that you can refer back to it to answer further questions.

   a. Where were you?
   b. What were you doing at the time?
   c. What were you trying to solve?
   d. How long did it take to solve?
   e. What were the results of your creativity or innovation?
   f. What was your emotional state or mood before, during, and after?
   g. What tools, resources, or help did you use/employ in the process?

   _____

   _____

   _____

   _____

   _____

4. Which qualities of Appreciative Intelligence appeared in these stories? Describe the example.

   a. Persistence of thought or behavior _____
   b. Self-confidence or belief that you could solve a challenge (or an instance of positive self-talk) _____
   c. Tolerance or management of risk, ambiguity (ideas that conflicted with your previous beliefs or knowledge), or uncertainty _____
   d. Irrepressible resilience (the ability to bounce back from a difficult time or to overcome an obstacle) _____

5. Reflect on your responses so far. When do you think you are most likely to reframe a situation? When do you most often appreciate the positive aspects of a person, product, or situation? When do you see concrete steps in the present that lead to future solutions? In what domains of your life? Under what conditions are you the most effective, innovative, creative, or successful? Of persistence, convictions that your actions matter, tolerance for uncertainty, or irrepressible resilience, which qualities are your strongest or occur most often? Bear in mind that there are no wrong answers. This is your personal and unique profile of Appreciative Intelligence.

_____
_____
_____
_____
_____

6. Describe a future scenario in which you are happy or effective in a new area (aspect) of your life or more successful or innovative in a current area. What qualities are stronger or show up more often? What are the stories you tell yourself? Are you generating more possibilities or reframing to see a more positive future? How have you helped others around you become more successful? (For example, what talents have been revealed? Are they benefiting from your reframing of situations for a better future?)

_____
_____
_____

7. How can you use the strengths and expand the profile you described in question 5 above to realize the scenario you described for question 6? This is how your future can unfold from the positive aspects of your current reality.

_____
_____
_____

Putting Your Knowledge into Practice

Once you understand what your personal profile of Appreciative Intelligence looks like (from question 5) and have a general sense of what you want it to look like in the future (from question 6), you enter quadrant 3 of the aforementioned model of Appreciative Intelligence. Now it's time to practice new behaviors and thought patterns.

It is no easy task to change a mindset or habits that you have held and reinforced over years. For most people, discomfort accompanies ambiguity, risk, and uncertainty. You may find out that what you have always believed may not be true (for example, if you believed that your intelligence is only hard-wired and cannot change, or if you learned that the only way to make change is by filling in gaps or fixing what is broken, rather than by expanding what works). You risk change in your relationships or satisfaction associated with the status quo as you change your mindset, behaviors, and levels of success. You may possibly feel uncertainty as you begin to see and experience a new future. With time and practice, however, change and increased comfort level with it can occur.

There are at least three different ways of working on the behaviors and thoughts associated with Appreciative Intelligence. First, you can change behaviors by working on them directly or changing how you think that leads to those behaviors. This is a typical way of changing a pattern. For instance, you may be accustomed to driving to work via a particular route everyday. If construction or closure of a bridge forces you to change routes, you will probably deliberately remind yourself to travel a new direction every morning until a new habit forms.

Second, you can change your thought processes directly. One of the ideas for which 1972 Nobel laureate Gerald Edelman is well-known is called "neural Darwinisim." He pointed out that our brains have some 30 billion neurons and a million billion synaptic connections. During the process of development and into adulthood, connections that are most used are kept, while the least used connections are destroyed or "pruned." According to Edelman, constant neural activation will influence neural growth and synapse formation. In other words, the more we use certain mental processes, the stronger they become. Therefore, if we intentionally work on feeling optimistic, those neural connections are strengthened. We can think of this like a mental workout—if we work the neural "muscles" of optimism, they get strengthened and we feel optimistic. If we decide to be happy, those "happy-synapses" get strengthened. In other words, by choosing to have a certain mind-set, you can end up having it.[7]

Third, you can change your mindset by changing your actions. To grasp the significance of this, try the following quick exercise. Smile. Hold that smile for a few minutes. (It may feel like a long time.) Within a few minutes you will begin to feel happier than you were before you began to smile. After a while, your smile will feel natural, you may relax, and you may feel genuine happiness. Because our brains do not distinguish between a smile (or other action) that is brought about by a mental state or brought about by moving our physical muscles, we can change our mindset through physical changes.

With that notion comes the implication that by practicing reframing, you can change your ensuing qualities and behaviors. Conversely, by changing quality-related behaviors (for example, persisting at a particular action), you can change your perspective. By working from both directions, you may experience faster change. If one way works best for your learning style, however, use it.

A wide variety of tools for changing behaviors and thought patterns are available from consultants, teachers, psychologists, and others. The following are just a few that lend themselves to practicing intentional high Appreciative Intelligence. You will probably find that as you change one aspect of your Appreciative Intelligence, others will be affected automatically. For instance, as your ability to reframe grows, your self-talk becomes more positive and your resilience may increase. Further, as your resilience increases, you may become more confident with taking risks.

Tool 1: Change Your Stories

The way the leaders we interviewed told themselves success stories or affirming thoughts (as Charlie Pellerin mentally reminded himself of the story of Davy Crockett and as Fleur Frascella said that the dancers in her community wouldn't dislike themselves after reading magazine advertisements that suggest that thin equals beauty equals happiness), you can also tell yourself positive stories. In their book, *The Power of Resilience*, psychologists Robert Brooks and Sam Goldstein contend that people can develop "a resilient mindset" by "rewriting negative scripts."[8]

To change your beliefs about your actions and resilience, pay attention to the comments your mind makes to yourself and the remarks you make to others. If you are telling yourself or others that you have failed, or envision stories in your mind that feature yourself as the victim, martyr, or underdog, replace those stories or rewrite them as a closed chapter of your personal story that eventually has a successful ending. We are not suggesting that those who have experienced terrible things or tragedies rewrite their stories as though the events did not happen or label the negative aspects of those occurrences as wonderful. Instead, ask yourself how painful memories could be written as history, not the present, and what story line would create a better future.

Find the story of a successful person you admire—famous or not. Or, imagine yourself in the role of a winning book character—real or not. Put yourself in the shoes of any of the leaders we have written about in this book, or borrow a page from Charlie Pellerin's book and repeat the story of Davy Crockett to yourself. Envision yourself in the role of a successful leader, able to see possibilities and overcome obstacles, and you will begin to take on his or her characteristics.

Tool 2: Change Your Reflections

You can also expand your resilience and find new possibilities by reflecting on your experiences.

Barbara Frederickson, the researcher whose interviews of people before and after the September 11, 2001, terrorist attack on the United States demonstrated the value of resilience and positive emotions for staving off depression and for learning, conducted an experiment. Over a period of a month, her research team asked a group of college students "to find positive meaning and long-term benefit from their best, worst and seemingly ordinary experiences each day." At the end of the month, the members of the group showed more resilience than what they had reported before.[9]

The concept of double loop learning, introduced by Harvard University professor Chris Argyris and his late colleague Don Schon, may also be useful for you. Double loop learning is the processing of examining the assumptions behind the assumptions or thinking about your thinking, in short a higher level of reflection than what is typical. In this process, you reflect on the assumptions that are used for reflection and appreciate how using different assumptions may lead to different outcomes.[10]

By reflecting on your assumptions, observations, and actions each day, practicing looking for new and positive possibilities in people, products, and situations, you will begin to see potential in your surroundings. If writing your reflections helps you capture your thoughts more clearly and provides for later review, keep a success journal, similar to the idea books kept by Gore associates to record their ideas, thoughts, and progress. And as the saying goes, what you seek, you will find.

Tool 3: Change Your Questions

Another way to learn to reframe, or to see more of the positive inherent generative potential, is to borrow and adapt a technique from relatively new and small schools of therapy called "solution-focused therapy" and "brief therapy."[11] Their key principles are that people's problems aren't present one hundred percent of the time but intermittently, and that therapy should focus on producing adaptive behaviors in a relatively short period of time. By learning to recognize moments when the symptoms of a problem are absent and using those experiences as the driver for change, individuals can work to make the moments without the symptoms more sustainable. The therapist helps the patient strengthen what is working by asking questions to help him or her reframe.

Those reframing techniques and questions can be used to enhance Appreciative Intelligence. First, become aware of the domains or small pockets of your life where you are already seeing opportunities. Then ask yourself what would make you successful? This is a reframing question if, up until now, you have been preoccupied by the question of why you are not more successful. The more you focus on why you are *not* more successful, the more those reasons come alive and expand. So change your question to what would make you more successful. Next, ask what would happen if you had a magic wand and wished that all failure disappeared. How would you know that it had happened? What would you do differently? How would others around you know? What would other people say that would acknowledge or validate the new success?

Please note that we have intentionally used more "what" than "why" questions here. "What" questions typically generate data and understanding, while "why" questions generally elicit an emotional or defensive response and generate interpretation as opposed to data. "What" questions generally make respondents more comfortable, while "why" questions create apprehension and hesitation.[12]

There are other questions that may help you notice pockets of improvement, even if you feel you are still not as successful as you would like to be. At the end of a week, if you still say "I failed this week," ask yourself whether there were times that you experienced less failure than the previous week (or weeks before). Then ask what made that small difference? Continue the process of looking for incremental improvements and stretching what went well.

As you begin to see yourself as being more successful—a new frame—you will begin to be more self confident, more persistent, more resilient, and able to take more risk.

Tool 4: Seek Diverse Ideas (Talk to Someone Different)

Consider the following story. Many years ago now, a friend, a quality control expert, was driving his seven-year-old daughter to school before catching a plane to Spain. He was headed out to look for a solution to the problem of stinkbugs that were hitchhiking to other countries on shipping pallets of cans. When the daughter demanded to know why he was traveling again, he explained the problem (one on which he had consulted help from exterminators from England to Hawaii) to her.

"Wake them up!" she suggested. "Blast them with cold air and get them out of there."

He replied, "Making them cold will only make them fall asleep and hibernate on the pallets. If we wanted to wake them up and make them go away, we'd have to heat them up." As he said it, he realized he had solved his problem in a way—through temperature, not pesticides or other alternatives (a new frame)—that had not been thought about before. Shortly thereafter, a form of his idea was implemented. The insight that led to the solution came about by talking with someone who had a completely different view of the situation and a different set of knowledge and skills.

By seeking diverse ideas and embracing ambiguity—actively seeking information or beliefs that conflict with your own—you can stretch your comfort level with contradictions. You can figure out how to make connections between seemingly dissimilar ideas in order to create new frames. Like Dean Kamen, who is solving the challenge of the decline in engineering graduates through culture, not education, and the Rotarians, who thought of polio eradication as an organizational and managerial challenge, not a medical one, you can jumpstart your innovative ideas and creative solutions by trying on new ideas, looking at what works, and making connections among diverse concepts.

Developing Your Own Tools for Enhancing Appreciative Intelligence

Finally, because we are introducing the construct of Appreciative Intelligence with this book, we expect that as people begin to think about it and use it, some people will develop further techniques and approaches for enhancing it.

As you practice the components of Appreciative Intelligence and seeking possibilities, remember that Appreciative Intelligence is not about simply calling a negative a positive. It is about seeing what is already present in a person, product, or situation—seeing an oak in an acorn, but not a tropical mango. Enhancing your Appreciative Intelligence will not make you happy all the time or keep you from making mistakes or from ever failing. What your Appreciative Intelligence can do is to help you learn new solutions from those mistakes, enjoy new achievements, and reframe your world for a better view of the future.

Employing and Enjoying Your Appreciative Intelligence

In the fourth quadrant of the model, you are able to use your Appreciative Intelligence unconsciously or unintentionally. As the adage "practice makes perfect" comes true—as you repeatedly tell yourself success stories, reflect on what works well, ask yourself new questions, and spark innovative ideas through seeking out new ideas—you will probably develop new habits without realizing it. You automatically frame for a great future. Creative ideas begin to appear without you deliberately considering them or asking yourself a list of questions. Sustaining your Appreciative Intelligence in this quadrant happens automatically, because each time you use it naturally, you are in effect practicing it, even though you are unaware of it. Over time, you see the mighty oak within the acorn as a matter of course.

In conclusion, although Appreciative Intelligence cannot be seen or directly measured, it can be described qualitatively and understood intuitively. Because the brain changes and intelligence is not static, Appreciative Intelligence can be developed and enhanced within individuals. We hope that by providing a model for others to enhance their abilities, they will see their own possibilities for the future that are waiting to be realized in the present. Through their learning to see the mighty oak within the acorn, we hope that people and their organizations, families, and businesses experience the benefits and advantages commensurate with a creative, satisfied, and appreciated workforce or community.

Chapter 9

The Case for
Appreciative Intelligence

We are what we think. All that we are arises
with our thoughts. With our thoughts, we make
the world.
—Buddha[1]

For some readers the introduction of new concepts, including the specific new construct of Appreciative Intelligence, will be accommodated or assimilated into knowledge or belief systems with a degree of ease. For others, the ideas presented in this book may generate discomfort or skepticism because they do not readily fit within the readers' worldview based on their experiences or understanding. Chapters 9 and 10 are for readers who want more information to resolve ambiguity or skepticism, those who come from various fields of the social sciences and want further explanations, and those who are curious about the case behind Appreciative Intelligence. This chapter and the next one provide more information for people who want to know more about how the construct of Appreciative Intelligence came about, why we believe it is another type of intelligence, and what the field of social cognitive neuroscience can provide to help explain the mental processes we discuss in this book. For those of you who prefer to focus on the practical application of Appreciative Intelligence, skip ahead to Chapter 11. For others of you, read on.

The Intuitive Proposition

One of us (Tojo) perceived intuitively that that the ability to appreciate—to see and realize hidden value in people and situations—and to construct a positive future seemed more related to a leader's overall success than did traditional IQ (a score that can successfully predict academic success) or subject matter expertise. He observed in particular cultures of academia and business that the most successful leaders possessed a distinctive manner of working with people and their environment. As these leaders looked for ways that ideas could be realized, they seemed to find them, thus leading to a high incidence of innovation and other competitive advantages. Like venture capitalists, they poured resources into ideas that worked, not those that didn't. Tojo perceived intuitively that there was a link between leaders' positive and appreciative approach, innovative and creative ideas, and successful organizations.

As shown in Figure 9.1, by putting together pieces of evidence from literature of positive psychology and intelligence, our thematic and conceptual analysis of success stories and firsthand interviews of successful leaders and innovators, and brain studies from the field of social cognitive neuroscience, we put together a case for Appreciative Intelligence.

Some of the initial pieces of the case behind Appreciative Intelligence were supplied by the fields of psychology and organizational science. Existing knowledge and theories about positive psychology and intelligence provided a foundation for the project.

The Positive Psychology Movement was spearheaded by well-known psychologist Martin Seligman, beginning with his 1998 presidential address to the American Psychological Association. He showed how psychology as a discipline was focused on deficits and problems. In the previous 30 years, psychology journals had published 45,000 articles on depression, but only 400 on joy.[2] Seligman himself had a celebrated career as a result of his famous theory on "learned helplessness." His perspective changed when a fellow passenger on a trip asked him about studying optimism instead of pessimism. That was a turning point for Seligman; his 1991 best-selling book was called *Learned Optimism*![3]

According to Seligman, when psychology began developing as a profession, it had three goals: to identify genius, to heal the sick, and to help people live better, happier lives.[4] After World War II, however, psy-

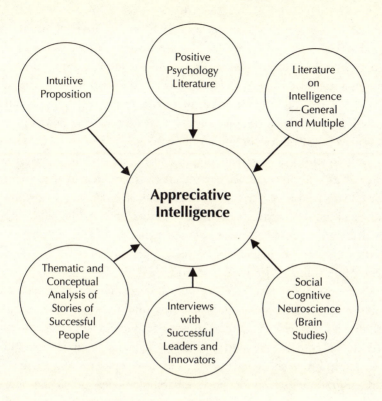

Figure 9.1. **Evidence for Appreciative Intelligence.**

chological theories generally focused on damage, coping mechanisms, and intervention techniques. He began to change that by focusing on the three central aspects of people's lives: love, work, and play. Along with Mihaly Csikszentmihalyi, well known for studies on the psychology of optimal experience, or *flow*,[5] Seligman created a research alliance to study Positive Psychology in 1998, which led to a flurry of research and publications.

One such example is psychologist Barbara Fredrickson's "broaden-and-build theory" of positive emotions that suggests that positive emotions broaden people's modes of thinking and action, eventually leading to lasting personal and social resources. In turn, they help people cope and thrive. In other words, one's experiences of positive emotions such as joy, pride, contentment, and gratitude can contribute to optimal individual and organizational functioning.[6] In earlier research, her team at the University of Michigan Positive Emotions and Psychophysiology

Laboratory studied the "undoing effect" of positive emotions on physiological reactions, including blood pressure and heart rate, against anxiety. Watching films of waves or puppies—eliciting contentment and amusement, respectively—produced quicker recovery from cardiovascular aftereffects of negative emotions in subjects than did watching films that elicited sadness. These findings suggest that experiencing positive emotions plays a critical role in human flourishing.[7]

Subsequently, a new field of positive organizational behavior has emerged as one of the most vibrant areas of research in management today. Just as positive psychology is focused on understanding optimal individual human psychological states rather than pathological ones, positive organizational behavior is geared to understanding optimal organizational states.[8] It has identified several key concepts for exploration such as hope[9] and subjective well-being.[10]

For developing our construct of Appreciative Intelligence, such pieces of information provided the background for examining what works well that leads to personal and organizational success, rather than what is broken and requires intervention. They provided an approach to looking at leaders' positive characteristics, such as hope, appreciation, passion for work, or joy. Studies from the positive psychology field provided evidence of the effect of optimism and other positive characteristics on stressful or challenging situations and as factors leading to health and success.

The Changing Understanding of Intelligence

Many pieces of information behind our work were about the concept of intelligence. Some pieces, including evidence that traditional intelligence doesn't always correlate with success, existed before we asked our first questions. Other pieces of the intelligence picture helped form a basis for our thematic analysis of success stories.

The first chapter's story of encountering two intelligent classmates at a high school reunion demonstrated how the author's classmates' definition of intelligence changed over time. Just as the classmates' definition changed, so has our society's.

In an early attempt to define, explain, and measure intelligence, at the London Exhibition in 1884 naturalist Sir Francis Galton measured visitors' head size, memory, and other variables that he thought might correlate with intelligence. "To his disappointment he discovered that eminent British scientists could not be distinguished from ordinary citizens on the basis of their head size."[11]

In the early 1900s, a string of psychologists, including Alfred Binet, Lewis Terman, and David Wechsler, devised intelligence tests for children in various attempts to predict who would or wouldn't perform successfully in school. Psychologists who opposed these standardized IQ (Intelligence Quotient, the traditional and numerical score of measured intelligence in an individual) tests, numerical assessments of the construct, and the classic definition of intelligence as cognitive reasoning abilities, however, believed the tests and scores were inadequate in generalizing across different cultures or predicting success in life. For example, in a landmark study during the 1940s, George Vaillant tracked the lives of 95 Harvard students into middle age and compared their life successes with their IQs. He found that IQ had no bearing on salary, productivity, professional status, satisfaction, or happiness in later life.[12]

As time marched on through the later 1900s, psychologists and researchers began to point to various abilities other than the standard notion of analytical intelligence as critical for effective job performance and success. Intelligence could no longer be considered a static, well-defined entity. Then, in the 1980s, a significant change came about in how people viewed intelligence.

Multiple Intelligences

In the early 1980s, Harvard University professor Howard Gardner's influential theory of multiple intelligences challenged the notion of a single definition of what it means to be smart. Gardner argued that intelligence isn't a single ability, or solely a general intelligence related to rational reasoning, but rather a number of capacities. Based on findings from the fields of anthropology, psychology, brain research, and cognitive science and on biographies of exceptional individuals, he concluded that there were at least seven types of intelligences: linguistic, bodily-kinesthetic, spatial, musical, logical-mathematical, intrapersonal, and interpersonal.[13] Sixteen years later, Gardner added naturalist intelligence to his original seven and discussed the possibility for a ninth type, called existential intelligence.[14] The notion that there were many different types of intelligence, not just one type that related to left-brain logic and reasoning, opened the door for additional intelligences (including Appreciative Intelligence) and the recognition that a broader portion of the population could be considered highly intelligent.

Emotional and Social Intelligence

In the 1990s, further changes in the widespread notion of the meaning of intelligence crystallized with the subjects of emotional and social intelligence and their supporting evidence.

Psychologists Peter Salovey and John Mayer, usually credited with providing the first definition of emotional intelligence more than fifteen years ago, initially defined it as "the subset of social intelligence that involves the ability to monitor one's own and others' feelings and emotions, to discriminate among them, and to use this information to guide one's thinking and actions."[15] A few years later, Daniel Goleman's best selling book *Emotional Intelligence* popularized the construct. Goleman defined emotional intelligence, or EI, as the capacity for recognizing one's own emotions and those of others. He highlighted the dimensions of self-awareness, self-management, self-motivation, empathy, and social skills. Goleman also asserted that "EQ" is more important than IQ for success in business and relationships and that EQ can be increased.[16] This additional intelligence gave further evidence and credibility to the notion that various types of intelligence exist and that they can be developed and enhanced.

Related to EI is social intelligence. Although there were various definitions for the concept as early as the 1920s, one by Ronald Riggio and co-researchers—the ability to perceive and interpret social situations, along with behavioral flexibility or adaptability[17]—is widely accepted. Studies of social intelligence added to the body of literature about intelligence and answered more questions about the link between success and effective leadership and other skills. For example, in a 1994 study of more than 1,000 military leaders, researcher Jannelle Gilbert found that social intelligence and social knowledge structures predicted leader effectiveness better than verbal skills and divergent thinking. The evidence suggested that the importance of social intelligence for effective leadership increases as one moves higher in an organizational hierarchy, where the complexity of social situations likewise increases. Together with emotional intelligence, social intelligence allows leaders to perceive the environment, interact, solve problems, and manage a diversity of complex and dynamic social domains.[18]

Still, we were left with the notion that there was a missing link between intelligence and success. To find missing parts of the puzzle after applying information from our literature search to Tojo's intuitive proposition, we began to examine real-world examples of successful people.

Developing the Construct of Appreciative Intelligence

To develop the construct of Appreciative Intelligence further, we began a long process of collecting and analyzing data on leaders and their organizations. We used a variety of sources—both primary (original interviews) and secondary (others' stories and research)—with thematic and conceptual analysis.

As we began the study of successful individuals and organizations, we examined over one thousand stories from the business publication *Investor's Business Daily*, "Leaders and Success" column, from January 1995 to 2004. These stories contained information about leaders, at least half of them historical, and how they surmounted obstacles in life and came to have an impact on society in many ways. Most of these leaders were financially and professionally successful, founding companies or reaching the position of chairperson or president. Often they were responsible for inventions, unique innovations, services, or processes that changed an industry or community. The stories were well researched and rich with details of the lives of these individuals, often starting from childhood or revealing aspects of their personalities that shaped who they became later in their lives.

After we deleted stories that were repeated or redundant, our final "population" of stories was reduced to 960. Within that group, we looked for a sample size of 480, half of the population of 960 stories. In these stories we examined the characteristics of the successful leaders.

Further in the process, we used a method called thematic analysis. Thematic analysis is one of the most widely used qualitative research methods in the social sciences. It is employed to find commonalities, patterns, or trends in a group of subjects for the purpose of answering questions or forming theories about the group as a whole. In the 1998 research methods book *Transforming Qualitative Information: Thematic Analysis and Code Development*, author Richard Boyatzis shows how the method has been used effectively since the 1950s. Another book, *Motivation and Personality, Handbook of Thematic Content Analysis*, edited by Charles P. Smith, makes a strong case for the validity of using the method for deriving new constructs. Some of the most well-known concepts in psychology, including the fear of success (proposed by Martha Horner in 1968) and the need for achievement (popularized by David McCleland in the 1950s), were discovered using thematic analysis. Even when it is not specifically called thematic analysis, the method is inherent as a step in most qualitative research approaches.

In thematic analysis, a *theme* can be defined as a statement of meaning that runs through most of the data or that occurs for a minority of the participants but carries heavy emotional or factual impact.[19] Jodi Aronson's article, "A Pragmatic View of Thematic Analysis,"[20] examines additional definitions of themes and practical uses for them. Themes are also defined as units derived from patterns such as "conversation topics, vocabulary, recurring activities, meanings, feelings, or folk sayings and proverbs."[21] They are identified by "bringing together components or fragments of ideas or experiences, which often are meaningless when viewed alone . . . but . . . fit together in a meaningful way when linked together."[22] M. A. Constas, another expert on thematic analysis, makes a convincing case that this "interpretative approach should be considered as a distinct point of origination"[23] in theory development, in other words, as a means of identifying new concepts, rather than solely as a tool to measure concepts identified through other methods.

Our first step was to build a valid argument for choosing the themes. We accomplished this by reading extensively and analyzing the literature on intelligence. By referring to the existing literature, we gained knowledge that allowed us to make inferences from the successful leaders' stories. Once we had collected themes and studied the literature, we were ready to formulate theme statements to develop a story line—a sort of "who did what, why, and how." As we gathered the various subthemes of the potential concept of Appreciative Intelligence to obtain a comprehensive view of the construct, it was easy to see a pattern emerging.

The next step in the thematic analysis was to identify all data that related to the already classified patterns. All of the interview data or story text that fitted under the specific pattern was identified and placed with the corresponding pattern.

Specifically, when reviewing leaders' stories, we looked at themes such as emotional reaction to failure or obstacles, capacity to reinterpret traumatic events into learning opportunities, ability to work from "rags to riches," and childhood attitudes toward earning money. We looked at themes that seemed to have direct bearing on their ability to achieve goals. We found subthemes including resilience, creativity, innovative solutions, holding high expectations for people, and giving people freedom to excel. As we pieced together themes that emerged, we began to form a comprehensive picture of these leaders' common experiences and attitudes. That picture was one of a unique ability to reframe reality, to appreciate the positive, and to see how resources and capabilities in the present could connect to future events.

Another method we used was conceptual analysis. Traditionally, content analysis has most often been thought of in terms of conceptual analysis. In conceptual analysis, a *concept* is chosen for examination, and the *analysis* involves quantifying and tallying its presence. The focus here is on looking at the occurrence of selected terms within a text or texts, although the terms may be implicit as well as explicit. While explicit terms are easy to identify, coding for implicit terms and deciding their level of implication is complicated by the need to base judgments on a somewhat subjective system. In the case of our examination and conceptual analysis of the most successful leaders, the number of times terms such as "opportunity," "appreciation," "hope," and "challenge" were tallied.

The same steps of thematic and conceptual analysis used to identify patterns and constructs in the "Leaders and Success" stories were used for interviews with 15 senior managers and leaders of various companies, government agencies, schools, and nonprofit organizations.

Clarifying Success

We selected leaders for interviews based on their observable signs of success, the definition of which we acknowledge is highly subjective. For one person "success" means high quality and longevity of personal relationships, for another it means attaining a position of influence or prominence within an organization (often indicated by a certain title), and for yet another it means attaining a level of personal financial wealth. Even within the same category or attribute, different people assign a label of success at different benchmarks; for example, "financial wealth" could mean accrued assets of a million or a billion dollars, or a yearly salary of $100,000 or $500,000 for five, 15, or 20 years (or any other dollar figure or number of years). In addition to being subjective, success is relative.

But the odd thing about success, like other intangible concepts, is that when it is not limited to a specific definition, observers usually agree on its presence in an individual or context. The difficulty of defining success, but the ease in identifying it, is similar to the paradox in the classic book by Robert M. Pirsig, *Zen and the Art of Motorcycle Maintenance*, in which the same students who could not answer the question, "What is *quality* in thought and statement?" could point out with near consensus which written compositions were examples of high quality in ideas, organization, and writing and which were not.[24]

Thus, rather than struggling to assign arbitrary limits on who could be considered successful, we chose to define "success" broadly and qualitatively for the selection of interview candidates, for purposes of our study, and for examples in this book. We considered these leaders successful because of peer recognition and awards (that is, acknowledgment of success by those who understand what is valuable or important in their own fields), ability to get along with others, levels of financial wealth that fit their needs and circumstances, position of influence in an organization, and, most importantly, the ability to achieve their goals and accomplish projects important to themselves and others. These attributes in our interview candidates were repeated or existed over a long period of time, such as taking numerous important projects to fruition, or collaborating or working well with others for many years. While these leaders also experienced setbacks or failures, the challenges were temporary or led to new avenues to success.

Exploring Appreciative Intelligence

In semi-structured interviews, fairly conversational but based on a certain set of parameters, conducted by telephone or in person, we asked the following questions:

- Tell me a story about a recent challenge in or to your organization. How did you handle it?
- How did you perceive this challenge?
- What was your initial emotional reaction to this challenge? What was your ultimate reaction? What were your thought processes as you learned about and solved the challenge?
- Have you always dealt with challenging situations in this way? Please provide an example or two.
- Are there situations when you saw an opportunity, or a talent in other people, when others did not?
- What, if anything, do you communicate to your organization about challenging situations? In what ways do you communicate to people around you?
- How do you manage feedback from others? What do you tell yourself if and when you get negative feedback from others? If self-doubt is created in your mind because of feedback from another, how do you deal with it? Can you give an example?
- How do you typically provide feedback to others?
- What, if anything, do you do to make your organization as innovative and productive as possible? How do you work with people around you to achieve maximum value for your organization?

Depending on the answers, additional probing questions were asked to learn more about the events, the deeper thoughts and emotions behind the actions, and other events or situations that would support (or not) the answers given by the leaders.

To learn more about leaders and their organizations, we made use of primary and secondary data collection. In addition to the primary data collection through interviews, when possible we engaged in participant observation by watching the leaders in action and joining in some of their activities. We also talked to people who knew them. For secondary data collection, we examined media articles, Web sites, and other sources.

Thematic and conceptual analysis of the "Leaders and Success" stories and interviews pointed to a picture of individuals with unique abilities. In crisis, need, or ordinary situations, they noticed opportunity. They saw positive aspects in people and situations. In so doing, they created significant advantages for their organizations.

As we analyzed the interview data and developed our own findings about Appreciative Intelligence, researchers in the fields of psychology and social cognitive neuroscience provided supporting evidence for our propositions: that the ability to perceive the positive inherent generative potential—to reframe, appreciate the positive, and see how the future unfolds from the present—is a newly identified type of intelligence and that, as we discuss in the next chapter, it is a function of particular parts of the brain.

Chapter 10

The Brains Behind
Appreciative Intelligence

If the human brain were so simple that we could
understand it, we would be so simple we couldn't.
—Emerson M. Pugh[1]

Appreciative Intelligence is a mental ability that affects how the world
is perceived and, in turn, deliberately thought about and acted upon.
Although it's difficult to demonstrate fully how our minds work and to
determine whether a mental process is conscious or unconscious, whether
it is innate or developed, or whether it is a characteristic, a mindset, an
attitude, or a trait, researchers in the past decade have made strides in
the areas of brain functioning and psychology. New diagnostic imaging
techniques provide fresh insights about the links among the brain, attitudes, emotions, intelligence, and behaviors. To explain the existence of
Appreciative Intelligence and show evidence for specific parts of the brain
as responsible for the mental processes that constitute its components, we
turn to other researchers' brain studies, or research in the social cognitive
neuroscience field. To help readers make sense of the studies we cite and
to provide a context for talking about specific brain areas and functions,
we begin with some basic information about the human brain.

A Quick Tour of the Brains behind Appreciative Intelligence

The human brain is one of the most fascinating organs on earth. It has evolved over millions of years and continues to adapt in infinite ways to meet challenges of everyday life.

Like the CEO of an organization, who sets an emotional tone, makes decisions, issues commands, directs actions, and coordinates numerous divisions and functions in order for a company to survive and thrive, the brain holds the ultimate responsibility for the body. It controls speech, movement, sensory perception, breathing, personality, emotions, dreams, heart rate, body temperature, breathing, memory, consciousness, and learning.

The brain can be diagrammed and labeled in many ways (see Figure 10.1). The different areas, bumps (referred to as gyri), and grooves (called sulci or fissures) can have multiple names based on who identified the function of a particular region, where the region is located, or what the area controls.

The three main areas of the brain are the forebrain, the midbrain, and the hindbrain. The forebrain, made up primarily of the cerebrum, is responsible for higher brain functions such as thinking, perception, attitudes, and complex actions. Functions of the midbrain include muscle movement and balance. The hindbrain is responsible for basic life functions such as breathing, blood pressure, and heart rate.

The cerebrum is divided into the left and right hemispheres, which (for the most part) control the right and left sides of the body, respectively, and are connected by a bundle of nerve fibers called the corpus callosum.

Through complex pathways and processes, the brain accomplishes an untold number of functions. Although many regions control specific movements or attitudes, and although damage to some regions does not cause a person's death, other brain sections work together interactively and cannot function separately. Hence, the regions of the brain we associate with the components of Appreciative Intelligence do not operate separately from others. The parts of the brain we propose are responsible for Appreciative Intelligence may not be, by far, the only areas responsible for these attitudes and perceptions. But for the purpose of this quick and simplified tour, we shall identify and describe the functions of the areas as separate parts.

Located in the forebrain, the predominant areas associated with the components of Appreciative Intelligence are the following:

- *Amygdala:* The amygdala is an almond-shaped part of the limbic system that lies beneath the surface of the front, medial part of the temporal lobe. It controls conscious and unconscious emotions and signals the release of hormones as humans respond to emotion-provoking situations. It works in conjunction with the prefrontal cortex (and orbito-frontal cortex) for conscious emotions. As related to Appreciative Intelligence, it plays a role in the way people perceive and respond to situations and people they encounter.

- *Prefrontal cortex:* The prefrontal cortex, a large part of the frontal lobe, is involved in abstract thought, personality, appropriate social behavior, spontaneity, insight, and problem solving. It is of primary importance in framing, perception, and other mental processes that are components of Appreciative Intelligence.

- *Orbito-frontal cortex (OFC):* The orbito-frontal cortex (part of the prefrontal cortex), located "directly behind the eyes, is responsible for integrating emotional responses generated in the limbic system with higher cognitive functions, such as planning and language, in the cerebral cortex's prefrontal lobes."[2] In relation to Appreciative Intelligence, the OFC takes part in processes required for framing, reappraising situations, resilience to negative situations, people perception, and successful interactions with other people.

- *Superior temporal gyrus (STG):* The STG, part of the cerebral cortex located at the edge of the temporal, parietal, and occipital lobes, is involved in auditory association, formation of language, and higher-order thought. It plays a role in Appreciative Intelligence with perception, appreciation of people, and the ability to deal with complex social situations and to solve challenges using insight.

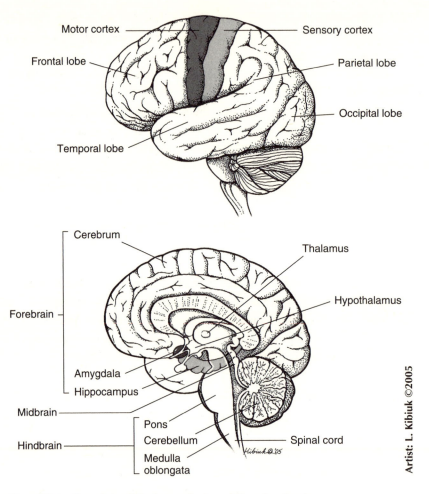

Motor cortex — Sensory cortex

Frontal lobe — Parietal lobe

Occipital lobe

Temporal lobe

Cerebrum — Thalamus

Hypothalamus

Forebrain

Amygdala
Hippocampus

Midbrain

Pons
Hindbrain — Cerebellum — Spinal cord
Medulla oblongata

Artist: L. Kibiuk ©2005

Figure 10.1. Two views of the human brain and its major structures.

In the same way that the definition of what it means to be smart has evolved, the explanation of the physical nature of intelligence has also changed dramatically in recent history.

For quite some time, humans have looked to physical attributes and brain anatomy for answers to questions about intelligence. As mentioned earlier in this book, over a century ago Sir Francis Galton measured the head size of people in an attempt to correlate it with intelligence. But in the past decade, technology developments have provided a new window to the brain and its functions. Although this area of research is still blazing trails, there is much we can draw from recent studies.

Neurologists, psychologists, medical researchers, neuroscientists, and sociologists are making strides in understanding how the human brain works and what regions of the brain are responsible for our behaviors, emotions, thought patterns, attitudes, and personality. In particular, the relatively new, interdisciplinary field of social cognitive neuroscience attempts to explain how perception, perspective taking, and human empathy (processes closely related to the reframing and appreciative aspects of Appreciative Intelligence) occur.

As the name suggests, social cognitive neuroscience explores relationships between the brain, specific thought processes, social factors, and ensuing behaviors. Social cognitive neuroscience researchers Kevin Ochsner of Columbia University and Matthew Lieberman of the University of California, Los Angeles, described how this emerging field is different from previous approaches that correlated only social factors and thought processes. They provided the example of what happens when we look at another person's face. A cognitive neuroscientist would ask what part of the brain is responsible for the feeling we have when we see that face. A social psychologist would ask what the personal, social, and cultural factors are that generated those feelings. Ochsner and Lieberman see social cognitive neuroscience as bridging the gap between the two disciplines.[3]

Medical diagnostic tools have contributed significantly to understanding how the human mind operates. Such tools include electroencephalograms (EEGs), scalp-electrode recording techniques to measure event-related brain potentials (ERPs), and the most common imaging techniques: positron emission tomography (PET) and functional magnetic resonance imaging (fMRI). Ochsner and Lieberman explained the workings of PET and fMRI as follows.

> PET involves inhalation of a radioactive gas or injection of a radioactive solution that is metabolized by brain areas. The more active a given brain region is during task performance, the more radioactive substance is present there and the greater the PET signal at that location. fMRI uses powerful magnetic fields to alter the orientation of atoms in the brain and

measures signals given off by these atoms as they return to their normal orientation. Brain areas that are used for performance of a given task use more blood and therefore produce a stronger signal that is detected by the fMRI scanner.

Experiments using PET or fMRI typically compare brain activation in two different psychological states (e.g., happy vs. sad), during the performance of two different kinds of tasks (e.g., remembering as opposed to passively viewing words) or for members of two different groups (e.g., depressed vs. nondepressed individuals). Whatever two tasks or conditions are being compared, it is important that they differ only in their reliance on the specific processes under investigation. When studies are designed in this way, one can infer that differences in brain activity between the two conditions reflect the operation of the processes of interest.[4]

Studies of people with brain injuries, illnesses, and abnormalities also shed light into the inner workings of the mind. By comparing behaviors of people with healthy brains to those who have damage to a specific region in the brain, scientists can often correlate specific areas of the brain with specific functions. An early example is from the nineteenth century: A railroad worker named Phineas Gage suffered damage to his forebrain when an accidental explosion drove an iron bar through his skull. Although he survived, he experienced changes in personality including loss of industriousness, responsibility, self-control, and mature social skills.[5]

The in-depth body of work based on social cognitive neuroscience studies using various medical imaging techniques such as fMRI is what we use to draw inferences about brain functioning in the leaders we observed and studied and to support our construct of Appreciative Intelligence.

Although these research projects examine different types of intelligence (e.g., social) and use different psychological terms than we employ to describe the components of Appreciative Intelligence (e.g., "evaluation" instead of "framing" or "reappraisal" instead of "reframing"), their findings support the notion of connections between neural functions and the mental processes of Appreciative Intelligence. Table 10.1 shows the relationships between the terms used for some key concepts studied by social cognitive neuroscientists (column 1), the authors' terms as related to Appreciative Intelligence (column 2), and the parts of the brain (column 3) associated with the thought processes set out in columns 1 and 2.

Concept Studied	Related Appreciative Intelligence Component	Brain Regions
Social intelligence	Appreciation of people, understanding of the social environment that is key to seeing how the future unfolds from the present	Orbito-frontal cortex, superior temporal gyrus, amygdala
Stereotyping	(Nearly opposite of appreciation of people)	Amygdala, right ventrolateral prefrontal cortex
Person perception	Appreciation of people	Orbito-frontal cortex, superior temporal gyrus, amygdala, prefrontal cortex, medial prefrontal cortex
Emotion, cognition, reappraising negative emotions, evaluative attitude	Irrepressible resilience, reframing, perception	Ventral medial frontal cortex, orbito-frontal cortex, amygdala, prefrontal cortex
Insight	Suddenly seeing connections and solving problems, insight, perception	Right temporal lobe, prefrontal cortex, right hemisphere anterior superior temporal gyrus, amygdala

Table 10.1: Relationships between Concepts Studied, Authors' Terminology, and Associated Brain Regions

Various studies from the field of social cognitive neuroscience provide evidence that suggests that social and general intelligences affect different parts of the brain, a notion that is encouraging for the possibility of separate areas of the brain controlling general and Appreciative Intelligence. Further, they point to complex neural networks, processes, and areas associated with perception, social evaluation, reappraisal, and insight. Predominantly, they identify the amygdala, the superior temporal gyrus, the prefrontal cortex, and the orbito-frontal cortex as the areas responsible for those functions.

Ultimately, studies suggest that people have the ability to put their brains into a state in which insight occurs, indicating the possibility for developing and enhancing our neural networks, which in turn holds further implications for increasing Appreciative Intelligence in individuals.

Evidence from Social Cognitive Neuroscience: Social Intelligence, Stereotyping, Person Perception, and Insight

As previously mentioned, research evidence from the new field of social cognitive neuroscience is what we used to support our construct of Appreciative Intelligence. Although these studies examine different types of intelligence and use different psychological terms than we employ to describe the components of Appreciative Intelligence, their findings support the notion of connections between neural functions and mental processes of Appreciative Intelligence. During our exploration of evidence for Appreciative Intelligence, we found numerous research articles and books on the following constructs and their neurological roots:

- Social intelligence
- Stereotyping
- Person perception
- Insight

The following subsections highlight studies that were recent, provided clarity of understanding, represented a larger body of work, or were most salient. The subsections also discuss how the constructs are related to, and their implications for, Appreciative Intelligence.

Social Intelligence

In the early 1990s, psychiatrist and researcher Leslie A. Brothers proposed that a network of neural regions constitute the "social brain." According to Brothers, the orbito-frontal cortex (OFC), the superior temporal gyrus (STG), and the amygdala work together to deal with the social environment.[6]

Testing the work of Brothers and building on that of Nicholas Humphrey, who in 1976 argued that social intelligence exists independently of general intelligence, Simon Baron-Cohen and co-researchers examined two groups with different levels of social intelligence. They compared normal subjects with patients with high functioning autism or Asperger Syndrome, who typically have difficulties relating to other people. Using fMRI and a test of judging what someone else is thinking or feeling by the expression in the other's eyes, they found that the STG and the amygdala showed increased activity when judging others' thoughts and feelings. Some areas of the prefrontal cortex also showed activation. On the contrary, patients with autism did not show activation in the amygdala. Hence, the researchers concluded that social intelligence has its roots in the STG and the amygdala.[7]

Although social intelligence and Appreciative Intelligence are not the same constructs, they are related through the notions of appreciation of people and comprehension of the social environment that is key to seeing how the future unfolds from the present. What Baron-Cohen referred to as social intelligence—as shown by the judgment of others' feelings based on expressions—is closely related to the perception and evaluation that occur in Appreciative Intelligence, as when Brownie Wise looked for fire in the eyes of job candidates or when Estee Lauder evaluated potential customers. Such studies about social intelligence hold a number of implications for Appreciative Intelligence. First, although social intelligence is not the same as Appreciative Intelligence, evidence that suggests that social and general intelligences involve different parts of the brain is encouraging for the possibility of separate areas of the brain controlling general and Appreciative Intelligence. Second, they provide evidence that could explain the neural functioning and role of the amygdala, the STG, and the OFC behind the appreciative evaluation of situations and people.

Stereotyping

As mentioned previously, successful leaders with high Appreciative Intelligence deal with each person in a unique way. They seem to embody the adage, "Don't judge a book by its cover." Looking past outward appearance or traditional signs of socioeconomic status, they seem to see a core of an individual that others do not. Furthermore, these leaders have a knack for seeing potential strengths, talents, and other positive useful attributes. They set the stage for talent to be revealed, developed, and valued. Such thinking is nearly the opposite of stereotyping and prejudice.

Stereotypes are attributions assigned to a particular social or ethnic group. Examples of stereotypical thinking range from positive to negative assumptions and may not be based on facts. Consider the following example of a stereotype that has shaped the employee demographics of Fortune 500 companies: that Asian Americans are smart in computer programming and analytical tasks, but don't make effective leaders. Researchers found that although the U.S. national percentage of Asian Americans is 4 percent, in Fortune 500 companies 12 percent of computer programmers were Asian Americans but only half of one percent held a management position of vice-president or above.[8]

Because people usually cannot explain their rapid mental processes, it is methodologically difficult to determine whether a person with high Appreciative Intelligence does not form as many stereotypes as others do or whether he or she has a better ability to see past initial stereotypical thoughts. But new imaging methods have provided insight into processes behind stereotyping and identified brain regions involved in emotions, thoughts, and behaviors associated with stereotyping.[9] For example, Allen Hart and co-workers[10] and Elizabeth A. Phelps and co-workers[11] related the amygdala to perception—and automatic stereotyping—of faces of a different race. Others have taken that work further.

Reaction based on amygdala processing can occur faster than a person even becomes aware that he or she has witnessed an object or event. Recent research by social cognitive neuroscientists Mary Wheeler and Susan Fiske has suggested, however, that despite the speed at which a reaction to seeing another person might occur, it is possible for individuals to suppress stereotypical responses intentionally. Using fMRI, they compared participants' brain activity in the amygdala when they showed them photos of unfamiliar African-American and European-American faces and asked them to perform three different tasks. They found that when the task required participants to look at the person in the photograph as an individual (deciding whether or not the person would like a given vegetable not associated particularly with one culture or the other), participants showed less amygdala response, stereotyping, and prejudicial thought than when the task required participants to assign the person in the photograph to a category (over 21 years old or not).[12]

Their findings are consistent with an fMRI study conducted at UCLA's Ahmanson-Lovelace Brain Mapping Center and published in 2005 by Matthew Lieberman and his colleagues. They asked African-American and European-American study participants to match people's races in photographs of expressionless African-American and European-American male faces. They also asked the participants to match the word "Caucasian" or "African-American" to the photographs. They found that while both African-American and European-American individuals showed greater amygdala activity in response to the African-American photographs to be matched than to European-American ones, race-matching through words (verbal encoding) led to less amygdala stimulation. They suggested that the right ventrolateral prefrontal cortex may have been inhibiting the amygdala.[13]

Such findings also give strong support to our contention that individuals with high Appreciative Intelligence might have the ability to intentionally reframe a situation so as not to see the automatic stereotypes. The other common thread in these studies is that there is a clear neural basis that accounts for stereotyping and similar perceptual processes. The amygdala and the prefrontal cortex, which have emerged as a center for perception of other people, could also point to the neural basis of Appreciative Intelligence.

Person Perception

People understand each others' short- and long-term emotions, desires, values, and personalities through the process of person perception.[14] This ability to generate realistic inferences is essential for making accurate predictions about how they might behave. The leaders we studied, such as William Coleman, Brownie Wise, and NASA's Ed Hoffman, masterfully predicted successful behavior of potential employees, customers, and colleagues. In this way, we propose that person perception is tied to Appreciative Intelligence.

As with stereotyping, a socio-cognitive neuroscience network can be found for the capacity for effective person perception. Reiterating the aforementioned study of Baron-Cohen, children with autism or Asperger

Syndrome show abnormal amygdala activation when interpreting the social meaning of eye gaze.[15]

In 2003, another group of researchers led by Reuven Bar-On, a pioneer in the work of emotional intelligence, proposed that the ventro-medial prefrontal cortex, the amygdala, and the insular regions are part of a neural system involved in emotional signaling, decision making, and, ultimately, emotional intelligence. They showed that emotional and social intelligence are different from cognitive or general intelligence, as are the neural systems behind them.[16]

Again, such a line of thinking, proposed by influential cognitive neuroscientists, may support our contention that Appreciative Intelligence is different from general (cognitive), emotional, and social intelligence and that it may have its own unique supporting neural system, although not far from those for social and emotional intelligence.

Insight

Another commonality of leaders with high Appreciative Intelligence was that each had unique insights or perceptions that led to creative and innovative solutions: Coleman lanterns, Coca-Cola as a beverage, unique pieces of laboratory equipment, new processes for freezing food, and new organizations. Opportunity and necessity—as the mother of invention—knock at the door for many people, but Appreciative Intelligent leaders seem more often to be prepared to hear the knock and open the door. They make their "Aha!" or "Eureka!" moments have significant impact on their businesses, organizations, and communities.

How such unique answers to questions and "Aha!" moments come about and the origin of insight in the brain were the topics of a recent study by Mark Jung-Beeman, John Kounios, and their research team.[17] Using EEG and fMRI, they found patterns of brain activity surrounding the moment that an answer to a word puzzle entered their subjects' minds. The study participants were asked whether they felt an answer had "just popped into their heads," indicating they had an insight, or whether they used a more methodical, noninsight approach.

The EEG measured the moment the answer popped into their heads, while the fMRI indicated the location of brain activity. In the cases where subjects reported getting the answer with insight, the EEG showed a burst of brain activity in the right hemisphere just before the subjects hit a button indicating they had solved the puzzle. The fMRI, meanwhile, showed a small spot in the right hemisphere anterior superior temporal gyrus that lit up more when the subjects got their answers with insight. Furthermore, the researchers found that before subjects even saw a question, those who solved puzzles with insight showed some increased brain activity on the EEG. It appeared that the brain state before the problem is presented predicts whether the subjects solve it with insight or not. In other words, the subjects who used insight put their brains into a state in which they were more likely to have a flash of insight.

The work of Jung-Beeman and his colleagues, identifying the right hemisphere anterior STG as the key region responsible for insight, provides yet another pointer to it as a region highly active in those with the components of thinking we refer to as Appreciative Intelligence. This research also suggests the possibility that if people have the ability to put their brains into a state in which insight occurs, people may have the ability to put their brains into an intentional state of Appreciative Intelligence. If so, the further implications for developing and expanding Appreciative Intelligence as they learn to enter a brain state or mindset has exciting possibilities for increasing Appreciative Intelligence in individuals and their organizations.

Tying together the various social cognitive neurological studies, the complex processes associated with perception, social evaluation, reappraisal, and insight that relate to the components of Appreciative Intelligence seem to come from the amygdala, the superior temporal gyrus, the prefrontal cortex, and the orbito-frontal cortex.

In conclusion, we collected a wide variety of pieces of information: existing knowledge from the field of psychology on intelligence, positive psychology, and positive organizational behavior; new social cognitive neuroscientific research identifying the role of the amygdala, the superior temporal gyrus, and the prefrontal cortex; and study and observations of historical and current organizational leaders who possess a rare ability to reframe or reappraise reality, appreciate the positive, and see how the future unfolds from the present. Assembling these pieces into a coherent whole, we found the picture of the missing link between intelligence and success: Appreciative Intelligence.

Chapter 11

Moving Forward for an Extraordinary Future

First, say to yourself what you would be; and then
do what you have to do.
—Epictetus (2nd century A.D.)

It is difficult to imagine that before the 1800s, there weren't standard names or classifications of clouds. Humans have always watched the skies, but it wasn't until 1802 that amateur meteorologist Luke Howard classified and labeled cirrus, cumulus, and stratus clouds.[1] His identification and naming conventions provided a foundation for scientists and the general population alike to categorize all clouds as a variety of three basic forms, disseminate knowledge about them, study them further, and apply the information to weather prediction. The language itself gave people a way to make sense of the natural phenomenon of clouds. Over time, many people have forgotten or have never known that cloud names or the scientific study of clouds did not always exist.

Similarly, the ability to see the mighty oak in the acorn has always been at play, and throughout history it has shaped leaders, innovators, entrepreneurs, and their success. Like farmers and sailors who developed their own systems for understanding clouds as signs of warning or fair weather, leadership scholars and innovation experts have seen and noted successful people's novel perspectives and vision. Introducing Appreciative Intelligence, identifying it, and labeling it as a distinct form of intelligence, however, as in this book, have significant ramifications for individuals and organizations.

As with clouds or any newly pinpointed and named construct, the language around Appreciative Intelligence allows and generates discussion about it that leads to its description, study, prediction, teaching, and development. By identifying and naming Appreciative Intelligence, we can ask more questions about it, look more carefully at people who exhibit its qualities, attempt to make predictions about future leaders and inventors or their behaviors, and develop or expand it within our organizations and ourselves. Consistent with the most accepted understanding of intelligence as a changing capacity that can be enhanced and nurtured rather than as a static entity, the possibility of recognizing and cultivating it means the ability to affect prosperity, health, and success on individual and organizational levels. If we understand what constitutes the missing link between intelligence and success, then the implications are that we can shape the future we desire by applying what we know about Appreciative Intelligence.

In this final chapter, we look at possibilities for a future in which your Appreciative Intelligence is recognized, identified, developed, and enhanced. We lay out the implications of Appreciative Intelligence on the individual, organizational, and societal level. Last, we offer three steps to start you on the journey of creating your own successful future through Appreciative Intelligence.

Implications of Appreciative Intelligence

Taking an umbrella to work on a morning when the sun is shining brightly but the day's weather forecast calls for showers is a small action for most of us. Yet it is a significant consequence of the identification of clouds that opened the way for thousands of people now to know something new ("A front is coming in, so it will probably rain this afternoon") and take action accordingly (carry an umbrella, although the sun is shining). What if, by identifying, naming, and studying Appreciative Intelligence, people's daily lives were changed in similarly small, yet significant, ways?

What if more schools adopted principles similar to those of Delaware Valley Friends School? What if more salespeople saw potential good customers in people who walked into a shop, as Estee Lauder did?

What if more employers, managers, or directors helped bring out the best in their team members the way Ed Hoffman looks for talent in NASA's leaders or Gore associates encouraged Matt Schreiner to work on a new project? What if more students came up with innovative solutions, like those of Westtown School's FIRST team who reframed and recycled used boards from an old wooden tank as material to build a shipping crate for their robot? What if more corporations, nonprofit organizations, and government agencies sought to identify people who exhibit high levels of Appreciative Intelligence? What if society harnessed the power in Appreciative Intelligence for future success?

Now that Appreciative Intelligence has been identified, labeled as a construct, and described and a method for its development and enhancement has been prescribed, we believe that is just what will happen. It has implications at the individual, organizational, and society level.

For individuals, in its simplest case the identification of Appreciative Intelligence provides the opportunity for some who do not sport a high IQ to become recognized as intelligent. On a deeper level, the construct begins to explain what makes some people exemplary leaders or successful in various facets of life, and how focusing on the development of Appreciative Intelligence can improve effectiveness in both. It opens up possibilities for those with high levels to refine and hone their natural abilities and for those with lower levels to work with and expand the abilities already possessed.

Throughout the book we have given examples of how people with high Appreciative Intelligence set high standards and expectations for those around them and treat people as individuals of inherent high worth, thereby bringing out the best in others. In turn, their interactions set the tone for reciprocated respect and appreciation. Hence, those with higher levels of Appreciative Intelligence may create "high-quality connections"—that is, interactions in which people experience a sense of vitality, positive regard, and mutuality.[2] According to researchers Ryan Quinn of Washington University and Jane Dutton of the University of Michigan, such interactions endow individuals with psychological, social, physiological, and energetic resources which can support superior performance and a high level of personal competence.[3] Hence, they may enjoy better-quality relationships with colleagues, subordinates, and superiors than will people who have lower degrees of Appreciative Intelligence.

Similarly, their positive beliefs in themselves and their abilities become a self-fulfilling prophecy, and they enjoy increased triumphs and achievements. Additionally, because they believe that their actions matter, they have the ability "to enter into potential stressful situations with confidence and assurance and thus to resist stressful reactions."[4]

Because of their effective interactions, quality relationships, capacity to innovate, resistance to negative stressful reactions, and ability to see talent and bring out the best in others, people with Appreciative Intelligence become valued members of any organization and often rise to top positions or ranks as leaders. Because of their persistence, conviction that their actions matter, tolerance for uncertainty, and irrepressible resilience, they are often at the forefront of new ventures and startups. Such people often enjoy the tangible rewards of top positions as well as recognition and personal satisfaction.

We have also shown that Appreciative Intelligence contributes to higher incidence of innovation and creative solutions at the organizational level. It also lies behind employees with top talent, better retention rates, and less stress and the ability to respond effectively to lumps and bumps in a volatile economy or challenging environment. In an economy where analysts rank innovativeness and ability to attract and retain talented people in the top ten intangibles that matter to the success of a company,[5] the benefits associated with Appreciative Intelligence contribute significantly to an organization's survival, longevity, and long-term success.

The ability to see the positive part of reality informs organizations' strategy and tactics. Strategically, leaders can set long-term mission and goals based on the positive end state they perceive. Tactically, organizations experience a boost in innovation and creativity to carry out tasks toward long-term goals when a leader can reframe reality, appreciate what is positive, and see how the future unfolds from the present. Appreciative Intelligence sparks entrepreneurship, new products, services, knowledge, and solutions to operational challenges that can improve the profitability of the company by increasing revenue or reducing expenses. The ability to see hidden potential, and to realize that value, results in redefined products, such as Gore-Tex as a superior dental floss or a mediocre children's book edited into a successful short picture book.

Another advantage for organizations is the potential for increased talent and expertise in their employees, springing from the ability to see the hidden potential in people and to bring out untapped abilities. Increased talent isn't necessarily the result of leaders setting out to find people who are already the most accomplished performers. Instead, like distinguished talent scouts or coaches in the sports, entertainment, or job recruitment fields, leaders with high Appreciative Intelligence have a knack for seeing undeveloped or unpolished raw ability in the employees around them. By seeing talent within, rather than always recruiting from the outside, organizations spend fewer dollars on recruiting, relocating, and training new employees. Their members spend less time waiting for newly hired employees to learn the existing operations, policies, and politics. Groups are more likely to have a talent pool at hand exactly when needed, not weeks or months after a candidate or consultant search.

Leaders with Appreciative Intelligence also create a fertile environment for cultivating previously undiscovered or untested talent. Using the same mindset that allows creative solutions to emerge, they encourage talent and excellence to emerge and flourish. When individuals and groups are assumed to possess talent, competence, and high value inherently, leaders are more likely to remove barriers that inhibit creativity, provide resources to support new ideas, and offer freedom for people to excel. Such a culture allows risks that accompany exploration and opens the door for innovation. In a pointed example, William Coleman, the founder of the Coleman Company, was once a salesman with poor eyesight and no technical training. But he had a talent for surrounding himself with technically gifted employees and an eye for opportunity and creative solutions. Coleman thus built the company that bore his name and introduced the Coleman lantern to the world.[6] Because organizations led by people with high Appreciative Intelligence offer environments with resources to fund new ideas and freedom to excel, they enjoy high rates of employee satisfaction and retention, in addition to high rates of innovation.

One of the most significant implications of Appreciative Intelligence for organizations is the ability to bounce back from a difficult situation. The ability to reframe or reinterpret a given situation enables leaders to perceive that a positive consequence can be built from even the most unpromising circumstances. Rather than experiencing a position of impossibility, and therefore a situation without hope or remedy, the intelligent leader has the capacity to see what is possible and to set a plan of action with tangible steps to create the envisioned positive state. People with high levels of Appreciative Intelligence are adept at turning around an organization in trouble, leading it out of a crisis or disaster, or handling a defining, critical moment.

Many companies in a tough situation already possess the talent and resources to overcome obstacles; they just don't realize it. One difference between a company with leaders having high Appreciative Intelligence—and the ensuing irrepressible resilience—and one without them is that the former sees the talent and expertise that can help it through the situation. Furthermore, the appreciation and the positive light cast onto talented team members keeps them from jumping ship during tough times. Yet another difference is that in the former company the leader is able to redefine the situation for team members who have never experienced a similar obstacle or one of the same magnitude. Using words like "recapitalize" instead of "bankruptcy" or "challenge" instead of "disaster" helps replace team members' fears with hope and energy, and enables them remain to calm enough to concentrate on the task at hand. Finally, because of the appreciative process and the ability to convey the vision of a positive end state, organizations with leaders with high levels of Appreciative Intelligence have the ability to move more quickly into a productive mode following a tragedy or mistake. In contrast, in companies with leaders with low Appreciative Intelligence, people may not recognize that solutions and talent are right under their noses, and organization members waste time and energy by waiting to find out what to do or worrying.

We have also shown in this book that, ultimately, Appreciative Intelligence has a potential impact on organizations' survival and longevity. In a circular process discussed in detail in Chapter 7, leaders build an environment or culture that spreads their own Appreciative Intelligence to others. The previously discussed advantages of talent increase, innovation, employee retention, long-term resilience, and quality of leadership have a beneficial impact on organizations' finances, position in the marketplace or environment, and effectiveness—all drivers in organizations' goals of longevity and sustainability.

In the same circular process that spreads Appreciative Intelligence from the individual to the organization and back again, leaders with high Appreciative Intelligence and their organizations can have a profound influence on society. Showing up in a cultural enjoyment of rags-to-riches stories, a high regard for entrepreneurship and invention, a propensity for applying resources to new ideas, and freedom that shows up in public policy and the workings of the capital markets, Appreciative Intelligence becomes a magnet for further talent as well as a cultural competitive advantage. Consider the historical impact of Appreciative Intelligence on the farming community of Enterprise, Alabama, when they perceived the devastation the cotton-eating boll weevil insect inflicted on the cotton crop as an opportunity to diversify their agriculture. (Peanuts and other crops more than made up for the lost cotton, and today the town contains a monument to the insect "in profound appreciation of the Boll Weevil and what it has done as the Herald of Prosperity.")[7] Consider the role of Appreciative Intelligence in the more recent phenomena of Silicon Valley. The California technology center drew bright programmers, engineers, entrepreneurs, and venture capitalists from around the world, resulting in collaborations that have produced an immense number of electronics and computer innovations. Knowing that Appreciative Intelligence is such a force on society opens up a wide range of implications for the need to identify highly intelligent children and provide educational opportunities to hone their intelligence and associated behaviors for future life success. It also has implications for predicting who will make the best leaders in our society and what we can do as parents and families, caregivers, educators, and policy makers to enhance those natural abilities.

We believe that Appreciative Intelligence influences large-scale entrepreneurship and capacity for invention, a propensity for applying resources to new and potentially successful ideas. Appreciative Intelligence also takes on significance for the current economic and labor markets within the context of globalization of businesses and other organizations. Globalization has had an impact on everyone in one way or another, culturally, politically, or economically. As the dynamics of our society and the job market change, discomfort associated with ambiguity and uncertainty have followed in certain cases. U.S. and other national/international corporations large and small have set up shop in India, China, Brazil, and elsewhere. Many have outsourced jobs to workers in other countries or created expatriates of others, leaving some employees uncertain about the future of their own positions, looking for new jobs or lines of work, or adjusting to new companies or countries. As the culture, styles, and norms of differing countries influence each other, workers can be left with the uncertainty of what different communication styles or actions mean.[8] By using Appreciative Intelligence, workers and leaders can reveal and seize hidden opportunities to enhance their competitive advantage and manage fears and risk. Companies and countries, business leaders and policy makers can reframe their roles in a global context as places of intellectual capital and creative talent. Leaders with high Appreciative Intelligence will look to discover the untapped potential of the globalization of businesses and talent that already exist.

We believe this book is just the beginning of many discussions about Appreciative Intelligence. Intelligence is a dynamic concept. We're learning more about the brain as a continually changing organ. As researchers are moving into new exploration of intelligence and the brain, they are focusing on finding improvement, rather than simply fixing problems. We cannot guess all the ramifications of Appreciative Intelligence, but we hope that by providing a model for others to enhance their abilities, people will see their own possibilities for the future that are waiting to be realized in the present.

Step into the Future

Everyone has Appreciative Intelligence. Although some seem to be born with it and some appear to have higher levels than others, all can expand what they have. Like venture capitalists who allocate resources to what works rather than chisel away at what seems broken, people can reveal their own intelligence and expand their successful experiences.

By learning to reframe, appreciate the positive, and see how the future unfolds from the present, you can build and strengthen your Appreciative Intelligence, increase the incidence of innovative solutions, expand your possibilities, and cultivate your own genius. You can begin making these sorts of changes by taking three steps as soon as you put down this book.

1. At your next morning work meeting, reframe a colleague's idea to see the best way it could work for both of you and for your organization.
2. This afternoon or evening, have a new conversation with your child (or a student or a young friend).
3. Tonight, take time to reflect on the successes of your day.

1. Reframe at Work

Go to your Monday morning (or the next morning) meeting with a resolution to see a colleague's idea in a new way. When, or if, an idea proposed by a colleague seems impossible, impractical, or strange to you, pause for a moment. Take a deep breath and temporarily suspend judgment. Mentally ask yourself the following questions: How could I see this idea in a new light? What is my colleague seeing that makes this idea have merit? What else can I find in this idea that is good for me, my colleague, and our organization? What resources could I contribute that would make the idea possible, or how could I help achieve this goal? Instead of running through mental scenarios to determine how the idea could fall short, explore how the idea could work. If your opinion is elicited, instead of concluding that the idea could run into problems, ask what resources are available and what concrete steps could make it happen.

2. Talk with a Child

This afternoon or evening, when you talk with your child (or a student, a young friend, or someone you occasionally mentor), carefully consider the conversation. Although the issue at hand or the details of the situation may be different, determine how you might adapt the ideas and questions in the following scenario to come to a successful conclusion.

Suppose that your child mentions that he would like to become a painter (musician, writer, or other) when he grows up. You have some concerns that the occupation may not be lucrative (or practical, or some other value). Instead of immediately mentioning that there are problems associated with that field, stop for a moment to examine your current beliefs, values, and frame of reference. Temporarily put aside your fears of your child becoming a proverbial starving artist and think of at least one successful painter whose works, financial status, and lifestyle you admire. Ask your child if he has ever heard of the artist. Talk about what you know about the artist's path to success, what sorts of efforts it took, whom she knew and how she overcame challenges. Ask your child in what kind of galleries he would like to display his own work, whom he might get to know or to help him, and what studies might be necessary to follow in the footsteps of the successful artist.

If you learn that your child exhibits no real interest in taking action to become a successful painter, ask what it is about becoming a painter that seems attractive. Explore the answers to the question, again considering what is valuable and positive from your child's perspective. You may learn that your child loves engaging in the creative process or being in the presence of artists, for instance. Ask whether he has ever heard of other types of work that employ the creative process (such as advertising, graphic art, or Web site design) or working around artists (such as an attorney specializing in intellectual property rights, agent, or gallery owner) and talk about how successful professionals in those lines of work accomplish what your child likes. By reframing the conversation to explore such positive possibilities, you are honoring the needs, desires, and potential talents of your child, as well as your own experience and values. By pointing out concrete steps to achieve his goal, you help him see how the future could unfold from the present. You send the signal that you respect your child's ideas and want his success in a way that makes him happy.

3. Reflect on Your Day

At the end of the day, take stock. Write the answers in a success journal, as suggested in Chapter 8, or engage in mental reflection on the following questions: What did I do today that was my personal best? What of value did I reveal in projects or in other people at work or at home? What were my moments of success? When did I ask more questions instead of jumping to a negative conclusion? What did I learn today? At what points did I reframe, appreciate, or see the generative potential? Include the results of your morning work meeting or afternoon conversation with your child, as well as any other experiences during your day. Do not omit incremental progress or undervalue small successes. Again, remember to take an appreciative approach to your thinking, focusing on what worked rather than on what did not.

Each of the three steps helps you reframe the present idea or situation, see and appreciate its valuable aspects, and see how what is positive and available at present could create a better future for you and others. The three steps encompass three aspects of life—professional, family, and personal—and different times of the day—morning, afternoon, and night. Although they may seem simple, they can operate at different depths for different degrees of Appreciative Intelligence. As a college professor once said about an exam given to both undergraduate and graduate students, "The questions are the same. It's the answers that change." The steps provide an easy way to start using your Appreciative Intelligence. Over time, they can help you refine, enhance, and renew your ability to see the positive inherent generative potential in the present.

The three steps can also lead you to better ideas and solutions and stronger relationships with your colleagues, family, friends, and others. They help you better understand what you do well, how you are already successful, and how you can keep growing. By taking the three steps you begin a journey to create a future that is extraordinary for you and simultaneously honors the perspective of others.

A Closing Invitation

In this book we have laid out a path for concrete action for improving effectiveness in leadership, human relationships, and life by focusing on the development of Appreciative Intelligence. We expect that organizations will develop new questions for choosing employees, funding innovators, or grooming leaders in order to shape the future they desire. We invite consultants, teachers, human resource practitioners, psychologists, business leaders, policy makers, inventors, government workers, parents, and others to develop further practices and approaches to evaluation, development, and predictions of the construct. The number of healthy, mighty oaks and acorns that can sprout from the knowledge of this intelligence is boundless.

We conclude that the most effective and successful people exhibit the ability to perceive reality in a way that brings out the positive inherent generative potential. It is more important than IQ, subject matter expertise, environmental context, or resources at hand. A high level of the newly identified intelligence that exists within them—called Appreciative Intelligence—is the ability to see the mighty oak within the acorn.

Notes

Foreword
1. Steve Sternberg, "Scientists Ready to 'Map' Gene Variations, Diseases," *USA Today*, October 27, 2005.
2. Howard Gardner, *Frames of Mind: The Theory of Multiple Intelligences*, 2nd ed. (New York: Basic Books, 1993), xi.

Chapter 1
1. Hubble European Space Agency Information Centre, www.spacetelescope.org (accessed February 16, 2005).
2. World Health Organization, http://www.polioeradication.org/content/general/casecount.pdf (accessed May 11, 2005).
3. Peter Krass, "Tupperware's Brownie Wise Built and Prepped Her Army with Methodical Goal Setting," *Investors Business Daily*, August 28, 1998, sec. Leaders & Success.
4. Michael Tarsala, "Coca-Cola's Asa Candler: How He Took a Fizzling Brain Tonic and Made 'The Real Thing' Fizz," *Investors Business Daily*, February 1, 1999, sec. Leaders & Success.
5. Peter Krass, "Entrepreneur Estee Lauder: How She Created World's Largest Prestige Cosmetics Firm," *Investors Business Daily*, April 8, 1998, sec. Leaders & Success.
6. Dean Kamen, interview by author, May 12, 2005.
7. Fred Kerlinger, *Foundations of Behavioral Research* (New York: Holt, Rinehart and Winston, 1973), 28–29.
8. George Washington Carver as quoted from Jon Barnes, "Botanist George Washington Carver: Rather Than Give In to Poverty, He Used It to Spur Inventiveness," *Investor's Business Daily*, November 4, 1998, sec. Leaders & Success.
9. Viktor E. Frankl, *Man's Search for Meaning* (New York: Washington Square Press, 1963), 104.

Chapter 2
1. Rick Carter, "W. L. Gore & Associates, Inc. . . Quality's Different Drummer," *Industrial Maintenance & Plant Operation* (January 2002), 10–16.
2. W. L. Gore & Associates, www.gore.com (accessed August 11, 2005).
3. Alan Deutschman, "The Fabric of Creativity," *Fast Company*, Issue 89 (December 2004), 55.
4. Deutschman, "The Fabric of Creativity," 58.
5. W. L. Gore & Associates, www.gore.com (accessed August 11, 2005).
6. Matt Schreiner, interview by author, August 24, 2005.
7. George Shaw, interview by author, August 16, 2005.
8. Paul C. Judge, "How Will Your Company Adapt?" *Fast Company*, Issue 53 (December 2001), 128–138.

9. Procter & Gamble News Release, September 17, 2003, www.pg.com (accessed August 15, 2005).

10. Judge, "How Will Your Company Adapt?" 128–138.

11. Procter & Gamble News Release, September 17, 2003, www.pg.com (accessed August 15, 2005).

12. Ed Hoffman, interview by the author, December 20, 2004.

13. Jonathan W. Schooler et al., "Epilogue: Putting Insight into Perspective," in Robert Sternberg and Janet Davidson, eds., *The Nature of Insight* (Cambridge, MA: MIT Press, 1995), 575.

14. The Zeigarnik Effect, http://www.fasthealth.com/dictionary/z/Zeigarnik_effect.php, copyright 1997-2004 (accessed May 11, 2005).

15. Greg Radford, interview by the author, West Chester, PA, May 13, 2005.

16. Herb Pigman, interview by the author, January 28, 2005.

17. World Health Organization, http://www.polioeradication.org/content/general/casecount.pdf (accessed May 11, 2005).

18. William James, *The Principles of Psychology* (New York: H. Holt and Company, 1890/1918), 310.

19. Adam Di Paula and Jennifer Campbell, "Self-Esteem and Persistence in the Face of Failure," *Journal of Personality and Social Psychology*, 83, no. 3 (2002), 711–724.

20. Bill Sergeant, interview by author, February 9, 2005.

21. Stajkovic and Luthans defined self-efficacy as "an individual's conviction (or confidence) about his or her abilities to mobilize the motivation, cognitive resources, and courses of action needed to successfully execute a specific task in a given context." A. D. Stajkovic and F. Luthans, "Social Cognitive Theory and Self-Efficacy: Going Beyond Traditional Motivational and Behavioral Approaches," *Organizational Dynamics*, 26, no. 4 (1998), 66.

22. Albert Bandura, *Social Foundations of Thought and Action: A Social Cognitive Theory* (Englewood Cliffs, NJ: Prentice Hall, 1986).

23. Albert Bandura, "The Self-System in Reciprocal Determinism," *American Psychologist*, 33 (1978), 344–358.

24. F. Pajares and D. H. Schunk, "Self-Beliefs and School Success: Self-Efficacy, Self-Concept, and School Achievement," in R. Riding and S. Rayner, eds., *Perception* (London: Ablex Publishing, 2001), 239–266.

25. Robert K. Merton, "The Self-Fulfilling Prophecy," *Antioch Review*, 8 (1948), 193–210.

26. Warren G. Bennis and Patricia Ward Biederman, *Organizing Genius: The Secrets of Creative Collaboration* (Reading, MA: Addison Wesley, 1997), 15.

27. Domenic Carnuccio, interview by author, June 3, 2005.

28. William Isaac Thomas, *The Child in America* (New York: Knopf, 1928), 257.

29. Charles Pellerin, interview by author, January 12, 2005.

30. Fleur Frascella, interview by author, West Chester, PA, May 16, 2005.

31. Kirk Hallahan, "Seven Models of Framing: Implications for Public Relations," *Journal of Public Relations Research*, 11, no. 3 (1999), 205–242.

32. Albert Bandura, "Cultivate Self-Efficacy for Personal and Organizational Effectiveness," in E. A. Locke, ed., *The Blackwell Handbook of Principles of Organizational Behavior* (Oxford, UK: Blackwell, 2000), 120.

33. Robert J. Sternberg, and Todd I. Lubart, "An Investment Perspective on Creative Insight," in Robert Sternberg and Janet Davidson, eds., *The Nature of Insight* (Cambridge, MA: MIT Press, 1995), 535.

34. Wanda J. Orlikowski, "Learning from Notes: Organizational Issues in Groupware Implementation," MIT Sloan School Working Paper, #3428-92, May 1992.

35. J. L. Denis, A. Langley, and L. Cazale, "Leadership and Strategic Change under Ambiguity," *Organization Studies*, 17, no. 4 (1996), 673–699.

36. D. Ghosh and M. R. Ray, "Risk, Ambiguity, and Decision Choice: Some Additional Evidence," *Decision Sciences*, 28, no. 1 (1997), 81–104.

37. Howard Schultz and Dori Jones Yang, *Pour Your Heart into It: How Starbucks Built a Company One Cup at a Time* (New York: Hyperion, 1997), 1.

38. Joshua Correll, Steven Spencer, and Mark Zanna, "An Affirmed Self and an Open Mind: Self-Affirmation and Sensitivity to Argument Strength," *Journal of Experimental Social Psychology*, 40 (2004), 350–356.

39. Dean Kamen, interview by author, May 11, 2005.

40. George Shaw, interview by author, August 16, 2005.

41. Michael Philip Hand, "Psychological Resilience: The Influence of Positive and Negative Life Events upon Optimism, Hope, and Perceived Locus of Control," Doctoral Dissertation, Walden University, 2003.

42. Paul Pearsall, *The Beethoven Factor: The New Positive Psychology of Hardiness, Happiness, Healing and Hope* (Charlottesville, VA: Hampton Roads Publishing Company, 2003).

43. Salvatore Maddi and Deborah Khoshaba, *Resilience at Work: How to Succeed No Matter What Life Throws at You* (New York: AMACOM Books, 2005).

44. This new book provides a clear example of how resilience can be cultivated in individuals. Al Siebert, *The Resiliency Advantage: Master Change, Thrive under Pressure, and Bounce Back from Setbacks* (San Francisco: Berrett-Koehler Publishers, 2005).

45. B. L. Frederickson, M. M. Tugade, C.E. Waugh, and G. Larkin, "What Good Are Positive Emotions in Crises?: A Prospective Study of Resilience and Emotions Following the Terrorist Attacks on the United States on September, 11th, 2001," *Journal of Personality and Social Psychology*, 84, no. 2 (2003), 365–376.

46. E. C. Klohnen, "Conceptual Analysis and Measurement of the Construct of Ego-Resiliency," *Journal of Personality and Social Psychology*, 70 (1996), 1067–1079.

47. P. Salovey, B. T. Bedell, J. B. Detweiler, and J. D. Mayer, "Coping Intelligently: Emotional Intelligence and the Coping Process," in C. R. Snyder, ed., *Coping: The Psychology of What Works* (New York: Oxford, 1999), 141–164.

48. Barbara L. Fredrickson, "The Role of Positive Emotions in Positive Psychology: The Broaden-and-Build Theory of Positive Emotions," *American Psychologist: Special Issue*, 56 (2001), 218–226.

Chapter 3

1. W. Warren Wagar, *The City of Man: Prophecies of a Modern Civilization in Twentieth-Century Thought* (Baltimore: Penguin, 1968, 1963).

2. Phrase coined by Jonathan Mooney in *Learning Outside the Lines*, a book about ADD and dyslexia, and used by educators at DVFS to describe the way students with these differences often have been incorrectly labeled in traditional educational systems.

3. Katherine Schantz, interview by author, Paoli, PA, June 1, 2005.

4. Delaware Valley Friends School, http://www.dvfs.org (accessed May 22, 2005).

5. Katherine Schantz, interview by author, Paoli, PA, June 1, 2005.

6. Bill Keeney, interview by author, West Chester, PA, May 28, 2005.

7. Delaware Valley Friends School viewbook, "Freeing Creative Minds," designed by students, DVFS, 2004.

8. Source: U.S. Department of Education, National Center for Education Statistics, Integrated Postsecondary Education Data System (IPEDS), Spring 2003, Winter 2001-02, and Fall 2003, http://nces.ed.gov/programs/digest/d04/tables/dt04_169.asp.

9. Dave Brubaker, interview by author, June 1, 2005.

10. Bill Keeney, interview by author, West Chester, PA, May 22, 2005.

11. Bill Keeney, interview by author, West Chester, PA, May 22, 2005.

12. Delaware Valley Friends School viewbook, "Freeing Creative Minds," designed by students, DVFS, 2004.

13. Delaware Valley Friends School, http://www.dvfs.org (accessed May 22, 2005).

14. Bill Keeney, interview by author, West Chester, PA, May 22, 2005.

15. Delaware Valley Friends School, http://www.dvfs.org (accessed May 22, 2005) and Katherine Schantz, interview by author, June 1, 2005.

16. Lucia Herndon, "Mentors Making a Big Difference," *The Philadelphia Inquirer*, April 25, 2004, sec. M, p. 2.

17. Bill Keeney, interview by author, West Chester, PA, May 25, 2005.

18. Bill Keeney, interview by author, West Chester, PA, May 25, 2005.

19. Glenn Heck, interview by author, June 13, 2005.

Chapter 4

1. Alan Deutschman, "The Fabric of Creativity," *Fast Company*, Issue 89, December 2004, 54.

2. Michael Mink, "He Shined a Light 'Round the Old Campfire," *Investors Business Daily*, September 22, 2004, sec. Leaders & Success.

3. For Inspiration and Recognition of Science and Technology, http://www.usfirst.org/ (accessed October 6, 2005).

4. For Inspiration and Recognition of Science and Technology, http://www.usfirst.org/ (accessed October 6, 2005).

5. Max Alexander, "Wow, Isn't That Cool!" *Smithsonian*, 34, no. 6 (September 2003), 95–96.

6. Ed Hoffman, interview by author, December 20, 2004.

7. Bill Sergeant, interview by author, February 9, 2005.

8. Kenneth Gergen and Tojo Thatchenkery, "Organization Science as Social Construction: Postmodern Potentials," *Journal of Applied Behavioral Science*, 40, no. 2 (2004), 228–249.

9. David Snow and Robert Benford, "Framing Processes and Social Movements: An Overview and Assessment," *Annual Review of Sociology*, 26 (2000), 611–639.

10. D. A. Snow, E. B. Rochford, S. K. Worden, and R. D. Benford, "Frame Alignment Processes, Micromobilization, and Movement Participation," *American Sociological Review*, 51 (1986), 464–481.

11. Margaret A. Neale and Max H. Bazerman, "The Effects of Framing and Negotiator Overconfidence in Bargaining Behaviors and Outcomes," *Academy of Management Journal*, 28, no. 1 (1985), 34–49.

12. Robert M. Entman, "Framing: Toward Clarification of a Fractured Paradigm," *Journal of Communication*, 43, no. 4 (1993), 51–58.
13. Harold H. Kelley, "The Warm-Cold Variable in First Impressions of Persons," *Journal of Personality*, 18 (1950), 431–439.
14. John Kounios, interview by author, Philadelphia, PA, April 22, 2005.
15. Robert Sternberg and Janet Davidson, eds., *The Nature of Insight* (Cambridge, MA: The MIT Press, 1995).
16. Charles Pellerin, interview by author, January 12, 2005.
17. Mark Jung-Beeman, John Kounios, et al., "Neural Activity When People Solve Verbal Problems with Insight," *PLoS Biology*, 2, Issue 4 (April 2004), 500–510.
18. Mark Jung-Beeman, Karuna Subramaniam, et al., "Mood Effects on Creative Insight Problem-Solving," poster presentation at Cognitive Neuroscience Society meeting, April 2005.
19. Annette Bolte, Thomas Goschke, and Julius Kuhl, "Emotion and Intuition: Effects of Positive and Negative Mood on Implicit Judgments of Semantic Coherence," *Psychological Science*, 14, no. 5 (September 2003), 416–421.
20. Dan Lovallo and Daniel Kahneman, "Delusions of Success: How Optimism Undermines Executives' Decisions," *Harvard Business Review*, Reprint R0307D (July 2003), 3.
21. Adam Nossiter, "Bush Tours Hurricane Ravaged Areas," http://aolsvc.news.aol.com/news/article.adp?id=20050824033709990005 (accessed 9/13/05).
22. Greg Radford, interview by the author, May 13, 2005.

Chapter 5

1. Matt Krantz, "Howard Schultz: Keeping His Passion as Fresh as the Morning Brew," *Investors Business Daily*, Feb. 2, 1999, sec. Leaders & Success.
2. David Cooperrider and Suresh Srivastva, "Appreciative Inquiry in Organizational Life," *Research in Organizational Change and Development*, 1 (1987), 129–169; Karl Weick, "Affirmation as Inquiry," *Small Group Behavior*, 13 (1982), 441–442.
3. R. Rosenthal and R. Lawson, "A Longitudinal Study of the Effects of Experimenter Bias on the Operant Learning of Laboratory Rats," *Journal of Psychiatric Research*, 2 (1964), 61–72.
4. Lucien Cordaro and James R. Ison, "The Psychology of the Scientist: X. Observer Bias in Classical Conditioning of the Planarian," *Psychological Reports*, 13 (1963), 787–789.
5. Robert Rosenthal and Lenore Jacobson, *Pygmalion in the Classroom* (New York: Holt, Rinehart and Winston, 1968).
6. Mitchel G. Adler, "Conceptualizing and Measuring Appreciation: The Development of a Positive Psychology Construct," Doctoral Dissertation, Rutgers University, 2002.
7. Mitchel G. Adler and Nancy S. Fagley, "Appreciation: Individual Differences in Finding Value and Meaning as a Unique Predictor of Subjective Well-Being," *Journal of Personality*, 73, no. 1 (2005), 79–114.
8. Adler and Fagley, "Appreciation," 82.
9. Max Alexander, "Wow, Isn't That Cool!" *Smithsonian*, 34, no. 6, (September 2003), 95–96.
10. Geoffrey Vickers, *Value Systems and Social Process* (London: Penguin, 1968), 139.

11. Geoffrey Vickers, *Freedom in a Rocking Boat* (London: Allen Lane, 1970; London: Penguin Books, 1972), 102.
12. Adler, "Conceptualizing and Measuring Appreciation," Doctoral Dissertation. Rutgers University, 2002, p. 7.
13. Adler and Fagley, "Appreciation," 79–114.
14. Sandra L. Schneider, "In Search for Realistic Optimism: Meaning, Knowledge, and Warm Fuzziness," *American Psychologist*, 56, no. 3 (2001), 250–263.
15. Peter Krass, "Tupperware's Brownie Wise Built and Prepped Her Army with Methodical Goal Setting," *Investors Business Daily*, August 28, 1998, sec. Leaders & Success.
16. Peter Krass, "Entrepreneur Estee Lauder: How She Created World's Largest Prestige Cosmetics Firm," *Investors Business Daily*, April 8, 1998, sec. Leaders & Success.
17. Dan Goldin, in Cheryl Dahle, "NASA's Mr. Team: The Man behind NASA's Academy of Program and Project Leadership," *Fast Company*, Issue 29, November 1999, 322.
18. Ed Hoffman , interview by author, December 20, 2004.
19. Greg Radford, interview by author, West Chester, PA, May 13, 2005.
20. Matt Schreiner, interview by author, August 24, 2005.
21. Fleur Frascella, interview by author, May 16, 2005.
22. Nick Turner, "Entrepreneur Michael Dell: How He's Made His Firm the Fastest-Growing Computer Maker," *Investors Business Daily*, March 1, 1999, sec. Leaders & Success.
23. John. M. Darley and Russell H. Fazio, "Expectancy Confirmation Processes Arising in the Social Interaction Sequence," *American Psychologist*, 35 (1980), 867–881.
24. Darcy Reich, "What You Expect Is Not Always What You Get: The Roles of Extremity, Optimism, and Pessimism in the Behavioral Confirmation Process," *Journal of Experimental Social Psychology*, 40, no. 2 (2004), 199–215.
25. Fred Luthans, "Positive Organizational Behavior: Developing and Managing Psychological Strengths," *Academy of Management Executive*, 16, no. 1 (2003), Kim Cameron, Jane Dutton, and Robert Quinn, *Positive Organizational Scholarship: Foundations of a New Discipline* (San Francisco: Berrett-Koehler Publishers, 2003).
26. Appreciative Inquiry is "based on a socio-rationalist paradigm which treats organizational reality as a social construction and a product of human imagination." Kenneth Gergen and Tojo Thatchenkery, "Organization Science as Social Construction: Postmodern Potentials," *Journal of Applied Behavioral Science*, 40, no. 2 (2004), 228–249.
27. David Cooperrider and Diana Whitney, "Appreciative Inquiry: A Positive Revolution in Change," in Peggy Holman and Tom Devane, eds., *The Change Handbook: Group Methods for Shaping the Future* (San Francisco: Berrett-Koehler, 1999), 245–261, 247–248.

Chapter 6
1. Tojo Thatchenkery, *Appreciative Sharing of Knowledge: Leveraging Knowledge Management for Strategic Change* (Chagrin Falls, Ohio: Taos Institute Publishing, 2005), 73–74.
2. Raja Meenakshi, People's Project Coordinator of the Pulse Polio Immunisation Programme, interview by author, Chennai, Tamil Nadu, India, November 17, 2004.

3. George Shaw, interview by author, August 16, 2005.
4. Innovation in Canada, "Case 7, Research in Motion," http://innovation.ic.gc.ca/gol/innovation/site.nsf/en/in04212.html (accessed September 23, 2005).
5. Brad Stone, "BlackBerry: Bring It On!" *Newsweek*, September 26, 2005, E8–E14.
6. Innovation in Canada, "Case 7, Research in Motion."
7. Lloyd Sandelands and Robert Drazin, "On the Language of Organization Theory," *Organization Studies*, 10, issue 4 (1989), 457–478.
8. Herbert E. Simon, "Organizations and Markets," *Journal of Economic Perspectives*, 5 (1991), 25–44.
9. Richard L. Daft and Karl E. Weick, "Toward a Model of Organizations as Interpretation Systems," *Academy of Management Review*, 9, no. 2 (1984), 284–295.
10. Susan Case and Tojo Thatchenkery, "Market, Enactment, and Learning from Ambiguous Events: A Case Study of a Small Investment Firm," paper presented at the Entrepreneurship division of the National Academy of Management, Cincinnati, Ohio, August 9–14, 1996.
11. Karl E. Weick, *The Social Psychology of Organizing*, 2nd ed. (Reading, MA: Addison-Wesley, 1979), 147–156.
12. Gary Hamel and C. K Prahalad, "Corporate Imagination and Expeditionary Marketing," *Harvard Business Review*, July-August 1991, 3–11.
13. Case and Thatchenkery, "Market, Enactment, and Learning from Ambiguous Events."
14. Sony History, "Why No Record Function?" http://www.sony.net/Fun/SH/1-18/h2.html (accessed September 28, 2005).
15. Weick, *Social Psychology of Organizing*, pp. 149–150.
16. Weick, *Social Psychology of Organizing*, p. 149.
17. Case and Thatchenkery, "Market, Enactment, and Learning from Ambiguous Events," 9.
18. David L. Cooperrider, "Positive Image, Positive Action: The Affirmative Basis of Organizing," in S. Srivastva et al, eds., *Appreciative Management and Leadership* (San Francisco: Jossey-Bass, 1990), 94.
19. C. Perrow, *Complex Organizations: A Critical Essay*, 3rd ed. (New York: Random House, 1986), 212.
20. Weick, *Social Psychology of Organizing*, p. 149.
21. Kenneth Gergen, *An Invitation to Social Construction* (Thousand Oaks, CA: Sage, 1999), 116.
22. Gergen, *An Invitation to Social Construction*, p. 116.
23. Gergen, *An Invitation to Social Construction*, p. 117.
24. Term coined by Thomas Kuhn in his book *Structure of Scientific Revolutions* (Chicago: University of Chicago Press, 1962).
25. It is not just psychologists who have asked for generative theory in social sciences. Sociologists too have underscored the importance of it. For example, Lynn Smith-Lovin has pointed out that, as sociologists develop theories, they make a choice between the detail of accurate prediction and the generative nature of the theory. She argued strongly for the latter. Lynn Smith-Lovin, "Simplicity, Uncertainty, and the Power of Generative Theories," *Contemporary Sociology*, 29, issue 2 (2000), 300–307.
26. Joel Barker, *The New Business of Paradigms: Classic Edition Transcripts* (St. Paul, MN: Star Thrower Distribution Corp., 2001).

27. Denning, Stephen, *The Springboard: How Storytelling Ignites Action in Knowledge-Era Organizations* (Boston: Butterworth & Heinemann, 2000), 55.
28. George Shaw, interview by author, August 16, 2005.
29. W. L. Gore & Associates, http://www.gore.com (accessed August 11, 2005).
30. Brad Lemley, "The Super Bowl of Smart," *Discover*, February 2005, 56.

Chapter 7
1. Brad Lemley, "The Super Bowl of Smart," *Discover*, February 2005, 56.
2. Woodie Flowers, "Gracious Professionalism, A FIRST Credo," in *2005 FIRST Robotics Competition Manual*, Section 0—Introduction, 1.
3. Dean Kamen, interview by author, May 11 2005.
4. Matt Schreiner, interview by author, August 24, 2005.
5. Matt Krantz, "Howard Schultz: Keeping His Passion as Fresh as the Morning Brew," *Investors Business Daily*, February 2, 1999, sec. Leaders & Success.
6. David W. Johnson and Frank P. Johnson, *Joining Together* (New York: Allyn and Bacon, 2003), 26.
7. "The Power of Persistence," *Fast Company*, March 2003, http://www.fastcompany.com/fast50_02/people/persistence/gruner.html (accessed October 10, 2005).
8. Howard Schultz and Dori Jones Yang, *Pour Your Heart into It: How Starbucks Built a Company One Cup at a Time* (New York: Hyperion, 1997), 8.
9. A, Bandura, D. Ross, and S. A. Ross, "Transmission of Aggression through Imitation of Aggressive Models," *Journal of Abnormal & Social Psychology*, 63 (1961), 575–582.
10. Albert Bandura, *Social Learning Theory* (Englewood Cliffs, NJ: Prentice-Hall, 1977), 22.
11. Bandura, *Social Learning Theory*.
12. E. Coleman, *The Riches of Osceola McCarty* (Morton Grove, IL: Albert Whitman, 1998).
13. Max H. Bazerman, *Judgment in Managerial Decision Making* (New York: Wiley, 1990).
14. Certain neurolinguists, including L. Michael Hall and Robert B. Dilts, have categorized and named different types of frames of reference, such as blame, aim, solution, or positive intentions. L. Michael Hall, "When Bandler Played the Paranoid Blame Game," http://www.neurosemantics.com/Articles/paranoi.htm (accessed August 30, 2005).
15. Greg Radford, interview by author, May 13, 2005.
16. Herb Pigman, interview by author, January 28, 2005.
17. Ron Gruner, interview by author, December 22, 2004.
18. Matt Schreiner, interview by author, August 24, 2005.
19. Patricia Spackman, interview by author, Westtown, PA, February 7, 2005.
20. Matt Krantz, "Lydall's Leonard Jaskol—Training Employees to Work, Not Worry, on the Job," *Investors Business Daily*, January 17, 1995, sec. Leaders & Success.
21. Dean Kamen, interview by author, May 11, 2005.
22. Ann Harrington, "Who's Afraid of a New Product?" *Fortune*, November 3, 2003.
23. In the social sciences, this view is called anthropomorphism, which is attributing human qualities to nonhuman entities.

Chapter 8

1. Ed Hoffman, interview by author, December 20, 2004.
2. Nick Turner, "Entrepreneur Michael Dell: How He's Made His Firm the Fastest-Growing Computer Maker," *Investors Business Daily*, March 1, 1999, sec. Leaders & Success.
3. R. J. Herrnstein and C. Murray, *The Bell Curve: Intelligence and Class Structure in American Life* (New York: Free Press, 1994).
4. John Kounios, interview by author, Philadelphia, PA, April 22, 2005.
5. Alan Chapman, "Origins of Conscious Competence Model," http://www. businessballs.com (accessed April 21 2005).
6. Trish Hall, "Seeking a Focus on Joy in Field of Psychology," *The New York Times*, April 28, 1998, sec. Science Desk.
7. Gerald Edelman, *Wider Than the Sky: The Phenomenal Gift of Consciousness* (New Haven, CT: Yale University Press, 2004); Gerald Edelman, *Neural Darwinism: The Theory of Neuronal Group Selection* (New York: Basic Books, 1987).
8. Robert Brooks and Sam Goldstein, *The Power of Resilience: Achieving Balance, Confidence, and Personal Strength in Your Life* (New York: McGraw-Hill, 2004).
9. Barbara L. Frederickson, "The Value of Positive Emotions," *American Scientist*, 91 (July-August, 2003), 330–335.
10. Chris Argyris and Don Schon, *Organizational Learning: A Theory of Action Perspective* (Reading, MA: Addison-Wesley, 1978).
11. Peter De Jong and Insoo Kim Berg, *Interviewing for Solutions* (Pacific Grove, CA: Brooks/Cole Publishing, 2002); S. de Shazer, *Keys to Solution in Brief Therapy* (New York: W. W. Norton, 1985); S. de Shazer, *Clues: Investigating Solutions in Brief Therapy* (New York: W. W. Norton, 1988); S. de Shazer, *Putting Difference to Work* (New York: W. W. Norton, 1991); and S. de Shazer, *Words Were Originally Magic* (New York: W. W. Norton, 1994).
12. Tojo Thatchenkery, *Appreciative Sharing of Knowledge: Leveraging Knowledge Management for Strategic Change* (Chagrin Falls, OH: Taos Institute Publishing, 2005), 45.

Chapter 9

1. http://www.quoteland.com (accessed October 10, 2005).
2. Trish Hall, "Seeking a Focus on Joy in Field of Psychology," *The New York Times*, April 28, 1998, sec. Science Desk.
3. Martin Seligman, *Learned Optimism* (New York: A.A. Knopf, 1991).
4. Martin Seligman, "Building Human Strength: Psychology's Forgotten Mission," *APA Monitor*, 29, no. 1 (January 1998), http://www.apa.org/monitor/jan98/pres.html.
5. According to University of Chicago psychologist Mihaly Csikszentmihalyi, the state of "flow" is one in which a person is in full happiness, synchronicity, and harmony with himself or herself. Mihaly Csikszentmihalyi, *Flow: The Psychology of Optimal Experience* (New Yori: HarperPerennial Publishers, 1991).
6. Barbara L. Fredrickson, "The Role of Positive Emotions in Positive Psychology: The Broaden-and-Build Theory of Positive Emotions," *American Psychologist* Special Issue, 56 (2001), 218–226.
7. B. L. Fredrickson, R. A. Mancuso, C. Branigan, and M. M.Tugade, "The Undoing Effect of Positive Emotions," *Motivation and Emotion*, 24 (2000), 237–258.

8. Fred Luthans, "Positive Organizational Behavior: Developing and Managing Psychological Strengths," *Academy of Management Executive*, 16, no. 1 (2003), Kim Cameron, Jane Dutton, and Jane and Robert Quinn, *Positive Organizational Scholarship: Foundations of a New Discipline* (San Francisco: Berrett-Koehler Publishers, 2003).

9. C. R. Snyder, ed., *Handbook of Hope* (San Diego: Academic Press, 2000).

10. Ed Diener, "Subjective Well-Being: The Science of Happiness and a Proposal for a National Index" *American Psychologist*, 55, no. 1 (2000).

11. Rita Atkinson et al, eds., *Hilgard's Introduction to Psychology* (Fort Worth: Harcourt Brace College Publishers, 1996), 413.

12. George Valliant, *Adaptation to Life* (Boston: Little, Brown, 1977).

13. Linguistic intelligence is the ability to understand the phonology, syntax, and semantics of language and its pragmatic uses to convince others of a course of action, help one to remember information, explain or communicate knowledge, or reflect upon language itself. Storytellers, orators, poets, and writers exhibit linguistic intelligence in abundance. Bodily-kinesthetic intelligence is the ability to control one's bodily motions and the capacity to handle objects skillfully. Actors, craftsmen, athletes, dancers, and sculptors are proficient in this intelligence. Spatial intelligence is the ability to perceive the visual world accurately, to perform transformations and modifications upon one's initial perceptions, and to re-create aspects of one's visual experience. Architects, mapmakers, surveyors, inventors, and graphic artists must have this intelligence to do well in their fields. Musical intelligence is the ability to understand and express components of music, including melodic and rhythmic patterns, through figural or intuitive or formal analytic means. Logical-mathematical intelligence is the capacity to understand and use logical structures, patterns, relationships, statements, and propositions, through experimentation, quantification, conceptualization, and classification. As we can imagine, scientists, mathematicians, computer programmers, and statisticians will have this intelligence highly developed. Intrapersonal intelligence is the ability to access one's own emotional life through awareness of inner moods, intentions, motivations, potentials, temperaments, and desires, and the capacity to symbolize these inner experiences, and to apply these understandings to help one live one's life. Interpersonal intelligence, on the other hand, is the ability to notice and make distinctions among other individuals with respect to moods, temperaments, motivations, intentions, and to use this information in pragmatic ways, such as to persuade, influence, manipulate, mediate, or counsel individuals or groups of individuals toward some purpose. Howard Gardner, *Frames of Mind: The Theory of Multiple Intelligences* (New York: Basic Book, 1983).

14. Naturalist intelligence is the capacity to recognize and classify flora, fauna, and other natural phenomena. Existential intelligence was preliminarily defined as the ability to pose and ponder questions about life, death, and ultimate realities. Howard Gardner, *Intelligence Reframed: Multiple Intelligences for the 21st Century* (New York: Basic Books, 1999).

15. Peter Salovey and John D. Mayer, "Emotional Intelligence," *Imagination, Cognition and Personality*, 9 (1990), 185-211.

16. Daniel Goleman, *Emotional Intelligence: Why It Can Matter More Than IQ* (New York: Bantam Books, 1994).

17. R. E. Riggio, S. E. Murphy, and F. J. Pirozzolo, *Multiple Intelligences and Leadership* (Mahwah, New Jersey: Lawrence Erlbaum, 2002).

18. Jannelle Gilbert, "Leadership, Social Intelligence, and Perceptions of Environmental Opporunities: A Comparison across Levels of Leadership," Doctoral Dissertation, George Mason University, 1995.

19. M. Ely et al., *Doing Qualitative Research: Circles Within Circles* (Philadelphia: Falmer Press, 1991).

20. Jodi Aronson, "A Pragmatic View of Thematic Analysis," *The Qualitative Report*, 2, no. 1 (1994), http://www.nova.edu/ssss/QR/BackIssues/QR2-1/aronson.html.

21. S. J. Taylor and R. Bogdan, *Introduction to Qualitative Research Methods: The Search for Meanings* (New York: John Wiley & Sons, 1984), 131.

22. Madeleine Leininger, "Ethnography and Ethnonursing: Models and Modes of Qualitative Data Analysis," in Madeleine M. Leininger, ed., *Qualitative Research Methods in Nursing* (New York: Grune and Stratton, 1985), 33–72.

23. M. A. Constas, "Qualitative Analysis as a Public Event: The Documentation of Category Development Procedures," *American Educational Research Journal*, 29, no. 2 (1992), 253–266.

24. Robert M Pirsig, *Zen and the Art of Motorcycle Maintenance* (New York: HarperCollins Publishers, 1974, 1999), 184 and 208.

Chapter 10

1. http://en.thinkexist.com/quotes/emerson_m._pugh/ (accessed September 29, 2005).

2. Arthur Becker-Weidman, "Child Abuse and Neglect," http://www.mental-health-matters.com/articles/print.php?artID=581, 2001–2003 (accessed October 10, 2005).

3. Kevin N. Ochsner and Matthew D. Lieberman, "The Emergence of Social Cognitive Neuroscience," *American Psychologist*, 56, no. 9 (2001), 717–734.

4. Ochsner and Lieberman, "The Emergence of Social Cognitive Neuroscience," 718.

5. J. M. Harlow, "Recovery from the Passage of an Iron Bar through the Head," *Publications of the Massachusetts Medical Society*, 2 (1868), 327–347, cited in Antonio R. Damasio, *Descartes' Error: Emotion, Reason and the Human Brain* (New York: Avon Books, Inc., 1994), 4; Malcolm Macmillan, "The Phineas Gage Information Page," http://www.deakin.edu.au/hbs/GAGEPAGE/ (accessed November 21, 2005).

6. Leslie Brothers and Brian Ring, "A Neuroethological Framework for the Representation of Minds," *Journal of Cognitive Neuroscience*, 4, no. 2 (Spring 1992), 107–118.

7. Simon Baron-Cohen, Howard A. Ring, Sally Wheelwright, Edward T. Bullmore, Mick J. Brammer, Andrew Simmons, and Steve C. R. Williams, "Social Intelligence in the Normal and Autistic Brain: An fMRI Study," *European Journal of Neuroscience*, 11, issue 6 (June 1999), 1891–1989.

8. Tojo Thatchenkery, "Strategies for Addressing Asian-Pacific American Glass Ceiling: An Analysis of the Voices of the Invisible Minority in Corporate America and Federal Agencies," paper presented at the 23rd Annual Research Conference, Association for Public Policy Analysis and Management, Nov. 1–3, 2001, Washington, DC; Cliff Cheng and Tojo Thatchenkery, "Why is There a Lack of Workplace Diversity Research on Asian Americans?" *Journal of Applied Behavioral Sciences*, 33, no. 3 (1997), 270–276.

9. S. J. Breckler, "Empirical Validation of Affect, Behavior, and Cognition as Distinct Components of Attitude," *Journal of Personality and Social Psychology*, 47 (1984), 1191–1205.

10. A. J. Hart, P. J. Whalen, L. M. Shin, S. C. McInerney, H. Fischer, and S. L. Rauch, "Differential Response in the Human Amygdala to Racial Outgroup vs Ingroup Face Stimuli," *Neuroreport*, 11 (2000), 2351–2355.

11. E. A. Phelps, K. J. O'Connor, W. A. Cunningham, E. S. Funayama, J. Gatenby, J. Gore, and M. Banaji, "Performance on Indirect Measures of Race Evaluation Predicts Amygdala Activation," *Journal of Cognitive Neuroscience*, 12 (2000), 729–738.

12. Mary E. Wheeler and Susan T. Fiske, "Controlling Racial Prejudice: Social-Cognitive Goals Affect Amygdala and Stereotype Activation," *Psychological Science*, 16, no. 1 (2005), 56–63.

13. Matthew D. Lieberman, Ahmad Hariri, Johanna M. Jarcho, Naomi I. Eisenberger and Susan Y. Bookheimer, "An fMRI Investigation of Race-Related Amygdala Activity in African-American and Caucasian-American Individuals," *Nature Neuroscience*, 8 (2005), 720–722.

14. Stephen Franzoi, *Social Psychology* (New York: McGraw Hill, 2006), 95.

15. Simon Baron-Cohen, Howard A. Ring, Sally Wheelwright, Edward T. Bullmore, Mick J. Brammer, Andrew Simmons, and Steve C. R. Williams, "Social Intelligence in the Normal and Autistic Brain: An fMRI Study," *European Journal of Neuroscience*, 11, issue 6 (June 1999), 1891–1989.

16. Reuven Bar-On, D. Tranel, N. L. Denburg, and A. Bechara, "Exploring the Neurological Substrate of Emotional and Social Intelligence," *Brain*, 126, part 8 (2003), 1790–1800.

17. Mark Jung-Beeman, Edward M. Bowden, Jason Haberman, Jennifer L. Frymiare, Stella Arambel-Lin, Richard Greenblatt, Paul Reber, and John Kounios, "Neural Activity When People Solve Verbal Problems with Insight," *PLoS Biology*, 2 no. 4 (April 2004), http://biology.plosjournals.org.

Chapter 11

1. Richard Hamblyn, *The Invention of Clouds: How an Amateur Meteorologist Forged the Language of the Skies* (New York: Farrar, Straus and Giroux, 2001).

2. J. Dutton and E. Heaphy, "The Power of High-Quality Connections at Work," in K. Cameron, J. Dutton, and R. E. Quinn, eds., *Positive Organizational Scholarship* (San Francisco: Berrett-Koehler Publishers, 2003), 263–278.

3. Ryan Quinn and Jane E. Dutton, "Coordination as Energy-in-Conversation: A Process Theory of Organizing," *Academy of Management Review*, 30 (2005), 36-57.

4. Fred Luthans, "Positive Organizational Behavior: Developing and Managing Psychological Strengths," *Academy of Management Executive*, 16, no. 1 (2002), 60.

5. "Measures That Matter," Ernst & Young white paper (1997), 7.

6. Michael Mink, "He Shined a Light 'Round the Old Campfire," *Investors Business Daily*, September 22, 2004, sec. Leaders & Success.

7. Enterprise, Alabama—Boll Weevil Monument, http://www.roadsideamerica.com/tips/getAttraction.php3?tip_AttractionNo==19 (accessed November 22, 2005).

8. Ron Hira and Anil Hira, *Outsourcing America: What's Behind Our National Crisis and How We Can Reclaim American Jobs* (New York: AMACOM, 2005).

Bibliography

Anderson, Harlene, David Cooperrider, Kenneth Gergen, Mary Gergen, Sheila McNamee, and Diana Whitney. *The Appreciative Organization*. Chagrin Falls, OH: Taos Institute Publishing, 2001.

Andes, Jennifer. "Inventor Clarence Birdseye: His Search For A Better Way Helped Build A Food Empire." *Investor's Business Daily*, December 2, 1998, sec. Leaders & Success.

Argyris, Chris, and Don Schon. *Organizational Learning: A Theory of Action Perspective*. Reading, MA: Addison-Wesley, 1978.

Aronson, Jodi. "A Pragmatic View of Thematic Analysis," *The Qualitative Report* 2, no. 1 (1994), http://www.nova.edu/ssss/QR/BackIssues/QR2-1/aronson.html.

Atkinson, Rita, Richard Atkinson, Edward Smith, Darryl Bem, and Susan Nolen-Hoeksema. *Hilgard's Introduction to Psychology*. Fort Worth: Harcourt Brace College Publishers, 1996.

Bandura, Albert. "The Self-System in Reciprocal Determinism." *American Psychologist* 33 (1978): 344–358.

Bandura, Albert. *Social Foundations of Thought and Action: A Social Cognitive Theory*. Englewood Cliffs, NJ: Prentice Hall, 1986.

Bandura, Albert. "Cultivate Self-Efficacy for Personal and Organizational Effectiveness." In Locke, E. A., ed., *The Blackwell Handbook of Principles of Organizational Behavior*. Oxford, UK: Blackwell, 2000.

Barnes, Jon. "Botanist George Washington Carver: Rather Than Give In to Poverty, He Used It to Spur Inventiveness." *Investor's Business Daily*, November 4, 1998, sec. Leaders & Success.

Becker-Weidman, Arthur, Ph.D., "Child Abuse and Neglect," http://www.mental-health-matters.com/articles/print.php?artID=581.

Bennis, Warren G., and Patricia Ward Biederman. *Organizing Genius: The Secrets of Creative Collaboration*. Reading, MA: Addison Wesley, 1997.

Bennis, Warren G., and Robert J. Thomas, *Geeks & Geezers: How Eras, Values, and Defining Moments Shape Leaders*. Boston: Harvard Business School Press, 2002.

Block, J., and A. M. Kremen. "IQ and Ego-Resiliency: Conceptual and Empirical Connections and Separateness." *Journal of Personality and Social Psychology* 70 (1996): 349–361.

Boyatzis, Richard E. *Transforming Qualitative Information: Thematic Analysis and Code Development*. Thousand Oaks, CA: Sage Publications, 1998.

Brothers, Leslie. "The Neural Basis of Primate Social Communication." *Motivation and Emotion* 14, no. 2 (1990): 81–91.

Brothers, Leslie. "The Social Brain: A Project for Integrating Primate Behavior and Neurophysiology in a New Domain." *Concepts in Neuroscience*, 1 (1990): 27–51.

Cameron, Kim, Jane Dutton, and Robert Quinn. *Positive Organizational Scholarship: Foundations of a New Discipline*. San Francisco: Berrett-Koehler Publishers, 2003.

Carter, Rick. "W. L. Gore & Associates, Inc.: Quality's Different Drummer." *Industrial Maintenance & Plant Operation* (Jan. 2002): 10–16.

Cherniss, Cary, and Daniel Goleman. *The Emotionally Intelligent Workplace: How to Select for, Measure, and Improve Emotional Intelligence in Individuals, Groups, and Organizations.* San Francisco: Jossey-Bass, 2001.

Collins, Jim. *Good to Great: Why Some Companies Make the Leap . . . and Others Don't.* New York: Harper Business, 2001.

Constas, A. "Qualitative Analysis as a Public Event: The Documentation of Category Development Procedures." *American Educational Research Journal* 29, no. 2 (1992): 253–266.

Cooperrider, David, and S. Srivastva. "Appreciative Inquiry in Organizational Life." *Research in Organizational Change and Development* 1 (1987): 129–169.

Cordaro, Lucien, and James R. Ison. "The Psychology of the Scientist: X. Observer Bias in Classical Conditioning of the Planarian." *Psychological Reports*, 13 (1963): 787–789.

Csikszentmihalyi, Mihaly. *Flow: The Psychology of Optimal Experience.* New York: HarperPerennial Publishers, 1991.

Daft, R. L., and K. E. Weick. "Towards a Model of Organizations as Interpretation Systems." *Academy of Management Review* 9, no. 2 (1984): 284–295.

Denning, Stephen. *The Springboard: How Storytelling Ignites Action in Knowledge-Era Organizations.* Boston: Butterworth & Heinemann, 2000.

Deutschman, Alan. "The Fabric of Creativity." *Fast Company*, Issue 89, December 2004, 54–62.

Diener, Ed. "Subjective Well-Being: The Science of Happiness and a Proposal for a National Index." *American Psychologist* 55, no. 1 (2000): 34–43.

Dobbs, Lou. *Exporting America: Why Corporate Greed Is Shipping American Jobs Overseas.* New York: Warner Business Books, 2004.

Eden, D. *Pygmalion in Management: Productivity as a Self-Fulfilling Prophecy.* Lexington, MA: Lexington Books, 1990.

Ely, M., M. Anzul, T. Friedman, D. Garner, and A. McCormack Steinmetz. *Doing Qualititative Research: Circles Within Circles.* Philadelphia: Falmer Press, 1991.

Frankl, Viktor E. *Man's Search for Meaning.* New York: Washington Square Press, 1963.

Frederickson, B. L., M. M. Tugade, C. E. Waugh, and G. Larkin. "What Good Are Positive Emotions in Crises? A Prospective Study of Resilience and Emotions Following the Terrorist Attacks on the United States on September 11th, 2001." *Journal of Personality and Social Psychology* 84, no. 2 (2003): 365–376.

Fredrickson, B. L., R. A. Mancuso, C. Branigan, and M. M. Tugade. "The Undoing Effect of Positive Emotions." *Motivation and Emotion* 24 (2000): 237–258.

Fredrickson, B. L. "The Role of Positive Emotions in Positive Psychology: The Broaden-and-Build Theory of Positive Emotions." *American Psychologist* Special Issue, 56 (2001): 218–226.

Gardner, Howard. *Changing Minds: The Art and Science of Changing Our Own and Other People's Minds.* Boston: Harvard Business School Press, 2004.

Gardner, Howard. *Frames of Mind: The Theory of Multiple Intelligences.* New York: Basic Books, 1983.

Gardner, Howard. *Intelligence Reframed: Multiple Intelligences for the 21st Century.* New York: Basic Books, 1999.

Gardner, Howard. *Multiple Intelligences: The Theory in Practice*. New York: Basic Books, 1993.

Gergen, Kenneth, and Mary Gergen. *Social Construction: Entering the Dialogue*. Chagrin Falls, Ohio: Taos Institute Publishing, 2004.

Gergen, Kenneth. *An Invitation to Social Construction*. Thousand Oaks, CA: Sage, 1999.

Gergen, Kenneth. *Towards Transformation in Social Knowledge*. New York: Springer-Verlag, 1982.

Gilbert, Jannelle. "Leadership, Social Intelligence, and Perceptions of Environmental Opporunities: A Comparison across Levels of Leadership." Doctoral Dissertation, Department of Psychology, George Mason University, 1995.

Goleman, Daniel, Richard Boyatzis, and Annie McKee. *Primal Leadership: Realizing the Power of Emotional Intelligence*. Boston: Harvard Business School Press, 2002.

Goleman, Daniel. *Emotional Intelligence: Why It Can Matter More Than IQ*. New York: Bantam Books, 1994.

Goleman, Daniel. *Working with Emotional Intelligence*. New York: Bantam Books, 2000.

Halverson, A. M., M. Hallahan, A. J. Hart, and R. Rosenthal. "Reducing the Biasing Effects of Judges' Nonverbal Behavior with Simplified Jury Instruction." *Journal of Applied Psychology* 82 (1997): 590–598.

Hamblyn, Richard. *The Invention of Clouds: How an Amateur Meteorologist Forged the Language of the Skies*. New York: Farrar, Straus and Giroux, 2001.

Harrington, Ann. "Who's Afraid of a New Product?" *Fortune*, November 10, 2003, 189–192.

Hart, A. J., P. J. Whalen, L. M Shin, S. C. McInerney, H. Fischer, and S. L. Rouch. "Differential Response in the Human Amygdala to Racial Outgroup vs. Ingroup Face Stimuli." *Neuroreport* 11 (2000): 2351–2355.

Herrnstein, R. J., and C. Murray. *The Bell Curve: Intelligence and Class Structure in American Life*. New York: Free Press, 1994.

Innovation in Canada, "Case 7, Research in Motion." http://innovation.ic.gc.ca/gol/innovation/site.nsf/en/in04212.html.

Judge, Paul. "How Will Your Company Adapt?" *Fast Company*, December 2001, 128–138.

Kerlinger, Fred. *Foundations of Behavioral Research*. New York: Holt, Rinehart and Winston, 1973.

Krass, Peter. "Entrepreneur Estee Lauder: How She Created World's Largest Prestige Cosmetics Firm." *Investors Business Daily*, April 8, 1998, sec. Leaders & Success.

Krass, Peter. "Tupperware's Brownie Wise Built and Prepped Her Army with Methodical Goal Setting." *Investors Business Daily*, August 28, 1998, sec. Leaders & Success.

Learman, L. A., J. Avorn, D. E. Everitt, and R. Rosenthal. "Pygmalion in the Nursing Home: The Effects of Caregiver Expectations on Patient Outcomes." *Journal of the American Geriatrics Society* 38 (1990): 797–803.

Luthans, Fred. "Positive Organizational Behavior: Developing and Managing Psychological Strengths." *Academy of Management Executive* 16, no. 1 (2002): 57–75.

Leininger, M. M. "Ethnography and Ethnonursing: Models and Modes of Qualitative Data Analysis." In Leininger, M. M., ed., *Qualitative Research Methods in Nursing*. Orlando, FL: Grune and Stratton, 1985, 33–72.

Mink, Michael. "He Shined a Light 'Round the Old Campfire." *Investors Business Daily*, September 22, 2004, sec. Leaders & Success.

Mooney, Jonathan, and David Cole. *Learning Outside the Lines: Two Ivy League Students with Learning Disabilities and ADHD Give You the Tools for Academic Success and Educational Revolution*. New York: Fireside, 2000.

Ochsner, Kevin N., and Matthew D. Lieberman. "The Emergence of Social Cognitive Neuroscience." *American Psychologist* 56, no. 9 (2001): 717–734.

Pajares, F., and D. H. Schunk. "Self-Beliefs and School Success: Self-Efficacy, Self-Concept, and School Achievement." In R. Riding and S. Rayner, eds., *Perception*. London: Ablex Publishing, 2001, 239–266.

Perrow, C. *Complex Organizations: A Critical Essay*. 3rd ed. New York: Random House, 1986.

Peterson, Peter. *Running on Empty: How the Democratic and Republican Parties Are Bankrupting Our Future and What Americans Can Do about It*. New York: Farrar, Straus and Giroux, 2004.

Pigman, Herbert A. *Conquering Polio*. Evanston, IL: Rotary International, 2005.

Pirsig, Robert M. *Zen and the Art of Motorcycle Maintenance*. New York: HarperCollins Publishers, 1974, 1999.

Prahalad, C. K., and G. Hamel. *Competing for the Future*. Cambridge, MA: Harvard Business Press, 1994.

Quinn, Ryan, and Jane E. Dutton. "Coordination as Energy-in-Conversation: A Process Theory of Organizing." *Academy of Management Review* 30 (2005): 36–57.

Riggio, R. E., Susan E. Murphy, and F. J. Pirozzolo. *Multiple Intelligences and Leadership*. Mahwah, NJ: Lawrence Erlbaum, 2002.

Rogers, Doug. "Discount Broker Charles Schwab: Changing Brokerage Industry with Perseverance, Vision." *Investors Business Daily*, June 23, 1995, sec. Leaders & Success.

Rosenthal, R. "Pavlov's Mice, Pfungst's Horse, and Pygmalion's PONS: Some Models for the Study of Interpersonal Expectancy Effects." In T. A. Sebeok and R. Rosenthal, eds., *The Clever Hans Phenomenon*, Annals of the New York Academy of Sciences, Vol. 364. New York: New York Academy of Sciences, 1981.

Rosenthal, R. "Teacher Expectancy Effects: A Brief Update 25 Years after the Pygmalion Experiment." *Journal of Research in Education* 1 (1991): 3–12.

Rosenthal, R. *Experimental Effects in Behavioral Research*. New York: Appleton-Century-Crofts, 1966.

Rosenthal, R. *Experimenter Effects in Behavioral Research*, enlarged ed. New York: Irvington, 1976.

Rosenthal, R. *On the Social Psychology of the Self-Fulfilling Prophecy: Further Evidence for Pygmalion Effects and Their Mediating Mechanisms*. New York: MSS Modular, 1974.

Rosenthal, R., and K. L. Fode. "The Problem of Experimenter Outcome-Bias." In D. P. Ray, ed., *Series Research in Social Psychology*. Washington, DC: National Institute of Social and Behavioral Science, 1961.

Rosenthal, R., and L. Jacobson. *Pygmalion in the Classroom: Teacher Expectation and Pupils' Intellectual Development*. New York: Holt, Rinehart and Winston, 1968.

Sandelands, Lloyd, and Robert Drazin. "On the Language of Organization Theory." *Organization Studies* 10, issue 4 (1989): 457–478.

Salovey, Peter, and John D. Mayer. "Emotional Intelligence." *Imagination, Cognition and Personality* 9 (1990): 185–211.

Saxenian, Annalee. *Regional Advantage: Culture and Competition in Silicon Valley and Route 128*. Cambridge, MA: Harvard University Press, 1996.

Saxenian, Annalee. *Silicon Valley's New Immigrant Entrepreneurs*. San Francisco: Public Policy Institute of California, 1999.

Schultz, Howard, and Dori Jones Yang. *Pour Your Heart into It: How Starbucks Built a Company One Cup at a Time*. New York: Hyperion, 1997.

Seligman, Martin E. P. *Learned Optimism*. New York: A.A. Knopf, 1991.

Seligman, Martin. "Building Human Strength: Psychology's Forgotten Mission." *APA Monitor* 29, no. 1 (1998), http://www.apa.org/monitor/jan98/pres.html.

Simon, Herbert E. "Organizations and Markets." *Journal of Economic Perspectives* 5 (1991): 25–44.

Smith, Charles P., ed. *Motivation and Personality, Handbook of Thematic Content Analysis*. New York: Cambridge University Press, 1992.

Snyder, C. R., ed. *Handbook of Hope*. San Diego: Academic Press, 2000.

Stajkovic, A.D., and F. Luthans. "Social Cognitive Theory and Self-Efficacy: Going Beyond Traditional Motivational and Behavioral Approaches." *Organizational Dynamics*, 26, no. 4 (1998): 62–74.

Stavros, Jacqueline, and Cheri Torres. *Dynamic Relationships: Unleashing the Power of Appreciative Inquiry in Daily Living*. Chagrin Falls, OH: Taos Institute Publishing, 2005.

Sternberg, Robert J., Jacques Lautrey, and Todd I. Lubart, eds. *Models of Intelligence: International Perspectives*. Washington, DC: American Psychological Association, 2003.

Sternberg, Robert, and Janet Davidson, eds. *The Nature of Insight*. Cambridge, MA: The MIT Press, 1995.

Sternberg, Robert J., and Anna T. Cianciolo. *Intelligence: A Brief History*. Malden, MA: Blackwell, 2004.

Sternberg, Robert J. *Successful Intelligence: How Practical and Creative Intelligence Determine Success in Life*. New York: Plume Books, 1997.

Sternberg, Robert J., ed. *Why Smart People Can Be So Stupid*. New Haven: Yale University Press, 2002.

Sternberg, Robert J. *Wisdom, Intelligence, and Creativity Synthesized*. New York: Cambridge University Press, 2003.

Sternberg, Robert J., George B. Forsythe, Jennifer Hedlund, Joseph A. Horvath, Richard K. Wagner, Wendy M. Williams, Scott A. Snook, and Elena Grigorenko. *Practical Intelligence in Everyday Life*. New York: Cambridge University Press, 2000.

Sternberg, Robert J., and Jean E. Pretz, eds. *Cognition and Intelligence: Identifying the Mechanisms of the Mind*. New York: Cambridge University Press, 2005.

Stone, Brad. "BlackBerry: Bring It On!" *Newsweek*, September 26, 2005, E8–E14.

Tarsala, Michael. "Coca-Cola's Asa Candler: How He Took a Fizzling Brain Tonic and Made 'The Real Thing' Fizz." *Investors Business Daily*, February 1, 1999, sec. Leaders & Success.

Taylor, S. J., and R. Bogdan. *Introduction to Qualitative Research Methods: The Search for Meanings*. New York: John Wiley & Sons, 1984.

Thatchenkery, Tojo. *Appreciative Sharing of Knowledge: Leveraging Knowledge Management for Strategic Change.* Chagrin Falls, OH: Taos Institute Publishing, 2005.

Tonelson, Alan. *The Race to the Bottom: Why a Worldwide Worker Surplus and Uncontrolled Free Trade Are Sinking American Living Standards.* Boulder, CO: Westview Press, 2002.

Turner, Nick. "Entrepreneur Michael Dell: How He's Made His Firm the Fastest-Growing Computer Maker." *Investors Business Daily*, March 1, 1999, sec. Leaders & Success.

Valliant, George. *Adaptation to Life.* Boston: Little, Brown, 1977.

Vygotsky, L. S. *Thought and Language*, ed. and trans. by Eugenia Hanfmann and Gertrude Vakar. Cambridge: MIT Press, 1979.

Weick, Karl. *Social Psychology of Organizing.* New York: Random House, 1979. Weinreb, Michael. "Power to the People." *Sales & Marketing Management*, April 2003, 30–35.

Whitney, Diane, Amanda Trosten-Bloom, and David Cooperrider. *The Power of Appreciative Inquiry: A Practical Guide to Positive Change.* San Francisco: Berrett-Koehler, 2003.

Index

Appreciating Those Who Made This Book Possible

There are candles all around you, lighting the way
with warmth and support.
—Eric Metzker

Until one lives through the challenges of writing a book, one doesn't realize how many people are behind a finished product, how generous they are with their time and expertise, and how important they are to bringing a book to life. We believe that everyone has a book inside, but not everyone has a multitude of business partners, colleagues, and friends who are willing to help that book see the light of day. Through this process, we have learned how crucial it is to publicly acknowledge and appreciate that guidance, help, and, in some cases, sacrifices. We would like to thank the following people:

- David Cooperrider, who wrote the Foreword to our book and whose appreciation was at the outset of this work

- The authors and researchers whose words were quoted and works were cited, including Jim Collins for his brilliant perspectives and stories; Warren Bennis, whose writing style and previous works inspired Carol; Howard Schultz, whose book *Pour Your Heart into It* helped us persevere while providing an excellent source for study; and the numerous psychologists, social scientists, and social cognitive neuroscientists whose research laid the foundation for our book

- The men and women—the leaders and innovators—who graciously gave the time to talk with us about their experiences: Keith Barrett, Domenic Carnuccio, Fleur Frascella, Ron Gruner, Glenn Heck, Ed Hoffman, Dean Kamen, Bill Keeney, John Kounios, Eric Metzker, Herb Pigman, Charlie Pellerin, Greg Radford, David Rayburn, Katherine Schantz, Matt Schreiner, George Shaw, Bradley Smith, Patti Spackman, Bill Sergeant, the members of the 2004 Westtown School Robotics team, and others who shared their stories and experiences anonymously; all of whose stories and ideas made our work possible

- Others who helped with logistics, additional facts, and corroboration of information—Corey Field; Marian Murphy and Ken Freitas at FIRST; Carol Pandak and Vivian Fiore at Rotary International, who provided statistics and history of the Polio Plus program; Kathleen Sanger, Dave Brubaker, Ali Pincus, and Pritchard Garrett at Delaware Valley Friends School; and Victoria Dow, Executive Director of the West Chester Public Library

- Our editorial review board whose ideas were invaluable—Carl Ingram, Chris Lee, Carol Prescott McCoy, and Perviz E. Randeria

- The entire staff at Berrett-Koehler Publishers, particularly Steve Piersanti, whose suggestions gave our ideas clarity and structure, and Jeevan Sivasubramaniam, who answered every question quickly and as though it were intelligent and important

- Lydia Kibiuk, the illustrator of the diagrams of the brain in Chapter 10

We are also grateful to several colleagues who either endorsed the book or supported us in many ways, including Kenneth Gergen, Jane Dutton, David Boje, Robert Gephart, William Pasmore, Jay Conger, Warner Burke, Art Kleiner, Diana Whitney, Jacqueline Stavros, Jane Seiling, Dora Fried, David Barry, Nancy M. Dixon, Melinda Merino, Robert Kramer, Venkataraman Nilakant, Kingsley Haynes, Roger Stough, Sara Cobb, Ann Baker, Mark Addleson, Joel Foreman, June Turner, and Carl Wilhelm-Stenhammar.

Although there may be others whom we have not mentioned by name, we are sincerely grateful for your contributions.

From Tojo

Having an idea is not enough. A validation from the professional community is most important for new ideas to develop better and have positive impact. That was what I was looking for when I talked enthusiastically to Karl Weick in 1999 about my conceptualization of Appreciative Intelligence during a conference on *Language and Organizational Change* in Ohio. The legendary scholar and mentor of many academics in organization science had earlier supported my nonmainstream ideas, such as hermeneutics and organizations as texts. Karl Weick gently probed me, brought more clarity to my thinking, and encouraged me to work on it further and write about it. During the next six years I would share my thinking on Appreciative Intelligence with several of my academic colleagues, each of whom showed the same enthusiasm I had. I am grateful to you all.

Then there are my students. When I helped found the graduate program in organizational learning at George Mason University a decade ago, little did I realize that it would create a community of reflective practitioners who would stay engaged with the faculty long after they had graduated and moved on to occupy responsible positions. Many of the members of my "kitchen cabinet" who read the manuscript and gave insightful comments were graduates of our organizational learning program who saw themselves as members of the *learning community*—a graduate course they once took with me while in the program and which became a real community once they left school. The learning community has always been an "Appreciative Intelligence Laboratory" where students and faculty are encouraged to bring their ideas and find them come alive with the intentional affirmation provided by the mindfulness of its members. In addition to recognizing that intellectual climate, I acknowledge a few who read the manuscripts and provided useful feedback: Tom Walsh, Martin Hill, Karl Widmayer, and Brad Hendricks. Others in the kitchen cabinet who read the manuscripts and gave insightful comments include Ram Tenkasi, Bruce Hanson, William Rifkin, Con Kenney, Don Austin, and Rahul Verma.

I thank Carol Metzker, my coauthor, not only for accepting my invitation to write this book with me but for something different. Initially I was going to write an academic book on Appreciative Intelligence—the type of book that might put many of you to sleep! It was Carol, a graduate of our Organizational Learning Masters program, who encouraged me to try the reverse: to start with an applied book and write a "dense, scholarly" one later. The result you see here is a hybrid: a scholarly book that reads like a popular, easy-to-understand, applied book, made possible by Carol joining me as a co-author. I am grateful for Carol's total dedication to this book and her extraordinary attention to detail. She kept this writing project on track and made sure everything got done on time.

I also want to thank my wife, Tessy, and my daughter, Sruthi, for their constant encouragement and support. Sruthi lightened the otherwise stressful writing process by pointing out my Homer-like qualities! We watched the television show *The Simpsons* together almost every day, and she started calling me "Homer Simpson." True to the Pygmalion Effect described in the book, I have now become a Homer!

From Carol

Writing a book is an enormous undertaking. This one was no exception. Beyond the efforts of many, there was something more that supported my role in bringing this book to light: gifts of trust, patience, humor, spirit, care, grace, and understanding. These were given freely by people who granted interviews and by friends, colleagues, and family. The leaders and innovators who agreed to talk with me trusted me to listen carefully, to treat their stories with esteem and sensitivity, and to portray them with honesty and respect. Like candles lighting a path, advisors and colleagues guided my work with constructive feedback, patience, and humor. When the going got tough, friends and family treated me with grace and understanding.

Thank you to friends who formed the advisory committee we called the "kitchen cabinet": Dad (Bill Hart), dava money, Connie Harrison, Jay Holland, Annalie Korengel Lorgus, and Eric Metzker. I am grateful for your constructive suggestions as you read chapters and brought forth new perspectives on the practical merits of these ideas. I appreciate your willingness on a moment's notice to provide your educated and considerate opinions.

I would like to thank Tojo, as coauthor and friend, for your tireless efforts, even temper through thick and thin, and sense of humor during the period we referred to as "death by footnotes." Your mental flexibility and spontaneity have served as wonderful examples.

I would also like to thank Laura Bernstein, Marie and Jay Holland, Annalie Korengel Lorgus and Gary Lorgus, and Carolyn and Dave Rayburn, who provided feedback, interest, and encouragement as the book progressed. A special note of appreciation is extended to Annalie, who graciously gave of her time, energy, and spirit.

The ultimate candles lighting my way—throughout the arduous and transformative task of organizing ideas and notes, putting thoughts on paper, and revealing to the world thoughts that I believed were important enough to share and concepts that will make a positive difference in this world—were members of my family. They showed great Appreciative Intelligence, reframing reality to see this project as something positive and important for the future and to find ways to make it happen. Thanks to my parents for helping when I traveled, for sharing their knowledge, and for exploring ideas and values with me that influenced this book. Thanks to Elizabeth and Kathryn for their loving support when I needed to focus on writing, mirth when I needed to take a break, and the wisdom to see which time was which. Thank you to Eric for believing in me and the project every step of the way and allowing me to watch his amazing appreciation of others.

Appreciative Intelligence: Working for You

How effective and happy are you in various aspects of your life? By further exploring and enhancing your Appreciative Intelligence, you can make a lasting, positive difference in your workplace, home and community. To learn more, please visit our Web site at www.appreciativeintelligence.com.

How can Appreciative Intelligence help your organization? It can be applied to
- Identify high-potential individuals for succession planning
- Unlock creativity and innovation
- Capture and expand best practices
- Set goals and objectives tailored to your organizational culture
- Transform your organization for a successful future

Toward these outcomes, Tojo Thatchenkery and Carol Metzker offer small-group workshops, consulting, seminars, and speaking engagements for business, nonprofit, government, and educational organizations. For more information or to schedule an event, please contact us at info@appreciativeintelligence.com.

We invite you to share your Appreciative Intelligence-related success stories, lessons learned, or techniques that helped you or others develop and enhance their intelligence. Please e-mail us at successstories@appreciativeintelligence.com. Please let us know whether we may post your message on our Web site so that others may learn from your experiences.

For other inquiries, contact Tojo Thatchenkery at Tojo@appreciative intelligence.com or Carol Metzker at Carol@appreciativeintelligence.com. We look forward to hearing from you.

About the Authors

Tojo Thatchenkery

Tojo Thatchenkery, Ph.D., is a Professor of Organizational Learning and Knowledge Management at the School of Public Policy, George Mason University, Fairfax, Virginia. He is also a member of the NTL Institute of Applied Behavioral Science and the Taos Institute. He has over twenty years of experience in teaching at various MBA, public policy, organizational development, and executive programs in the United States, Europe, Australia, and Asia. Tojo founded the Organizational Learning Laboratory at the George W. Johnson Learning Center at George Mason University and served as its director from 1995 to 2000. His research has been funded by agencies such as the U. S. National Science Foundation and the U.S. National Security Agency

For more than fifteen years Tojo has been researching, consulting, and teaching in appreciative organizational design. Examples include Appreciative Inquiry, which he has been teaching to graduate students at George Mason University for over a decade, and Appreciative Sharing for Knowledge, a new knowledge management tool to leverage tacit knowledge in organizations. He has written extensively on appreciative processes in organizations, which include his doctoral dissertation, numerous refereed publications, and a recent book, *Appreciative Sharing for Knowledge: Leveraging Knowledge Management for Strategic Change.*

Tojo has extensive consulting experience in change management, organization design, and knowledge management. Past clients include IBM, Fannie Mae, Booz/Allen/Hamilton, PNC Bank, Lucent Technologies, General Mills, British Petroleum, Tata Consulting Services, the International Monetary Fund, the World Bank, United States Department of Agriculture, and the Environmental Protection Agency.

Tojo is on the editorial board of the *Journal of Applied Behavioral Sciences* and the *Journal of Organizational Change Management.* He is also the book review editor of the *Journal of Organizational Change Management* and the past Program Chair of the Research Methods Division of the 16,000-member-strong Academy of Management. Tojo has also used the appreciative lens to study diverse themes such as information communication technology (ICT), the economic development of South Asian countries (co-edited book), and the social capital and organizational mobility of Asian Americans in the United States.

Tojo lives in Chantilly, Virginia, with his wife and daughter and can be reached at Tojo@appreciativeintelligence.com.

Carol Metzker

For over 15 years, Carol Metzker has helped clients tap into their success stories to uncover best practices, share knowledge, and communicate clearly for successful outcomes. She has worked successfully in educational, nonprofit, and corporate environments. She has a Master's degree in Organizational Learning from George Mason University.

Stories she has written as contributing editor for *Investor Relations Update* about executives in *Fortune* 500 companies appear in monthly print and online publications of the National Investor Relations Institute. Her articles have appeared in numerous publications including *Global CEO, Journal of Organizational Change Management, Management Next,* and the Association for Financial Professionals' journals *Pulse* and *Exchange.*

Her past experience as Director of Client Services at Anderson Leadership Group, a leadership communication consulting firm, cultivated her interest in leadership development and gave her the opportunity for close observation and experience with top-level leaders. Her work as a writer and consultant has led to interviews of hundreds of executives about their successful and innovative practices, providing a closer look at companies and their members. Her work as an interviewer and writer for a National Science Foundation–sponsored study on the impact of information technology on India's development provided an exceptional view of a variety of social and business cultures.

Carol's volunteer service inspires her and also provides the subject for articles and frequent speaking engagements. She has served as a mentor for FIRST. As a Rotarian, in 2004 she experienced the polio eradication program firsthand, participating in and leading National Immunization Day trips to India.

She lives in West Chester, Pennsylvania, with her husband and two daughters and can be reached at Carol@appreciativeintelligence.com.

About Berrett-Koehler Publishers

Berrett-Koehler is an independent publisher dedicated to an ambitious mission: Creating a World that Works for All.

We believe that to truly create a better world, action is needed at all levels—individual, organizational, and societal. At the individual level, our publications help people align their lives and work with their deepest values. At the organizational level, our publications promote progressive leadership and management practices, socially responsible approaches to business, and humane and effective organizations. At the societal level, our publications advance social and economic justice, shared prosperity, sustainable development, and new solutions to national and global issues.

We publish groundbreaking books focused on each of these levels. To further advance our commitment to positive change at the societal level, we have recently expanded our line of books in this area and are calling this expanded line "BK Currents."

A major theme of our publications is "Opening Up New Space." They challenge conventional thinking, introduce new points of view, and offer new alternatives for change. Their common quest is changing the underlying beliefs, mindsets, institutions, and structures that keep generating the same cycles of problems, no matter who our leaders are or what improvement programs we adopt.

We strive to practice what we preach—to operate our publishing company in line with the ideas in our books. At the core of our approach is *stewardship*, which we define as a deep sense of responsibility to administer the company for the benefit of all of our "stakeholder" groups: authors, customers, employees, investors, service providers, and the communities and environment around us. We seek to establish a partnering relationship with each stakeholder that is open, equitable, and collaborative.

We are gratified that thousands of readers, authors, and other friends of the company consider themselves to be part of the "BK Community." We hope that you, too, will join our community and connect with us through the ways described on our website at www.bkconnection.com.

Be Connected

Visit Our Website

Go to www.bkconnection.com to read exclusive previews and excerpts of new books, find detailed information on all Berrett-Koehler titles and authors, browse subject-area libraries of books, and get special discounts.

Subscribe to Our Free E-Newsletter

Be the first to hear about new publications, special discount offers, exclusive articles, news about bestsellers, and more! Get on the list for our free e-newsletter by going to www.bkconnection.com.

Participate in the Discussion

To see what others are saying about our books and post your own thoughts, check out our blogs at www.bkblogs.com.

Get Quantity Discounts

Berrett-Koehler books are available at quantity discounts for orders of ten or more copies. Please call us toll-free at (800) 929-2929 or email us at bkp.orders@aidcvt.com.

Host a Reading Group

For tips on how to form and carry on a book reading group in your workplace or community, see our website at www.bkconnection.com.

Join the BK Community

Thousands of readers of our books have become part of the "BK Community" by participating in events featuring our authors, reviewing draft manuscripts of forthcoming books, spreading the word about their favorite books, and supporting our publishing program in other ways. If you would like to join the BK Community, please contact us at bkcommunity@bkpub.com.